Praise for *Truly Great Sec...*

This is exactly what I needed to read before embarking on my improvement work. As always, John weaves together theory, research and practice to focus on what really matters: getting teaching and learning right in the classroom. We've worked with John for several years now. He has supported us in school improvement with pragmatic wisdom and wit! He never loses sight of what matters: the children and the quality of their learning through expert teaching. As with John's previous books, *Truly Great Secondary Teachers* combines a genial warmth with astute observations. The warmth radiates off the pages: both John's warmth towards the teachers he profiles and the teachers' warmth towards their charges which permeates each case study. Most importantly, his portraits of teachers at the top of their game provide incredibly important learning for all of us interested in schools.

Samantha McMonagle, Executive Lead for School Improvement, Central Regions Schools Trust

The power of story to help us to understand how the world works is well-documented. The power of story to draw us in to new and unfamiliar territories is an underestimated element of professional learning. What we find in these wonderful accounts of stunning practitioners are insights, strands of gold and subtle nuances that invite us to reflect on our own practice. *Truly Great Secondary Teachers* is such a joy to read, to reflect on and to marvel at. Wherever we are in our professional lives, we will take some inspiration from these incredible colleagues, who have managed to get to the heart of the matter, bring their students with them, get great results and continue to be fascinated by the craft of teaching. Truly transformational.

Mary Myatt, educational consultant

There are few things more valuable to those of us in the world of education than hearing first-hand about the nuances, complexities and contradictions of truly excellent teaching. In *Truly Great Secondary Teachers*, John Tomsett has done us all a hugely valuable service – he's found 10 expert practitioners who can tell us what makes a great teacher – not in the simplistic language of data and outcomes, but in the delicate and subtle language of real classroom experience.

Sammy Wright, Head Teacher, Southmoor Academy, author of *Exam Nation*

I have always believed our great profession is packed full of expert teachers. Indeed, as John Tomsett says in the introduction to *Truly Great Secondary Teachers*, there are 'thousands of them' in our classrooms up and down the country. In this book, the author has brilliantly embodied that expertise through a series of detailed teacher profiles; each one contains a strong balance of theory and practical ideas to use in the classroom, whilst being packed full of personal connections and anecdotes. The tips and reflections from serving practitioners are profound, and the evidence base behind the claim that these colleagues are 'truly great' is extensive. The author also recognises all of the truly great teachers who could have been included if there were enough pages. I am already looking forward to *This Much I Know About Truly Great Secondary Teachers 2*!

Nigel Whittle, Principal, Waltham Toll Bar Academy

A brilliant book to inspire teachers, parents, pupils and the wider public at a time when we urgently need more people to enter – *and stay in* – the teaching profession. Being a 'truly great teacher' is about so much more than the mechanical delivery of results and ticking boxes. It requires a complex range of skills, joy and, above all, belief and interest in young people and how they learn. *Truly Great Secondary Teachers* reminds us that if we want to have a really equitable and excellent education system, attracting and developing the very best people, into what should be a life-enhancing career, must be a priority.

Fiona Millar, school governor and *Guardian* columnist

We can all name a teacher that stands out. Getting excellent results for the young people will always be one of the reasons why they are memorable, but *Truly Great Secondary Teachers* clearly shows that results are only part of the picture. John Tomsett's book shows why the Ofsted approach to quantifying teaching will never truly work. How do we measure how well a teacher connects with their students in the classroom? How do we put a number on a teacher's ability to see a group of learners struggling with a concept and know instantly what they need to do to get over that learning barrier? It is quite simple ... we can't! I loved reading about every teacher in this book and every one of them made me want to go and teach my next lesson a little better, with a bit more conviction and in a way that makes it memorable. Read *Truly Great Secondary Teachers*, be inspired and find your own way of doing the same.

Vic Goddard, author of *The Best Job in the World*

Truly Great Secondary Teachers is full of insights into what makes a truly great teacher. With a deep respect for the teachers profiled in this book, John Tomsett does a fantastic job of highlighting the key features of effective teaching. The lesson visits, student feedback and testimonials offer a powerful sense of the impact that a great teacher can have on young lives. The author's reflections on his own experience of great teachers are particularly compelling. The key elements are identified: high expectations, meticulous planning, good behaviour management, relentlessness and consistency. But, above all else, a deep commitment to young people is the key attribute that every outstanding teacher shares. This book is an inspiring and informative read for anyone interested in becoming a great teacher.

Brenda Landers, Executive Head Teacher, Swanlea School

John Tomsett's latest work is an extraordinary celebration of teaching, exploring what truly defines greatness in the classroom. Through captivating case studies of 11 diverse and deeply inspiring educators, Tomsett dismantles the notion of a one-size-fits-all metric for teaching excellence. Instead, he invites us to see teaching as an art form, powered by individuality, passion and humanity. The featured teachers are vibrant personalities whose enthusiasm, love for teaching and commitment to their students leap off the page. Tomsett's analysis is astute, identifying nine common traits that these educators share – from clarity and high expectations to the ability to build positive relationships. These characteristics form a practical yet profound guide for anyone in the profession. *Truly Great Secondary Teachers* is a must-read for teachers and leaders alike, reminding us that great teaching is as varied and rich as the students it serves. It's inspiring, thoughtful and deeply affirming.

Patrick Cozier, Head Teacher,
Highgate Wood School and Sixth Form Centre

THIS MUCH I KNOW ABOUT
TRULY GREAT SECONDARY TEACHERS

(AND WHAT WE CAN LEARN FROM THEM)

JOHN TOMSETT

FOREWORD BY PROFESSOR ROB COE

Crown House Publishing Limited
www.crownhouse.co.uk

First published by
Crown House Publishing Limited
Crown Buildings, Bancyfelin, Carmarthen, Wales, SA33 5ND, UK
www.crownhouse.co.uk

and

Crown House Publishing Company LLC
PO Box 2223, Williston, VT 05495, USA
www.crownhousepublishing.com

© John Tomsett, 2025

The right of John Tomsett to be identified as the author of this work has been asserted by him in accordance with the Copyright, Designs and Patents Act 1988.

First published 2025.

All rights reserved. Except as permitted under current legislation no part of this work may be photocopied, stored in a retrieval system, published, performed in public, adapted, broadcast, transmitted, recorded or reproduced in any form or by any means, without the prior permission of the copyright owners. Enquiries should be addressed to Crown House Publishing.

Crown House Publishing has no responsibility for the persistence or accuracy of URLs for external or third-party websites referred to in this publication, and does not guarantee that any content on such websites is, or will remain, accurate or appropriate.

Image p. 236: from J. Goodrich, *Responsive Coaching: Evidence-informed Instructional Coaching that Works for Every Teacher in Your School* (Woodbridge: John Catt Educational, 2024). permission kindly received from John Catt Educational.
Quote pp. 239–240: from G. Duoblys, Michael Young: What we've got wrong about knowledge and curriculum, *TES* (21 September 2022). Available at: https://www.tes.com/magazine/teaching-learning/general/michael-young-powerful-knowledge-curriculum. Permission for use kindly received from G. Duoblys.

EU GPSR Authorised Representative

Appointed EU Representative: Easy Access System Europe Oü, 16879218
Address: Mustamäe tee 50, 10621, Tallinn, Estonia
Contact Details: gpsr.requests@easproject.com, +358 40 500 3575

British Library Cataloguing-in-Publication Data

A catalogue entry for this book is available from the British Library.

Print ISBN: 9781785837418
Mobi ISBN: 9781785837593
ePub ISBN: 9781785837609
ePDF ISBN: 9781785837616

LCCN 2025931344

Printed and bound in the UK by
Gomer Press, Llandysul, Ceredigion

This book is dedicated to Tom Sherrington, who has taught me more about the frustratingly complex process of teaching and learning than he would ever know!

Foreword by Professor Rob Coe

I suspect this book may have come into being partly because of a misunderstanding, a failure of communication. As John describes in the introduction, it arose from a presentation Raj Chande and I gave about our National Institute of Teaching project to try to estimate value-added scores for individual teachers (anonymised) in order to learn more about what great teaching is and how it develops. John was in the audience and something about the idea of reducing the rich complexity of teaching to a single number seemed to grate with him – perhaps not unreasonably. He asked a question that I interpreted as challenging, and I am sorry to say I responded a bit confrontationally, trying to put him down and close down the challenge. As a result, I missed the opportunity to find common ground, to understand his concerns and to explain why what we were trying to do was not quite what he thought. My bad. But from that bad, came a brilliant thing: a pair of books.

This Much I Know About Truly Great Secondary Teachers (and what we can learn from them), alongside its accompanying title *This Much I Know About Truly Great Primary Teachers (and what we can learn from them),* is a wonderful celebration of the complex and beautiful art of classroom teaching. It brings to life the ways great teachers coordinate great learning in classrooms with a set of vivid case studies. The chosen examples cover a range of school types, social contexts, pupil ages and subjects. Each teacher is unique in the way they teach, and in how they talk about teaching; each has found their own way; each is brought to technicolour life in John's vignette. But they also have some common characteristics and behaviours, as John draws together, summarising what we can learn from them in the final chapter.

I first started thinking in a systematic way about what great teachers do when writing the report *What Makes Great Teaching?* in 2014.[1] The

---

1 R. Coe, C. Aloisi, S. Higgins and L. Elliot Major, *What Makes Great Teaching? Review of the Underpinning Research* (London: Sutton Trust, 2014). Available at: https://www.suttontrust.com/wp-content/uploads/2014/10/What-Makes-Great-Teaching-REPORT.pdf.

Sutton Trust and Gates Foundation had co-organised a conference in Washington DC at which they wanted to bring together some of the best teachers and school leaders from around the world. Lee Elliot Major had asked me to lead on creating the report that became *What Makes Great Teaching?* and to present it at the conference. I first knew John as one of the early edu-bloggers and through Twitter, and by that point was working with him directly as part of an Education Endowment Foundation (EEF)-funded project to evaluate the impact of training school research leads to interpret and apply research evidence, led by Huntington School where he was the head teacher (Research leads Improving Students' Education – RISE).[2] I think I nominated John to be invited to Washington as part of a small group of outstanding school leaders from England. My memory is that the report and its messages had a somewhat luke-warm reception in Washington. Although our hand-picked delegates from England liked it, the majority of teachers there were from the US and other places where the role of research evidence in teaching was not yet established. *What Makes Great Teaching?* went on to become the Sutton Trust's most downloaded research report, by some margin, and has since featured in the recommended reading for all trainee teachers in England through the *Initial Teacher Training and Early Career Framework.*[3]

In the report we defined effective teaching by its impact on valued student outcomes, acknowledging that a range of different outcomes could be valued (for example, academic attainment in examinations, future education and career trajectories, along with impacts on students' attendance, behaviours and attitudes). We also considered in some detail other approaches to evaluating the quality of teaching, including: classroom observations, by peers, principals or external evaluators; student ratings surveys; principal (or head teacher) judgement; teacher self-reports; analysis of classroom artefacts; and teacher portfolios. We presented the evidence about the convergence

---

2 See: https://educationendowmentfoundation.org.uk/projects-and-evaluation/projects/the-rise-project-evidence-informed-school-improvement.

3 Department for Education, *Initial Teacher Training and Early Career Framework* (January 2024). Available at: https://assets.publishing.service.gov.uk/media/661d24ac08c3be25cfbd3e61/Initial_Teacher_Training_and_Early_Career_Framework.pdf.

of these different approaches and concluded that 'their predictive power is usually not high'. To illustrate the strength of the relationships typically found in the best research studies, we gave a hypothetical example: 'If we were to use classroom observation ratings to identify teachers as "above" or "below" average in their impact on student learning we would get it right about 60% of the time, compared with the 50% we would get by just tossing a coin. It is better than chance, but not by much.'

Part of the reason classroom observation correlates only weakly with student progress measures is that observing classrooms is a lot harder than it seems. Most teachers and school leaders have a clear idea what great teaching looks like. When they watch a lesson, they have a strong sense that they can interpret what they see and hear, and that they can judge how good it is. In my experience, it is very hard to convince them that their judgements may not be as accurate as they intuitively feel. And yet, these judgements are mostly wrong.[4]

Among the reasons why it is so hard to judge effectiveness from observation is that many of the things that make a difference to students' learning are not visible, and even those that are may not be on display in any particular lesson. This creates a challenge for any researcher who wants to develop an evidence-based protocol for lesson observation and it applies to all the existing instruments (some of which we reviewed in *What Makes Great Teaching?*). But for teachers and school leaders, who are not trained and accredited in using a validated protocol and rely on their intuitive judgements, there is a further reason: different teachers do not completely agree about what great teaching is. As we said in the report, 'It might seem obvious that this is already well known: we surely know what great teaching looks like … In fact, there is some evidence that an understanding of what constitutes effective pedagogy – the method and practice of teaching – may not be so widely shared, and even where it is widely shared it may not actually be right.' A small section of the report pointed out some exam-

---

4 See, for example, R. Coe, Classroom observation: it's harder than you think, *Cambridge Insight* [blog] (9 January 2014). Available at: https://www.cem.org/blog/classroom-observation.

ples of 'popular teaching practices not supported by research evidence' to illustrate that describing great teaching is not just common sense. But the press release led with 'many common practices can be harmful to learning and have no grounding in research'[5] and I recall doing multiple radio and television interviews explaining the dangers of 'lavish praise for students'.

All of this is perhaps a slightly long-winded way of saying that identifying great teachers is tricky and trying to describe what they do that makes them great even more so. Many excellent researchers over the last 50 or more years have tried to do both, and yet our knowledge remains partial and uncertain. It is one of those questions about which practitioners will mostly feel frustration that researchers are making it so complicated. Surely, we know what great teaching is and is it really that hard to describe it? To which researchers may reply that, certainly, it is not hard to do it badly, but doing it well is very hard indeed.

What Makes Great Teaching? reviewed and quality-assured a wide range of research evidence about the components of teaching quality and presented an outline framework to summarise it. When I started working for Evidence Based Education in 2019, we thought it would be useful to update the review. But we soon realised that a summary of research findings about effective teaching, however authoritative and accessible, is not enough to help teachers to do more of it, more faithfully, more sustainably, more effectively, and at greater scale. For that, we needed a more diverse set of tools to support a coherent approach to professional development, hence the *Great Teaching Toolkit*. Nevertheless, the foundation of that Toolkit is an updated Evidence Review.

---

5 Sutton Trust, Many popular teaching practices are ineffective, warns new Sutton Trust report [press release] (30 October 2014). Available at: https://www.suttontrust.com/news-opinion/all-news-opinion/many-popular-teaching-practices-are-ineffective-warns-new-sutton-trust-report/.

The *Great Teaching Toolkit: Evidence Review* sets out a model for great teaching, based on the best currently available evidence.[6] The highest-level summary clarifies that great teachers do four fundamental things:

1. Understand the content they are teaching and how it is learnt
2. Create a supportive environment for learning
3. Manage the classroom to maximise opportunity to learn
4. Present content, activities and interactions that activate their students' thinking

Each of these four broad dimensions is then split into a total of 17 elements:

1. Understanding the content

    1.1. Deep and fluent content knowledge

    1.2. Curriculum knowledge: sequencing

    1.3. Knowledge of tasks, assessments and multiple explanations

    1.4. Knowledge of student thinking: misconceptions

2. Creating a supportive environment

    2.1. Relationships with students and cultural sensitivity

    2.2. Student–student relationships and climate

    2.3. Promoting learner motivation

    2.4. High expectations, challenge and trust

3. Maximising the opportunity to learn

    3.1. Managing time and resources to maximise productivity

    3.2. Clear and consistent rules, expectations and consequences

---

6 R. Coe, C. J. Rauch, S. Kime, and D. Singleton, *The Great Teaching Toolkit: Evidence Review* (Sunderland: Evidence Based Education, 2020). Available at: https://evidencebased.education/great-teaching-toolkit-evidence-review/.

3.3. Preventing and responding to disruption and showing awareness

4   Activating hard thinking

4.1. Structuring: matching tasks, scaffolding and signalling objectives

4.2. Explaining: presenting and connecting ideas and modelling examples

4.3. Questioning: promoting hard thinking and assessing

4.4. Interacting: giving, receiving and responding to feedback

4.5. Embedding: practising, reinforcing and spacing learning

4.6. Activating: building independence and supporting metacognition

Of course, these are just headlines, very abbreviated descriptions of complex practices that are, at best, inadequately captured in words. To be well-defined, in addition we need exemplification (rich and varied examples and non-examples) and operationalisation (clear processes for assessing whether an example represents the target practice). A big challenge with descriptors is that we can think we mean the same things by the same words when we actually have quite different understandings in practice, especially when the descriptors are quite abstract and general, as they inevitably must be.

The purpose of sharing this framework here is twofold. The first is to note that there is a lot of overlap between what the evidence suggests are the practices most associated with effective teaching and the practices described in the following chapters. John summarises ten behaviours of truly great teachers in the last chapter and I would say they are all represented in the model, and that other features of their teaching, described in the individual chapters, are also represented. Overall, I would say we are in pretty close agreement about what great teachers do.

The second reason is that each detailed vignette, based on an observation of one lesson and discussions with the teacher, their colleagues and pupils, brings these characteristics to life in a way no general framework can. We are left with a much richer picture of not just what these teachers do, but why: the choices and adaptations they make and the principles that guide them. In short, we need both: a generic, research-grounded framework, and specific, detail-rich descriptions of real examples.

So, does a single, numerical value capture everything that is worth knowing about great teaching? Of course not; no one has ever claimed it could or should. This might be an example of the perfectionist fallacy, that because something is not perfect it must be useless. Of course, most things are in-between. The key is to understand what uses and interpretations are valid.

In the assessment, measurement and psychometric tradition in which I was trained as a researcher, validity is not seen as a property of a particular score or measure. Instead, validity applies to specific uses and interpretations of that measure. Before we can judge whether it is appropriate to use assessment data (from a variety of commercial, bought-in assessments, school-made assessments, and national assessments and examinations) to estimate the impact of a teacher on pupils' learning, we need to know the purpose: what will it be used for, and what caveats are attached to its interpretation?

In the presentation that provoked John to put down a marker for truly great teaching, we were perhaps not as clear about this as we could have been. In our project, teacher value-added scores will be used for research purposes only, with fully anonymised data. We have a clear agreement with the teachers, schools and trusts who have provided the data that no consequences (good or bad) can be linked with these value-added scores. Moreover, the analysis we have done so far makes it clear that, even if people wanted to use the scores for things like selection, reward, or performance management, scores for individual teachers are mostly not really accurate enough to support those uses. Scores are probably accurate enough for us to find large-scale statistical patterns, which is what we have set up the project to do. We want to learn more, in a systematic and rigorous way, about what great teachers (i.e. those who help their students to learn more) do, know and believe and about how they became great, and how we can help all teachers to be more like them.

The teachers whose work is celebrated in the chapters of this book also contribute to the wider project. Not only do they spend their days doing the most inspiring, challenging and important job in the world, educating the next generation, but by sharing their practice with us in these pages, they illuminate the world of truly great teachers. Most of them seem to think that they are nothing special, that they just do their job and that many others do the same. While the last part of this may be true – there are many more truly great teachers who could have been featured – the first part is not: they are truly special, awe-inspiring individuals, and we all have a lot to learn from them.

Rob Coe

Preface

In order to write the teacher profiles that comprise this book, I visited each teacher's school during the autumn term of 2024 and the spring term of 2025. The schedule of visits was completely random, but what I learnt about these truly great teachers built over time. Consequently, I have ordered the profiles chronologically. They can be read one-by-one as individual narratives, or from beginning to end to give a more holistic sense of how my understanding of the professional behaviours common to these teachers grew.

Acknowledgements

In my experience, teachers are naturally modest. They usually focus upon what they *feel* they are getting wrong in the classroom, rather than what they are doing right. Consequently, persuading a teacher to feature in a book that celebrates how well they teach is difficult. Sincere thanks goes, then, to the teachers whose stories I tell here – Dave Williams, Suzy Marston, Michelle Goodger, Garry Littlewood, Chris McGrane, Tom Fraser, Louise Booth, Jack Bream, Jen Lewis, Mary Cawley and Mariam Sankar – for taking a metaphorical deep breath and agreeing to let me into their working lives, to see what they do so well. Inevitably, my words are an inadequate representation of their truly great teaching.

Over the years, Professor Rob Coe's impact upon my thinking has been immense. As the narrative of this book reveals, our challenging conversation about how best to judge teacher effectiveness at the researchED national conference in September 2024 spawned this book and its accompanying title, *This Much I Know About Truly Great Primary Teachers (and what we can learn from them)*. Without Rob, neither book would have been written. For him, then, to agree to write the books' forewords reflects huge generosity of spirit on his part. I cannot thank Rob enough.

I could not have written these books without the cooperation of the teachers' head teachers, colleagues and pupils. It has been fun zipping about the country, visiting such a range of diverse schools in such a short time. I felt welcome everywhere I've been, for which I am very grateful and my conversations with the pupils will, especially, stay with me for a long time.

It is good to be back at Crown House again, a decade after my first book with them. I am keen to thank publicly David Bowman and his colleagues for having faith in me and accepting my pitch for this project. His team have worked tirelessly with me to prepare these books for publication, particularly Beverley Randell.

Finally, I must thank my wife Louise for tolerating all those evenings I was unavoidably absent, either holed up in a hotel in a far-flung corner of these Isles, or next door in my office tapping away on my laptop.

Contents

Foreword by Professor Rob Coe i
Preface ix
Acknowledgements xi

Introduction 1
A Truly Great English Teacher: Dave Williams 9
A Truly Great Drama Teacher: Suzy Marston 21
A Truly Great Mathematics Teacher: Michelle Goodger 45
A Truly Great Food Technology Teacher: Garry Littlewood 67
A Truly Great Mathematics Teacher: Chris McGrane 93
A Truly Great English Teacher: Tom Fraser 129
A Truly Great History Teacher: Louise Booth 153
A Truly Great English/History/Media/EPQ Teacher:
Jack Bream 183
A Truly Great Science Teacher: Jen Lewis 205
A Truly Great Special School Teacher: Mary Cawley 227
A Truly Great Science Teacher: Mariam Sankar 257
What Might We Learn from these Truly Great Teachers? 281

Select Bibliography 303

'This job of teaching is so hard that one lifetime isn't enough to master it.'

Dylan Wiliam[1]

---

1 Speaking at The Schools Network (then known as the SSAT) National Conference 2010.

Introduction

The genesis of this book, and its accompanying title (*This Much I Know About Truly Great Primary Teachers*), is rooted in a conversation with Professor Rob Coe. At the national researchED conference in September 2024; I had listened to Rob and his colleague, Dr Raj Chande, talk about their quest to establish a single value-added progress score for a teacher's students to determine that teacher's effectiveness in the classroom.

What Rob and Raj want to do is find a reliable, easily accessible metric to assess teacher quality. In 2014 I went to Washington DC with Rob and several others, including luminaries like Professor Lee Elliot Major, to launch the Sutton Trust's publication, *What Makes Great Teaching?*, in which Rob et al. defined 'effective teaching as that which leads to improved student achievement using outcomes that matter to their future success'.[1] It's logical, in the light of that sensible definition, to choose one student value-added progress score if you are searching for a single metric.

I first met Rob over a decade ago when Alex Quigley, Stuart Kime and I ran a project for the Education Endowment Foundation.[2] We spent several afternoons in my office discussing how to set up the project. Rob made my head hurt. He genuinely transformed my professional outlook. He just kept asking the question, 'How do you know?' And most times, I couldn't answer him.

When we were chatting about his single value-added progress score project, I said to Rob that I thought there were other things they might do to determine how to measure teacher quality, rather than pursue a

---

1 R. Coe, C. Aloisi, S. Higgins and L. Elliot Major, *What Makes Great Teaching? Review of the Underpinning Research* (London: Sutton Trust, 2014). Available at: https://www.suttontrust.com/wp-content/uploads/2014/10/What-Makes-Great-Teaching-REPORT.pdf.
2 See: https://educationendowmentfoundation.org.uk/projects-and-evaluation/projects/the-rise-project-evidence-informed-school-improvement.

single, numeric pupil progress data point. Rob conceded that I *might* have a point, but then he asked me, 'Well, what should we be doing?'

I said that I would think about it. And I have. A lot.

My counter to Rob and Raj's argument is that being a truly great teacher goes way beyond value-added scores. The characteristics of truly great teachers will, in my experience, result in their pupils making great academic progress. But the impact this teacher can make upon their students' lives is surely measured in myriad ways, beyond the single metric Rob and Raj want to establish.

As you may already have realised, dear reader, the single metric Rob and Raj are pursuing sticks in my craw. Sammy Wright's remarkable book, *Exam Nation*, asks, amongst many things, how our education system became so obsessed with the single output measure of pupils' academic progress.[3] Don't get me wrong, examination success gives young people a choice about how they live their lives; that said, without wanting to provoke cries of 'the soft bigotry of low expectations', surely there are other measures of success which matter just as much, but in different ways. If we pursue a single value-added measure as the *only* outcome of education that *really* matters, then we have, perhaps, missed the point. As Bernard Andrews wrote in his provocative essay, 'How "efficiency" derailed education', 'if school encourages and enables students to be brave, kind, wise and so on, and if it does so with prudence, then it is time and money well spent.'[4]

If Rob and Raj did one thing, they got me thinking … about all the colleagues I worked with over 33 years, and about the hundreds of teachers I have had the privilege of watching teach as a peripatetic consultant since stepping down from headship. In answer to Rob's question, 'Well, what should we be doing?' I have concluded that we should try to ascertain what it is that truly great teachers do that makes

---

3   S. Wright, *Exam Nation: Why Our Obsession with Grades Fails Everyone – and a Better Way to Think About School* (London: Vintage Publishing, 2024).

4   B. Andrews, How 'efficiency' derailed education, *TES* (25 February 2025). Available at: https://www.tes.com/magazine/teaching-learning/general/how-efficiency-derailed-education.

them truly great. Consequently, I identified 19 teachers – eight primary and ten secondary colleagues, and a special school colleague – who I think could be described as truly great teachers and constructed a profile for each one of them. In the following pages you will find profiles of the ten secondary teachers. The primary teachers' profiles can be found in the sister book, *This Much I Know About Truly Great Primary Teachers (and what we can learn from them)*. I have included our special school colleague in both books, as the learning from her profile is educative irrespective of phase, making it eleven teacher profiles in all in *Truly Great Secondary Teachers*.

When it comes to pupils' attainment and progress, I too want pupils in the classes of truly great teachers to make brilliant progress and attain amazing examination grades. But any data on pupils' progress needs triangulating with other evidence. Consequently, to assure you that they are truly great, each teacher profile contains the following elements:

- A conversation with their head teacher/principal (if possible)
- Lesson observation reflections
- Interviews with pupils
- An interview with me
- Testimonials from colleagues, pupils and parents
- A summary of the traits that make them exceptional
- Pupil progress and attainment data

Having been involved in education, in one guise or another, for 54 of my 60 years on earth, I knew I couldn't include all the tremendous teachers I've known in that time. I would have featured more, but even eleven is probably too many. So, my sincere apologies to all those truly great teachers I could have included, but didn't because there just weren't enough pages to go round.

It wasn't so hard finding eleven truly great teachers – there are thousands of them in our country's classrooms. The challenge was to persuade them to let me include them in the book. Truly great teachers are a modest lot. They took some convincing to take part. And when a school leader asked me what I meant by a 'truly great teacher', I replied: *Nothing scientific . . . a teacher who you think is truly great, who really knows their stuff, who teaches great lessons, day-in, day-out, whose pupils get great outcomes and who is just consistently great in every sense.* Consequently, the teachers featured in this book are not intended to be representative of anything. They are merely a small group of teachers I happen to know or who have been recommended to me by people I know and trust. In the words of Sir David Carter, they teach 'consistently good lessons that are well planned and progress sequentially from the previous lesson.'[5] And that's it.

In the final chapter of this book, I identify the professional behaviours common to the teachers I have featured. I contextualise my conclusions within research findings from Barak Rosenshine.[6]

Now, I am acutely aware of the problem with labelling anyone a *truly great teacher*. No teacher is flawless. *Any* teacher can teach poorly, simply because the essential raw materials of a lesson are flesh and blood, not wood and steel. In every lesson there are literally hundreds of variables, each one of which can make any *teacher* look anything but truly great. As Chris Husbands so elegantly argues, 'it's teaching, not teachers, which matters.'[7]

That said, if I had focused upon *teaching* rather than *teachers* in the book's title, it would have not represented the content of the book, nor what motivated me to write it. The book is about *teachers*, and how those teachers teach in a way that means their students learn. If the book was entitled, 'This Much I Know About Truly Great Secondary *Teaching*', it would have suggested that it's about me and what I might

---

5 In a private conversation with the author.
6 B. Rosenshine, *Teaching Behaviours and Student Achievement*, no. 1 (IEA studies) (Slough: National Foundation for Educational Research, 1 November 1971).
7 C. Husbands, Great teachers or great teaching? Why McKinsey got it wrong, *IOE blog* (10 October 2013). Available at: https://blogs.ucl.ac.uk/ioe/2013/10/10/great-teachers-or-great-teaching-why-mckinsey-got-it-wrong/.

think about secondary teaching, when the book is about truly great secondary *teachers* and, crucially, *what we can learn from them*.

Beyond that important semantic nuance, I wanted to stress the *humanity* of the teaching and learning process. Focusing upon the teachers and what they actually do in the classroom in detail, underlined how teaching and learning is such a messy, joyful, human process. And I wanted, ultimately, to celebrate some of the best teachers I know, as I near the end of my professional career and hand the baton on to the truly great colleagues featured here.

I am both delighted and hugely grateful that Professor Rob Coe agreed to write the foreword to this book. He provides a brilliant, forensic counterpoint to my qualitative approach. It may be that any teacher whose pupils make extraordinary progress, only make that progress because that teacher exhibits the professional behaviours shared by the eleven truly great teachers featured here. The behaviours and the progress data are, perhaps, just two sides of the same coin.

The conversations that form the heart of this book have been genuinely inspiring. Gadamer said that, 'No one knows in advance what will "come out" of a conversation … a conversation has a spirit of its own, and the language in which it is conducted has a truth of its own so that it allows something to "emerge" which henceforth exists.'[8] We live in a world of binary intransigence. So, in the spirit of collaboration, I hope that the conversations you'll find in the following pages spark limitless discussions in schools across the country, and from those discussions clarity and truth emerge as we all work to provide our young people with the richest classroom experiences imaginable.

Of the eleven teachers, one is no longer practising his craft in the classroom. He is my own favourite teacher, Dave Williams.

---

8 H. Gadamer, translated by J. Weinsheimer and D. Marshall, *Truth and Method* (New York: The Crossroad Publishing Corporation, 1991).

After I was chucked out of school during my first term of A levels, I spent two fruitless years in pursuit of a career in golf. When that project failed, I returned to school. First time round, I'd made a science-centric choice of A levels. On my return, I chose mathematics, because I could do maths, economics because you didn't need the O level (the precursor to the GCSE) and, scratching around in some desperation for a third, chose English literature.

But Marion Greene and Dave Williams taught me how to read texts closely and how to write about texts critically. Without them, I wouldn't have studied English at university. Without them, I wouldn't have taught.

My memory recalls that Dave was firm, fair and fierce. He knew his stuff. He never once wandered round the room. We never did group work, or presentations. He explained every page of *The Return of the Native* and *Mill on the Floss*, every line of *The General Prologue* and *The Wife of Bath's Tale*, every nuance of Shakespeare's dense comedy *Love Labour's Lost*, and we dutifully made notes in our copies of the text, which still sit on my bookshelf.

Dave marked every essay in detail, gave us fabulous, witty feedback and never once failed to return them within the week. I still have those essays in my loft. You did the work because you wanted to reciprocate his commitment and, frankly, if you didn't, the consequences were dire. You have the right to be (mock) angry if your students aren't doing the work because you genuinely care about them doing the work. We cared because Dave cared.

And Dave was the funniest teacher I was ever taught by, bar none. We laughed a lot. I am still in frequent contact with him some 43 years since he began teaching me, and if I want 30 minutes of conversation that is astrologically predestined to make me chuckle non-stop, I'll give him a ring. Being taught by Dave Williams was both a joy and a challenge.

It was Dave who had the most influence upon my teaching style. Everything about the way he taught spoke to me. When I began teaching, after a less than educative PGCE, I mimicked much of Dave's pedagogic approach. It makes sense, then, to begin this book with an interview with David Eric Williams, who taught me over 40 years ago, and remains my very own truly great teacher . . .

A Truly Great English Teacher: Dave Williams

Dave Williams taught English at Uckfield Community College from 1979 until he retired in 2016. He taught me A level English literature from 1982 to 1984.

IRL[1]: Dave Williams

John Tomsett (JT): Did you teach anywhere else before you began at Uckfield?

Dave Williams (DW): No. I did my English degree at Cardiff, and then my one-year postgraduate training at Cheltenham. I left my application too late to do teacher training at Cardiff, so I

---

1 IRL = In Real Life

went to Cheltenham for the racing! I did a teaching postgraduate course because my girlfriend at the time decided she wanted to teach. I wanted a career in journalism. I applied for the Centre for Journalism Studies in Cardiff and got put on the reserve list. I spoke to some people who said I'd be better off just going straight to a newspaper. But I wasn't ready to go into the world of work, so did the postgrad.

I had a couple of teaching practices; the first was at Churchdown School, which was good preparation for Uckfield because it was similar – rural, comprehensive, similar catchment, similar size, similar location. The other teaching practice was a bit of a waste of time – Denmark Road High School for Girls, which was in the middle of Gloucester, and a proper old school. There was only one other bloke on the premises, and that was the caretaker. The pupils were brilliantly behaved. It was just a waste of a teaching practice. There was a little bar in the staff room with a couple of optics. If you wanted a drink, you helped yourself, any time of day, and just put the money in a bowl.

JT: **Amazing. I remember when I did my training at Lewes Priory in 1987, they had a full-sized snooker table in the staff room. So, the first school you taught at was very similar to Uckfield?**

DW: Yeah. Churchdown Comprehensive. It was midway between Cheltenham and Gloucester. I can't remember an awful lot about it … on one occasion, a fight broke out in one of my classes, and I just didn't know how to deal with it. I think I eventually went in and got between them. That made a bit of an impact on me. It was something that encouraged me to be reasonably firm about behaviour in my classroom. I had six or seven weeks there, which was a good grounding. And while I say the girls' grammar school was a waste of time, what it *did* do was cement further my love of teaching English literature. There was a lot of teaching proper, old-school, English literature there. The students just wrote everything down and did everything you wanted, and I enjoyed that.

When I was appointed at Uckfield in May 1979, I remember during the interview the head teacher asking me, 'How would you plan to teach a class of mixed ability, 3rd years (Year 9 in today's money)?' I was so *green*, Tommo! I knew nothing. I replied, 'Give me the job, and I'll show you in 6 weeks.' It was an answer born of desperation and cluelessness, and he thought it was a really smart response! Oh, dear …

JT: **I was in Year 10 when you joined there. I first met you in the English corridor. My mate Brophy was banging the lockers outside your room, and you came out and accused him of being John Bonham (Led Zeppelin's drummer), and we were quite impressed by your musical knowledge. You really bollocked us and sent us out into the rain.**

DW: Down with the kids! Marilyn Kellett, my career-long head of department, encouraged the firmness in me. When she died last autumn, a few of us did pieces for the local radio in her memory. I said that she saw something in me that I thought was never actually there, but fair play, she persevered with me. I was very young. I was 22 and, you know, didn't have much idea. She encouraged me to have this quite fierce persona, which I was only too happy to go along with.

Pat Wager, the head of PE, helped me a bit because he spread some rumour that I was an ex-Wrexham footballer called Dougie Williams. So, a lot of the ne'er-do-well 5th years (Year 11s) gave me instant respect for that. I don't know whether Pat did it to help me or whether it was a bit of a laugh. I'd been given the Year 12 O level resit class. So those kids would have been nearly 17 when I was teaching them, and I was just 22. I felt more affinity with the students, to be honest, than I did the staff. Because a lot of the staff seemed bloody ancient to me! And the staff room! We're talking about 1979. When you opened the door into the staff room, this huge cloud of cigarette smoke just rolled out! They called it 'The Smokers' Corner'. It's like saying you're only allowed to pee in one end of the swimming pool! 'It's okay. They only smoke *over there* …'

JT: I remember never wanting to go to the staff room to ask for a teacher. Never. It was terrifying. You knocked on the door and absolutely crapped yourself.

DW: The default position for any member of staff answering the door would be *put-upon exasperation*: 'Yes? *What?*'

JT: Exactly. So, when did you start feeling it was it was working in the classroom? When did you begin to feel more secure in the job?

DW: Good question. Those days, the bad days where you're driving home and you're thinking, 'Yeah, I'm not good at this.' You know? 'Perhaps I wasn't prepared enough. Perhaps I can't control the kids.' But you have those days all the way through your career. Keeps you honest, and I think as long as you've got that, that self-criticism and self-awareness and realisation that if it hasn't gone well, whose fault is it? 'Well yeah, it's *my* fault', you'll be OK.

I can remember Marilyn telling me early on, 'Get them writing, get the students with their heads down, just writing. And walk around the classroom.' That was it. I sort of grew into that. Once you've got the control, it gets easier. It's important. It's the analogy about riding a horse. Have the reins absolutely tight. The horse can't move its head and then gradually, just imperceptibly, loosen the reins and, in the end, you don't need the reins at all.

It's also about relationships. I remember, early on in my career, putting the word 'w-h-o-l-e' on the board as an example of a homonym. I pronounced it 'hoole', which you do in North Wales and some kid said, 'What's that word, sir? Say it again?' I realised they were having a pop at how I speak! I remember going in early one morning and writing on the chalkboard all the lyrics to 'Career Opportunities' by The Clash, because it tied in with something I was teaching. Little bits and pieces like that helped. So, just like me referencing the drummer with Brophy, keying into the students' culture, and always being aware of the kinds of things that would help me build those relationships. Like politicians, Sir Keir with his supporting Arsenal. It's always good to be *of the people*, isn't it? Always good to know that stuff.

JT: **It's so important. I used to remove all the naughty Year 10 lads from all the English classes, make them into a single class for myself, and teach them English GCSE. When Man United lost the league to City in the final kick of the season in 2012, I had them first thing Monday in the library. When I went in, they'd all made the effort to get there early and were stood in a line with the newspapers wide open with the backs of the newspapers facing me. It was just a wall of City light blue. It was absolutely brilliant! They completely stitched me up, and they loved it. They're working-class kids and if they think you're on their side, they'll do anything for you.**

DW: It sounds very cheesy and very corny, but it's about mutual respect. Even when I was being fierce with youngsters, it was all part of the drama, the role play. You know, one of my rules was always to return work properly marked, quickly. If I'm saying, you've got a week in which to do it, then I've got a week in which to return it. Later on in my career, a class might ask, 'Have you marked our stuff, sir?' And I'd say, 'I haven't quite, and I should have done by now. If it's not ready for the next lesson, I'll give each of you a pound.' I never had to do it because I'd set the alarm for quarter past 2 in the morning and do it.

JT: **Obviously.**

DW: Obviously.

JT: So, when you had a text to teach, what was your approach? What was your thinking about how to teach something like *Macbeth*?

DW: *Henry IV part 1* was my text. I started teaching that in my first year, in 1979, and it must have been on the syllabus for a good many years because I almost knew it off by heart. To begin with, I would familiarise myself with the exam paper and make sure I knew where we were heading from that standpoint.

So, with things like Shakespeare the language would be intimidating. They'd try to read it aloud and make a dog's dinner of it, and I'd say, 'Right, so this is difficult, but I know all this. I'm the font of all wisdom here. I know it inside out …'

JT: That resonates! It's 42 years since you taught me … Every. Single. Page. Of. *Mill. On. The. Floss* … [*laughing*].

DW: So, I would get to grips with the text. Know every word. I don't think, in the early years, I read many critical essays about the texts. As A level became more embedded in my teaching timetable I read more around the text.

I always try and get them interested, try and find things of historical interest or, as you know, bits of humour. I mean, even if you teach flipping *King Lear*, you can find plenty of humour … 'What *was* he thinking?' [*several seconds of unfettered laughter*]. 'It's obvious. He deserved all he got!' [*more laughter*]. With Shakespeare, it's about how damned cool Shakers was. He knew how we work. By the time we had studied the play, the students realised that he's writing about ordinary people. It's just the language is different. That's the thing … his understanding of people. That's the big selling point for Shakespeare, and all the other writers, I guess.

JT: Did you see lots of change across your career? If you look at that list of texts that you taught me – Chaucer, Hardy, George Eliot, Shakespeare – they're extraordinary in terms of the literary canon compared to what they teach now at A level. *The Kite Runner*'s fine, but it's not a patch on *The Return of the Native*, I don't think.

DW: By and large, with GCSE and certainly at A level, I tended to teach texts from the literary canon, traditional texts. In my very last year, they gave me a new GCSE Year 10 class, so I had a whole new syllabus to learn there, and they gave me Year 12 as well, which was, I think, a new syllabus and new texts. I suppose they knew I'd get stuck in. I had to prepare a lot. I said to Mandy (Dave's wife) this morning, 'Tommo's going to interview me. I hope he's not going be disappointed' …

JT: Not at all.

… because I was never someone who read manuals on how to teach. Sometimes you would go to a course, or somebody would come into the school and tell you stuff, and sometimes you'd think it's a bit interesting. But, I don't know … it was never arrogance. I just felt, 'I know what I'm doing. It seems to work'. The results were always good. Then there's the honesty of working hard and always making sure you're properly prepared and, therefore, the students are properly prepared. I think my mantra right the way through, especially with A level, was: 'Any answer that is rooted in the text will always be a good answer.' Make sure you have banks of quotations. That was the style. It didn't change in 40 odd years, and, thankfully, the results didn't change. They were always good.

JT: Summarising then, you worked really hard, you knew the texts inside out, you had great control of the classroom, you had enough time to have some fun, you commanded respect from the students, you respected them and you treated them fairly. And over time, not much changed because that formula worked.

DW: Yeah, and *high expectations* [with emphasis] both of myself and the students. In every sense. Like with the marking. I always gave personalised feedback. No short cuts. Even when we all had to do PIN (praise, improvements, next) – marking at Uckfield, I'd do that, but you'd always get the individualised comment from me. I always used their initials or their full name, which was something I picked up from my A level English teacher. He was an Oxford graduate, A. T. Jones. He looked like the bulldog in *Tom and Jerry*; heavy jowls. He was a lovely guy. He would break off in the middle of the double lesson and say, 'I'm just off to the staff room for a smoke. You can amuse yourselves.' He called everybody by their full name. I was always David Eric Williams. Like him, I always wore very formal clothes – suit and jacket – because I was so young, I had to create an older persona for myself.

Like I say, I would blame myself if the students didn't understand what I'd taught them, but if I *knew* I'd taught something well, and the class hadn't done terribly well as a whole because they hadn't made the effort, I'd call them out on it. I'd say, 'Look. I've done my bit here. I know what I'm doing. You do your bit.' I would tell them how good I was and how hard I worked, so I expected the same of them.

JT: **You were always the expert in the room, Willie. Unashamedly, the expert in the room.**

DW: But I was always very encouraging if a youngster, whatever age, made a good observation in their homework or in class. I'd say, 'Flipping heck, I would never have thought of that!' That kind of honesty or just that openness is key.

JT: **You're giving the students that faith in you.**

DW: Beginning of every new term in September, any new class, my line was always, 'In this room, if you do what I tell you, you will do all right. You will be fine. I will make you better at English. I will get you through.' Perhaps a bit of kidology, but it really worked because you're older and they're younger. It's a performance. You play the role.

JT: So, tell me about one or two things you remember, any great moments.

DW: What? A great lesson or a great moment in my career? I don't think I can remember great lessons. I can remember great classes, relationships. Not so much that was down to me, but maybe the mix of youngsters, the dynamic of the youngsters in the class. Sometimes they never gel, but most times they would. I'm not just talking about the bright classes. Towards the end of my career, I would give myself a few challenging classes, which were very rewarding. Mainly lads from the lower set English groups. It's more the atmosphere and the class dynamics that I remember. There was one GCSE class – I think a lot of them stayed on and did English literature A level – who were easy to teach. The standards they reached were fantastic. There were some individual students in maybe my last 5 or 6 years, at A level, where the quality of what they were writing was remarkable, and sometimes I'd think, 'You've done a bit of this, mate. You've helped them write this.' I didn't hide the praise for them. I would write in the comments, 'This is as fine a sixth form essay as I think I've ever encountered.'

I sometimes bump into the kids. You must get it too because you still live in the town where you taught. I went down the pub maybe 3 or 4 weeks ago. There were a couple of lads there, in their forties, rough and ready types, builders, and they spoke very affectionately of me and Brown (our mutual friend, Lloyd Brown) and their time in our lessons. I just love the fact that you can go into the pub and there're kids who are in their late fifties who say, 'Hello, sir.' Always, always about relationships. But, that would've been in whatever job I'd have done. It's about how you interact with other people, isn't it? Always.

JT: Always. That presence in the community is important. I mean, you taught me, my brother, my sister, and my nieces, and my brother-in-law. Whole generations.

DW: Blimey … I'll tell you something just before you come to the end. Jerry Gunn (Dave's colleague and my old PE teacher) popped in a couple of nights ago. His son Raff is on the senior team in his school, and he's all caught up with the kind of slogany stuff, all the jargon. I said to Gunners, when I look back on the teaching now, what I remember is just the teaching and the relationships with the students and the colleagues. All those thousands and thousands of hours in meetings and I don't remember any of it. My career is distilled down to what it really was, the classes and the relationships.

And Tommo, I'd like to think that you as a head, you valued the staff and you would clear away a lot of the pretence. I never subscribed to the guff. It was never that I didn't think people's opinion mattered. It was just that what worked for me seemed to work for me, and I could have presented that was being a *thing*, but it was just what I did.

JT: **You could've said that you had chosen a warm/strict approach – that's a phrase currently in the edu-ether – but you didn't need to label it. You were really strict, but you had some fun. It's common sense. It's not hard.**

DW: Common sense is a tricky one. Because one's opinion of what it is, might not be another's. It's not common. When it comes to teaching, you should get established, create your platform, and then it's natural … just be yourself.

JT: **There's a great line by Gandhi that says that happiness is when what you say, what you do, and what you think are completely aligned. I used to say, 'Look. I'm going to spend 12 hours in this building today. I'm not going to be anybody else but me. Right?' I always say to** deputies when they're applying for headship, 'Don't pretend to be someone else on interview because once you're the head, you've got to be the persona they've selected, not yourself, all the time. Don't pretend to be anything else. And if you don't get the job, it wasn't the right fit for you.' For 33 years, including 18 as a head, I was a round peg in a round hole. Just loved it. I went to work as though it wasn't work and had a lot of fun.

DW: In my last year or so of teaching, I was getting a bit older, getting a bit tired. I was director of sixth form. I never stinted. Ever. I don't think a lot of colleagues realise – even colleagues within the department – how long it takes if you mark properly. Think of how many years of my life I have spent marking. I don't begrudge it, but it's just quite a lot. So, I think the enjoyment element of my work was down to about 8 out of 10 in the last year. It got *as low* as 8 out of 10. The rest of it was 10. That's pretty good, isn't it?

You wouldn't remember a lady called Chris, the sixth form administration assistant? She had two sons, much younger than you. This moment would have been 15 years ago. I don't know what was on my mind . . . something. So, I would've been in my early fifties, and we were having a bit of a chat, and I said to her, 'Is it a life well lived, Chris?' I had the utmost respect for her. She was a bright woman who just hadn't bothered with her career after having the children. She replied, 'What do you mean?' I said, 'Well, I've been in this school all my working life. I don't know anything else. Should I not have gone to a different school? Should I not have tried something else?' She was a wise woman and she said to me, 'Well, have you enjoyed it? Are you still enjoying it?' I said, 'God, yeah!' So, she replied, 'Well, there's your answer.' Simple as that. Sometimes it's nice for somebody to state the bleeding obvious to you, isn't it?

JT: It's that moment when you realise all that yearning for something else is pointless. There isn't something else. It is what we have. 'Days are where we live', as Larkin said.

DW: When Chris retired, she got me a little book, *Don't Sweat the Small Stuff*.[2] For somebody like me – I'm on the spectrum, Tommo … the way I used to study those texts and go through them meticulously. Well, sometimes I would get a little bit overwrought about something pretty inconsequential, and here is my sixth form administration assistant putting me right. She was so lovely. I'd go in and chat to her about a bit of work, and then somehow, I'd start talking about this, that, and the other, and probably attempt a bit of humour. She'd sit there, and she'd look at me, and she'd have a little smile on her face, and she'd wait until I finished, and then she'd say, 'Off you go.'

It's going back to that thing we said right at the start. You can get a bad day any time in your career. It might just be a bad lesson in that day. Bloody hell! It would bring me low. Sometimes it's necessary to have somebody else to give you that little bit of perspective. In the end, you're answerable to your own conscience, which means that, hopefully, you'll stay honest.

JT: **That's a great way to end. Thanks Dave, for everything.**

---

2 R. Carlson, *Don't Sweat the Small Stuff and It's All Small Stuff: Simple Ways to Keep the Little Things from Taking Over Your Life* (London: Hachette Books, 2002).

A Truly Great Drama Teacher: Suzy Marston

Suzanne (Suzy) Marston is Director of Drama at Chesterton Community College, Cambridge, an 11–18 academy in the Eastern Learning Alliance.

The school leadership's view

I am sitting in the principal's office at Chesterton Community College, listening to Rolf Purvis tell me what I am going to find when I spend a few hours with Suzy Marston, drama teacher. 'Well, John, what you'll see today will be a *tour de force*. Suzy is a teacher with conviction. She always follows up. She cares. She is bothered. She never accepts nonsense. Teaching is in her blood. She has dedicated her life to teaching. I know it's a cliché, but she genuinely changes lives.' Rolf is sharp, urbane, and he has wisdom. He begins to chuckle. 'Whenever I go to observe her, I don't take any notes. I just watch and learn.' He tells me that everything Suzy does is planned to perfection, and that her preparation for my visit will have been meticulous.

Suzy was recommended to me by Lucy Scott, CEO of the Eastern Learning Alliance, based in Cambridge, who is sitting to my right, listening to Rolf. Lucy was a tremendous deputy head teacher when I worked with her in Yorkshire, before she rose rapidly to her current position. I trust Lucy; if she thought someone might be a truly great teacher, then I was pretty sure she'd be right.

Rolf continues: 'When you go to one of Suzy's lessons, you're going to *an event*! There is always seriousness. She is brilliant at making pupils feel comfortable. She has a fierce warmth. She is on a par with them. She treads that difficult line in terms of relationships with the students. She is, of course, the teacher, but she gives so much of herself to the students when she's teaching. She has a child-like love of the subject. And what she does is unteachable. It's beyond technical …'

'And she challenges the students', says Lucy. 'They are in the pit, grappling to get out. They can grasp stuff with their fingertips, haul themselves up and end up doing things beyond what they themselves think they can do.' Lucy talks from experience – her son is in Year 12 and has been taught by Suzy since he was in Year 7.

Rolf interjects, 'She ignores the targets we set for students – I know she does. She treats them as unique individuals, not numbers. The thing is, it's hard to argue against when you look at her drama students' value-added scores.'

Teaching Year 11

We talk for far longer than I'd planned. After a truncated tour of the school, Rolf hands me over to Nicola von Schreiber who is to be my guide. She's a friend of Suzy's and Chesterton's retired examinations officer; Rolf was correct – the plan for the day is precise and detailed. The performing arts block is brightly decorated. It proclaims the strength of its presence within the college, not just physically, but also philosophically. Where many secondary schools have sidelined the arts, Chesterton celebrates them.

We walk straight into Suzy teaching. She has identified a chair for me to sit at. Despite her diminutive physique, she is one of those teachers whose classroom presence inhabits the whole space. It is hard to take your eyes off her as she runs the room.

A group of Year 11 students are reading a *Guardian* newspaper article on poverty in the UK out loud, which has been projected onto the screen. Their expert prosody is impressive. They *feel* the desperation of the impoverished. Suzy doesn't need to ask them to take turns. They follow each other reading aloud without direction. That is a striking feature of Suzy's lessons – the students are incredibly well-trained. There is automaticity and efficiency to the way they operate. They don't waste a minute, a second, of the time they have with Suzy.

Seamlessly, Suzy sets up a role play. The students become a pack of news-hungry journalists harassing one of their peers who plays artist Gillian Wearing, whose photograph 'I'm Desperate' is their stimulus in devising. Suzy gives the journos old phones and recording gear to push into the face of the interviewee. Suzy is a journo too, acting with incredible zest. She stops every so often and helps the students refine what they are doing. Her questioning is precise and insistent. The pressure works – no one could possibly refuse to respond. The meta-thinking the students are doing while they are acting is truly impressive. And right in the centre of the throng of journalists is Suzy.

Importantly, Suzy doesn't allow the improvisation to go on too long – a minute, tops – before she stops and helps the students to analyse their performances. She questions, but she gives nothing away. She uses subject terminology and insists the students rehearse the words chorally. When she suggests a refinement to their acting, she is permission-based – 'Do you think we could do that?' The level of mutual respect between teacher and students is tangible.

The students are entirely absorbed in the process of learning. As they break out of their roles, Suzy questions the accessibility of the arts to the poorest in society. Chesterton Community College backs onto one of the most deprived council estates in Europe. But this is Cambridge, and the school has its share of students from relatively wealthy, middle-class, educated backgrounds. Suzy presses them. She asks them a question: 'A ticket to a West End show is the same as a weekly Universal Credit payment. Does it matter to you that art is just for the privileged few?' They pace the room thinking, until Suzy uses whatever is at her disposal to make a drum-beat and asks one of them for a response. The students respond sensitively. They are eloquent. They're under pressure. Teacher expectations are beyond high; they feel non-negotiable. Here is Rolf's 'fierce warmth' made real.

I look around the room. There is the random stuff you find in all thriving drama studios – a piano, a ceramic owl, a red leather settee, an egg box, a tennis ball, royal blue wooden seats, a mortar board, the word 'Joy' embossed on the lid of a biscuit tin. Behind her desk there's a sign with the imperative, 'Dare, always, dare'.

Suzy moves the students on. She cites four images from Ted Hughes' 'Tales from Ovid', an alternative stimulus for devising. Every time she declares the image, the students have to use their bodies to express a response.

1   His beauty had flowered
2   Like a cat in winter at a fire
3   Snatch their last words

4   With crackling torches

There is complete commitment to the activity. She asks one of the students to perform her response for the rest of the class and unpicks why she is so impressive: 'Look at her eyes. They move with the rest of her body. Her whole soul is invested in that.' When she said that last line, Suzy may as well have been talking about herself and her teaching.

To finish the session, she brings the students back to the work on poverty and combines the two improvisations. To gnarly background music, Suzy shouts a number and the students read current statistics about poverty to the audience from four makeshift placards – *There are 22% of people in the UK living in poverty in 2024* – which they then hold up, Brecht-style, one-by-one. At the same time the students assume their bodily poses to the Hughes images. Whilst it feels difficult to imagine written down, the effect of the two improvisations combined is startlingly impressive. It's intense, and the students' engagement is total. I write in my notes, 'Blimey, these kids are good!'

What the students think

Slightly behind schedule, Nicola leads me to a meeting room, populated by 14 students, ranging from Years 7 to 12 – a diverse group, including students with Free School Meals, SEND, EAL and an individual with a low reading age next to one with a string of grade 9s at GCSE. I have a list of names and the students have name tags. I explain that I am writing a book exploring whether a teacher can be judged on a single metric of a value-added score, or whether there is more to a teacher than the data. I don't have long. In good Think-Pair-Share style, I give them a couple of minutes to talk amongst themselves about what makes Ms Marston such a truly great teacher.

I begin with Years 7 and 8. The three youngsters talk about the energy Suzy brings into the room. They can't imagine the amount of planning she must do to produce such high-quality lessons. She gives individual feedback. One of them says that, 'Miss works 1:1 with you, but she also has a passion for all of us to improve. She brings everyone into the lesson.'

The Year 9s continue, 'She's so passionate about drama. She seems to enjoy herself. She pushes me. She sets high standards.' We explore the high standards theme. They are eloquent and insightful. 'Because she has high expectations of us, we have high expectations of ourselves', says one.

'It's true', says another. 'We learn our lines because she expects us to. We have a fear of her being disappointed. It motivates us.'

The Year 10 students built upon Suzy's work ethic. 'It's amazing that she adapts scripts according to who she has in the class. She spends weeks adapting scripts. Like *1984*, she tailors it for each of us in the class.'

This attention to the individual culminates in a comment from one of the older students. 'She's truly extraordinary. She knows each student. My mum came home from parents' evening and she said that Ms Marston knows me as a person, she knows my acting style, how my brain approaches each task. I think each pupil is a unique planet and Ms Marston's teaching allows us to express who we are.' What came through so strongly is that the students feel acknowledged, they feel *seen*.

Then one of the GCSE students says, 'Even if you muck up and forget a whole paragraph of your script she will be your loudest supporter in the audience.' They began laughing. So, for all the challenge and high expectations, the students feel utterly supported. They know they can fail and learn in a psychologically safe space.

Choosing GCSEs is an inexact science. Some choose a subject because they love the subject, some because it is the least-worse option and some because of the teacher. 'I chose drama as a GCSE because of the teacher not the subject.' I quickly ascertain that Suzy is the only drama GCSE teacher. The student goes on to say, 'I trust Miss with my full soul. It's futile not to trust her.' Nods of agreement across the room.

They have grown in confidence. I let the conversation loose, 'The great thing is, we get brilliant exam results. She teaches us exam technique. She shows us how to apply what we have learnt to answering exam papers. It's incredible.'

'But it's not just the grades at GCSE. It's the professional approach. We feel like actors. My self-belief and confidence have grown. She pushes you past all limits. I'm capable of doing stuff I didn't know I could do myself. She teaches us true lessons about life, and one of those is that hard work pays off.'

'It's true. There is such a professional attitude. We feel like adults. And 90% of the course is learning to fail. "Do it again", she says. And we do until we get it right. Like paid professional actors.'

'And those emails!' Laughter and headshaking erupt in equal measure. 'You know what you're doing at every step. My mum loves finding out what I am up to.'

'We know in complete detail what we're doing this working week, every week. She must spend so much of her life working. It's insane!'

I begin to draw things to a close. The clock is ticking ever nearer 11 am. I ask the sole Year 12 student what it is that he finds extraordinary about Ms Marston. His candid reply is illuminating. 'Well, when I got here in Year 7, I was quite shy. Like really shy. I didn't say very much and when I did talk, it was quite quietly. And then I got to drama and met Suzy. She noticed how shy I was. I'm not sure I had ever shouted in my life. It wasn't my style. She invited me to stand on a box in the middle of the room. And eventually I shouted as loud as I could. Like *really* shouted. And I have been able to shout ever since. She teaches you about life and prepares you for the world.' It was one of those moments in the classroom where things pause, where everyone in the room recognises we have been party to something special.

I finish with a simple task … the one word that best describes Ms Marston as a teacher (inevitably, they use more than the single word!): apotheosis (in the sense that Ms Marston helps you become the very best version of yourself), dedicated, driving force (a belief that you *can* and therefore you *will*), astonishing, inspirational, balanced (work and fun are kept in balance), and the classroom feels a free and safe place.

It's hard to prevent the talk opening up again, such is their enthusiasm for the subject matter … 'A family is built in those classes at GCSE. No one will judge you. We all understand this is a learning process.'

I thank them, and they file out expressing their thanks for the opportunity to discuss one of their favourite subjects … Ms Marston, who *is* drama to them.

Teaching Year 10

'I have to put you on the spot. We have to build the courage to respond because we're in the world of George Orwell's *1984*, a world where you have to answer questions …' It's Year 10. They are preparing to stage the play version of Orwell's famous dystopian vision of the future and Suzy is not letting anyone relax. The pressure is on. Any single student could be posed a question at any moment. In the warm-up we're exploring the inner truth of the character, discordant Shostakovich string quartets create a menacing mood.

In a Suzy Marston lesson, things are relentless. The lesson is tight and fast-paced. The students show such discipline. They are so well trained. To an untrained eye it looks effortless. It takes an expert to understand what Suzy must have done to achieve her students' behavioural automaticity. The spadework required to establish such order in the room has paid dividends. The students' behaviour allows for great teaching and purposeful learning.

With 100% attention from the students – some of whom I have just interviewed – she explains what she hopes they will learn. She is working on five pause techniques: the gasp; the ellipsis struggle to move; the missed beat; the astounded stagger; and, finally, the unpronounceable aposiopesis. She then intends to use these as they stage the opening of the play. But first they practise each one, again and again. There is a lovely moment when she explains how to act out the 'missing the beat' silence; the sideways look to the audience that communicates both incredulity and sudden enlightenment. Suzy acts it out and says that they can use the 'F' word. She reassures them, 'It's OK. You're not saying it. Just mouthing it silently.' I imagine it's the kind of adult type of treatment the students so appreciate.

As she works with the students, building up their skills, she is totally immersed in what she is doing. Her conviction is tremendous. I notice how she celebrates high-quality performance from the pupils. It's not prizes for all in a Suzy Marston class. The students would detect such insincerity. No, she lauds the genuinely good, in a way that everyone in the room is pleased for the recipient of her praise. One student acts out the falling into silence of aposiopesis particularly convincingly. Suzy stops the class and asks the student to act it out again for her peers. 'Isn't that beautiful?' she asks, rhetorically, and the students concur, smiles all round. They practise repeatedly until Suzy is happy with the quality of what she sees.

The lesson ends with a staging of the opening scene of the play. Everyone is involved. The three walls of the room are formed by the students. The actors have learnt their lines. The performance builds and builds. Suzy makes nuanced improvements here and here. The final attempt is impressive, but falls right at the end, when one student hesitates and delivers their lines haltingly. When it would have been far easier to have ignored the fact that he hadn't learnt his lines, Suzy holds him to account. Everyone needs to know that 'good acting means homework'. They won't make that mistake again.

Suzy has the right to be challenging, even slightly scary to some who aren't used to this. Her commitment is total, and she compels the students' attitudes to mirror her own.

IRL: Suzy Marston

John Tomsett (JT): **Tell me a bit about your move from theatre into teaching.**

Suzy Marston (SM): Can I just be completely honest?

JT: **Of course.**

SM: Well, I had always resisted becoming a teacher. My parents were both teachers and they had always been very pro-teaching, which – because I was the rebellious younger sibling – made me very anti the idea of going into the classroom!

I was an actor, a working actor, and I had bouts of success, particularly touring with a company called TNT theatre based in Munich. I did three years of Shakespeare with them. I played Ophelia in *Hamlet,* Juliet in *Romeo and Juliet,* and Hermia in *A Midsummer Night's Dream.* They were year-long tours, and we literally went across the world. That was a formative experience for me.

At that time in my life, I arrogantly saw teaching as a failure, haunted by the phrase, 'those who can, do and those who can't, teach'. I still feel today that many members of the public hold this prejudice against teachers and their 'long holidays'; it's a pity.

But I came home from three years touring and I was in a commercial production of *Twelfth Night.* I hadn't made it on television, but I had made it in the theatre and I'd managed to keep myself going. I had a moment, standing in the wings, where I thought, 'There's no creativity anymore in being an actor, just quite a lot of snobbery.' I stood backstage and I just thought, 'Enough, I've fallen out of love.' Not with Shakespeare, but with the industry.

So, I had to do something. While I was figuring things out, I came back home and my old school, Impington, needed a drama teacher for the second half of the autumn term. I was asked to be an artist in residence and, essentially, teach the lessons. I remember vividly, at the end of the first day of teaching, just curling up in the drama studio and sobbing and saying, 'That was hell!' Paul, my previous director, had offered me the chance to go back on tour in the New Year. When I got home to my husband, I said, 'I'm definitely going to take that contract, and carry on with acting. Even if I'm not known in this country, I'm still earning good money abroad.' But then I had a Year 7 lesson a couple of days later and it was like a new start. Naïve as it sounds, it hadn't occurred to me before that there would be students who didn't want to do drama, as with the first day of Year 9 lessons! But with the Year 7s, there was a universal puppy-like hunger for acting and being active, and that changed things: I thought, 'Actually, I like this.'

I then became very, very attached, I suppose, to the GCSE group and immediately began directing *Blood Wedding* with them. By Christmas, directing youth theatre – and teaching through directing – was my obsession, and it felt very purposeful – vital even – compared to some aspects of being an actor.

Sandra Morton, who was the head of Impington at that time, had also been my English teacher. That's why she'd asked me to be artist in residence. She said that they'd pay for me to do this graduate training programme scheme. I was paid to teach four days a week and then attend training one day a week. It allowed me to buy a house and stuff, and I suddenly felt like I was a proper person, which pleased my parents!

Most of all, I developed a deep conscience about the work; I love the play *Skylight* by David Hare, and there's an incredible monologue in that play from Kyra, who's a social worker. She says, 'What the hell does it matter why I'm doing it? Why anyone goes out and helps? The reason is hardly of primary importance. If I didn't do it, it wouldn't get done.' It's the same with teaching drama for me: teaching young people to speak up for themselves. It *has* to be done. I feel that someone's got to do it. I don't mean I'm a saint in thinking that, I just mean that is what motivates me, that this is important work.

It was a huge change. At Oxford, Rory Kinnear was a close theatre friend. It was poignant to find myself a few years into teaching, taking a coachload of students to see his Hamlet at the National, after which he kindly spoke to them at the stage door as I smiled proudly on. Rosamund Pike was also one of my best friends back at university. She's of course a big movie star now, and, again, she took the time to talk with my students over Zoom when we returned from lockdown: I thought 'how far apart our lives have become' but also, that the shared love of theatre remains the same, stronger even. I'm not name-dropping in a showy-offy way, but more because I've realised that success can take many forms, and that a creative lifestyle is portable and scalable. Now, and for the last, I suppose, 15 years, the ambition to be a famous actor has died in me. But a different ambition has taken over, right? I suppose that ambition is directed towards creating the best possible drama department/youth-theatre experience for young people that I can. An ambition to 'pass it on' as Alan Bennett puts it.

JT: **It's a really interesting transition there. I have a mate from university, Dave Maddock, who, until very recently, used to write for the *Mirror* newspaper. He ghost-wrote Robbie Fowler's autobiography, and often he used to say to me, 'I just want to be a teacher'. I would reply, 'Dave, you'll hate it because you quite like having your picture by-line in the paper every week, but the magic moments of joy that you have in teaching are anonymous, on a wet Thursday afternoon**

in November in the corner of a classroom. That's where the magic happens. And no one sees it. You just need to have that own self-satisfaction of having done that stuff.' That's a massive transition to make and you made it Suzy. It's sliding doors stuff, isn't it?

SM: Yeah. The path not taken.

JT: So, what are your thoughts when you plan a lesson, like I've just watched?

SM: You have to hold on to a sense of risk. I don't know precisely what's going to happen, but that's okay, and if you plan it too much, as though you're going to be in control – this will happen at this time and that will happen at that time, and there's no deviance from that plan whatsoever – the lesson will not work, the magic won't happen.

JT: It happened in there, just now.

SM: Yeah, to some degree it happened today. I'd give myself 8 out of 10 for today (actually, not as well planned as I'd have liked). I think what I did today, I planned about 50% of, and then 50% just came up.

JT: You could smell that. You could tell you were responding, that it wasn't totally planned.

SM: I think I'm always a bit, as you've said, 'off-piste', because you have to be in the moment, and that's where it's so much like theatre, in that it's about responding to the circumstances of that unique point in time. You don't know what the students are going to bring with them that day, and you don't know how the students are going to perform whilst someone's watching, particularly in drama, which can be quite personal and vulnerable.

JT: So how do you get them to be so vulnerable?

SM: Oh, gosh.

JT: **Because you do, amazingly.**

SM: Thank you … It comes from believing that that's a normal thing to ask, right? This quotation behind you, on my office wall, the circle of light from Stanislavski, 'This is called solitude in public'.[1] I teach that.

> 'In the circle of light on the state in the midst of darkness, you have the sensation of being entirely alone … This is called solitude in public … During a performance, before an audience of thousands, you can always enclose yourself in this circle, like a snail in its shell … You can carry it wherever you go.'

I teach Stanislavski as soon as they start the GCSE course. He is about keeping the fourth wall in place in a way that allows the actor to truly inhabit the character and to play the inner life of the role. I think if you are concentrated as an actor, then you don't even know you're being vulnerable, you aren't afflicted with anxiety because you're in the role, you're in that circle of light and I think that's very useful. On the whole, I think students appreciate being able to come into the drama studio and be vulnerable in a way that's an anomaly in the rest of their school experience. I try to conjure a completely psychologically safe space for them to explore. If someone's crying in role or crying because of an emotional memory that's come up, then I will always make sure that before they leave the studio, they're in a neutral place again. There are things you can do to step back from that intensity, which have become more and more important over the years.

JT: **Technically you do lots of interesting things in there, don't you? I love your choral stuff, getting their mouth around the words.** *Aposiopesis.* **That's really important. One of the things the Year 11s said, 'You know, we do this brilliant practical work, but she also preps**

---

1 K. Stanislavski, *An Actor Prepares* (Abingdon and New York: Routledge, 1989).

us for the exams, and she helps us get great results.' So, tell me about how you get that balance.

SM: We start with movement, starting with the practical and then moving to what might be described as theory. But, for me, it's very important that it's not described as theory because the two things are connected. The body, soul and brain are indivisible, so starting with the physical equalises everybody in that. Whether you are an EAL student or a student with dyslexia, you're all entering the physical response in a way that's not made problematic by those things. It's a universal language that then engages people and also gets them to respect each other as colleagues.

Then you bring in the text. What I've always done with GCSE groups is to perform the text even if the ultimate goal is to write about it in an exam, as it is these days. I make sure we begin with the practice. We stage the production so it's in their body. When I went to École Jacques Lecoq in Paris the big phrase there was, 'le corps sait tout', 'the body knows everything'. When they go into the written exam, they are going to be able to answer every question because of the lived experience they've had with this play. They know what lighting we had for the play. They were there, they did it. They went to all the rehearsals. They know ideas for how to block a particular scene because I was there directing them to do that, you know? Their body will know it. So, if they can just transfer that knowledge onto paper through lots of practising before the actual exam, then they will succeed.

It's OK having a model of memory involving the brain, but Simon McBurney's *Who You Hear It From*, is interesting regarding memory and the notion of learning things 'by heart'.[2] He says that to learn something 'by heart' comes from the Greeks who thought the heart was the organ of memory, not

---

2 S. McBurney and C. Courtney, *Who You Hear It From: Essays* (London: Complicite, 2012).

the brain, and that makes sense to me. The children remember the drama we study because, essentially, they *love* it.

Time after time students who have dyslexia, or students who perhaps aren't getting grade 9s in English, have got the grade 9s in drama because they are content driven, and if they've owned the ideas, practically, they can then write them down, incorporating the terminology.

JT: **You're brilliant on the subject terminology. You use it all the time.**

SM: That's a big thing, I suppose. They do need to know the terminology, but again, I'm using it through practice. If you've heard and said it, you can write it, to some extent. You might misspell it, but knowing it comes first, because there's no point writing out definitions if you don't know what the definition means. You have got to *feel* the thing. You can know it through your head, you can know it through your heart, through your hips, through your experience, as well as intellectually or academically, and the synthesis of all that is to me what is meant by 'deep learning'.

I'm also – and I don't mean this boastfully, it's just true – really hardworking and I mark lots and lots of mock papers. I'm a big believer in personalised feedback, even though it kills me! I'll just write it out every single time. I'll not just write, 'You need to add more terminology', I'll write, 'Reflect on how you might add this detail because of that specific point . . .', and then in the next mock that's what they do. So, it's about written and spoken personalised feedback in the context of a rehearsal.

But I'm lucky. I think a lot of teachers are very hardworking. I'm not placing myself out on a limb there. I'm privileged enough to be able to work this way because I don't have many students. I have 20–30 students in each GCSE cohort – that optimum number makes it manageable.

JT: OK, so what's been your favourite moment in teaching?

SM: Well, that's a moment that occurred just before lockdown. I had a Year 11 class. They were very bright, lots of them have since gone to Oxford and Cambridge, and we were having a laugh. We were looking at body language … we were all up on our feet. This body language theorist called Allan Pease talks about the three gazes, and we were acting them out and they were being playful and ironic. It was a very buoyant atmosphere in preparation for the written exam. It was March time, wasn't it?

JT: It was 20 March 2020. I remember it well.

SM: Yes, and all the practical for drama had been finished. We were transitioning those practical parts of drama to the written exam and doing final revision. So, the atmosphere wasn't stressed in the sense that the exam was tomorrow or something, and these actors had absolutely excelled themselves on stage and we were now thinking about how we could put that on paper.

I remember it not because it was anything remarkable as such, but because I didn't know that that would be the last time I would see them as a group. We were then called to a meeting with Lucy Scott, and she said the school's closing. I felt very tearful when she said that, and I came back to this room and I thought, 'Oh my God, I'm not going to see those students through now.' They were going to be my best ever cohort. They were going to absolutely ace that written exam as they already had the coursework, and the performances, but now … no grand finale … And I thought I have to do something positive before leaving the building.

We had just been to see *Leopoldstadt*, the play by Tom Stoppard, about a Jewish family in Vienna, most of whom ended up being sent to Auschwitz. These same students had come to see it and given it a standing ovation, and on the tube, on the way back to the train station, they were just crying. It had had a profound effect on them, and they'd written reviews. Lucy's then 12-year-old son had come to see the play too and he'd written a review.

So, I had three reviews that were really exceptional. Patrick Marber, the director, had loved Chesterton's version of his play *The School Film*, which he'd been to see a couple of years prior, so I sent the reviews to him by email thinking, 'Whatever happens after this, I've done something to make their work count.'

Without prompting, Patrick sent the reviews to Tom Stoppard: *Sir* Tom Stoppard. I had no idea he'd done that, but then, by post, a few days later, Sir Tom wrote to me to say:

> 'The fact that my play reached and affected three people so young – and who write about it with understanding – gives me more pleasure than anything else written about *Leopoldstadt* … These are tragic times, for teachers and pupils reciprocally. Patrick and I – and the *Leopoldstadt* company – are truly indebted to you.'

I then did a live Zoom production of *Henry V*, which Tom Stoppard came to watch online. He's kept in touch through postcards. It really was amazing to have the support of one's lifelong hero.

JT: **Well, you were amazing today.**

SM: Thank you. I'd say my teaching today was good enough, but not amazing. But I'd say that what I did today is genuinely what it's like every day, and there are some truly amazing moments in this studio.

JT: **You can't make that level of participation up, right? They were absolutely on it every nanosecond of the lessons.**

SM: Yes, that's universal and it's with all of my classes. I don't mean that boastfully, it's just as it is.

JT: **There is not a second wasted.**

SM: I think some students would prefer it if there were. My style is not for everyone, and sometimes I get it wrong. But the basic truth is that you've just got to do the work. Going back to the beginning, I was brought up to think it was okay – or even admirable – for a teacher to be angry, and as much as teaching trends and learning cultures have changed over the past two decades, I personally think – dare I say it – that controlled, reasoned and temporary anger can be good for kids! We're talking about making it clear to a student that not doing the work is not acceptable. They've got to know you care, and if they know you care, then they will care, which is what Sandra Morton taught me at the start of my career. I think that is a 100% true. They need to know you care. That's not *cuddly* care. It's the work. The work is too important. I'm going to give my all to this, and if I am, so are you. I think you can expect that from every single student, and usually that's what works for me. Nowadays, some people say that being professional is about not being emotional – teaching as a technical exercise – but I think that's nonsense. I am proud to be in a profession of emotional expression, whether acting or teaching.

I am not easily tameable, I suppose. I can be a bit high maintenance. I can expect the school hall to become a theatre overnight, rather than a canteen. Drama itself, the very nature of the subject, can be quite controversial. So, I'm very grateful that Lucy has given me this opportunity, and that she profoundly gets what art is, all kinds of art. She recognises that what I'm trying to do is to create art within a school, and she values that. I think there are heads out there who really don't. But if I could compress this interview into one sentence, one message, it would be that drama is a vital thing for kids to do.

JT: So just to wrap up, why do you think you are so effective at what you do?

SM: High expectations across the board, and at KS4/5, a sense that if you're walking in that door, there is an invisible contract that you sign to say, 'I'm going to give my best. And I'm not only going to give my best, but I'm going to become part of a company that wants to mirror professional practice, pursue excellence and *only connect*.' The alternative isn't to not give your best. The alternative is not to enter the room in the first place, but those who opt for drama at GCSE and A level, they've made that choice themselves.

I have one to ones with the students. I say, 'Look, if you're having a hard time with your maths revision or you've a bereavement, I can help you through this, you don't have to come to this extra rehearsal, that's okay.' It's not like I'm some intense, fiery dragon. You know, it's just a contract between the student, me and the subject that works.

JT: **You have the high expectations, but you also forgive because we're all fallible.**

SM: Oh completely. It's actually very important to accept that in myself too: I'm fallible. I go home every day and think, 'Should I have said that? I could have been better if I'd … I must go back tomorrow and put it right …' Teachers are all different, and my way is by no means *the* way, it's just something I've given my everything to. Look, it's about *love* isn't it? I love them, and I love drama: 'The play's the thing'. At one point in my career, a deputy head said to me, 'Do you want to be an assistant principal? You could become part of SLT and go right to the top.' I thought, 'Thanks, that's nice, but no, I'm not in the slightest bit interested in doing that.' I never will be. I'm interested in drama. These children that I'm working with doing drama are very giving of themselves, and they're doing it for love. I find that there is just so much endless creativity and fulfilment to be found through sharing drama with young people. I never get bored; I get exhausted, but I never ever get bored, and that – as a vocation – fills me with gratitude.

JT: **That's a lovely moment to finish. Thank you so much.**

Testimonials

'I often ask myself where I acquired my love for drama. But it is, of course, very obvious: it is down to *your* passion for the art form and *your* willingness to "give yourself" whole-heartedly, whatever the occasion.'

'You will always be my biggest inspiration and the voice in my head telling me I can do this.'

'Your confidence and encouragement resonate with every class you teach, creating an undying passion for the arts in generation after generation of today's youth.'

'Your energetic and passionate approach to learning has inspired us to step out of our comfort zone and care less about what others think.'

'I will never forget the final warm-up we did before our unit 2 exam. We had to go up to someone and say "I love you". It was the most bittersweet feeling; I have never felt so much warmth and love whilst tears were streaming down my face – knowing it was the last performance I would do at Chesterton.'

'Thank you for making us exceed what we thought was possible to achieve and for "dignifying young people".'

'You believed in me when I didn't believe in myself, which means more to me than you know.'

'You are a real-life *superhero*! They only give you the title of drama teacher because superhero is not an official job title at Chesterton.'

'The drama studio has been such a happy place for our daughter and offered her a home outside of home and a family outside of her family … she has always had a community to feel part of and something to focus on, that she is really passionate about, that enables her to feel valued and that brings her joy.'

'From one mum to another . . . I have to believe that your little boy will, in time, meet people that will affect his life in the positive way that you affect our children's lives.'

'I just wanted to thank you for welcoming me into your classroom. As a teacher who had been out of the system for so long, I needed inspiration and I really feel that I was blessed to have been given the opportunity to watch you work and experience your creative process.'

'Great work deserves recognition, and you certainly deserve yours . . . Rest assured that the incredible amount of effort and emotion you have put into making events like that happen is successfully fostering a sense of appreciation for the performing arts in a world that sometimes places overwhelming emphasis on STEM subjects. Industry without art is brutality! Whatever (my son) and his peers end up doing with their lives, your passion has helped steer them in a direction every parent will inevitably be proud of.'

'You are a marvel. You never cease to amaze me with the fire and beauty you bring out of people.'

So, what can we learn from Suzy Marston?

When I read through this chapter and reflected upon my time in Suzy's orbit, it was clear that her high expectations of her students are at the core of her effectiveness. In fact, it is the first thing she identified when I asked her why she is a truly great teacher.

Closely related to her limitless expectations of what her students can achieve in drama, comes her love of her discipline. She is, primarily, an actor. Her depth of experience on the stage informs her practice. Repeatedly, Suzy and her students talk about being professionals. At one point she calls her Year 11 class, 'actors'. Her knowledge of dramatic technique is comprehensive, and she's able to communicate that expertise to her students.

Suzy's enthusiasm for drama is matched by her enthusiasm for teaching her students how to act. To watch her teach is to watch someone entirely in their element. Her energy and work rate are simply further manifestations of her passion for the work. Like every dedicated subject teacher, she considers learning the discipline to be essential to her students' lives, not just the route to a good grade. She is a woman of conviction.

That sense of conviction is key to Suzy's effectiveness, as is her principal's attitude towards her. Rolf has the wisdom to see that there is nothing to lose and everything to gain by allowing Suzy the space to pursue her craft, unfettered by the prosaic features of our education system, such as data targets!

Finally, her success is based upon the professional relationships she fosters with her students, who feel acknowledged by Suzy. She balances the intensity of the work with a sense of fun. If there is one thing that comes through again and again, it's the strength of the bonds that Suzy fosters with cohort after cohort of her students. As she says in the final exchange in her interview, it's ultimately about love.

Suzy Marston's students' progress and achievement data

- Award from the Good Schools Guide at Impington Village College – the highest performing school in the country for girls in AS Drama (2015).
- In 2016: Results at Chesterton went from 0% grade A*/As to 62% A*s/As (with a cohort of 36) with Suzy being appointed head of drama.

- In 2018: Drama outcomes at Chesterton were 100% 9–5 (with the new grading system), with 79% of the cohort achieving 9–7 grades (only 24% achieving this nationally; 15 of the 29 candidates achieved grade 9).

- In 2022, 2023 and 2024 with cohorts of around 20, Subject Progress Index data was, on average, +2.5 (in layman's terms, that equates to something like 2.5 grades above expectations per student, based on their KS2 results) with an average of 50% of the cohort achieving grade 9 and 100% a 9–5 pass.

Beyond the curriculum, Suzy prepares students for summer seasons with National Youth Music Theatre and National Youth Theatre (in 2024, 12 of Suzy's current students were given coveted places in these companies). In 2024, Suzy's students also entered, for the first time, the Audience Choice Award at the ESU's 'Performing Shakespeare' Competition, held at the Globe Theatre, London, *and won*! Finally, she is most proud to be a mother of two children, who – having grown up being carted to her weekend rehearsals and Edinburgh shows – also live for theatre: her 10-year-old daughter has just been cast as Jane Banks in the UK tour of *Mary Poppins*.

A Truly Great Mathematics Teacher: Michelle Goodger

Michelle Goodger is a mathematics teacher at Ysgol Cwm Brombil in Port Talbot.

The school leadership's view

Our friend Simon is a professor of Romantic studies. Whenever we are out walking in the countryside, he will explain the Romantics' concept of the beautiful, the picturesque and the sublime in relation to defining different types of landscape. It is generally agreed amongst scholars that the sublime instils a feeling of awe in us, which can be terrifying. Whilst the Romantics were talking about nature, when it comes to industrial landscapes, there is nothing, in my experience, more sublime – that is, awesome and terrifying – than the view as you walk out of the front door and into the car park of Ysgol Cwm Brombil in Port Talbot. There, in front of you, stands the town's steelworks; proud, dark and magnificent. They work, day and night, producing steel. Or, at least they did, until 1 October 2024, when the last blast furnace was shut down.

The steelworks provided employment for 4,000 of the town's working population. Only 2,000 employees remain. I stood there once, at the end of the day, chatting to three women, all of them cleaners at the school. Their grandfathers, fathers and brothers worked, or had worked, at the steelworks. None of them knew what would happen when the furnaces shut. Port Talbot has above average levels of deprivation compared to the rest of Wales and public health is generally poor. Asthma is particularly bad. When Ysgol Cwm Brombil's future Year 11s walk out the school door for the final time, the landscape they see will have changed utterly. If they are going to compete for jobs nationally and internationally, they need a rich, challenging and ambitious education, along with great qualifications.

Luckily for those Year 11s, their head teacher is Shaun Clarke. Shaun is pleased. In fact, he's more than pleased. The school's 2024 GCSE results were the best they have ever been in the school's history, and the best in the LA. Every measure sees the school wildly outperform predictions. The percentage of 5 A*/A grades, for instance, was predicted to be 11% and they attained 21.2%. They have worked hard on the core business of teaching and learning, and it is paying off handsomely. Success is breeding success. The young people who are venturing out into a hugely uncertain world are increasingly well-prepared thanks to Shaun and his team.

I am sitting in Shaun's office, talking to him and assistant head teacher Annelise Taylor, about a truly great Ysgol Cwm Brombil mathematics teacher, Michelle Goodger. When I asked Annelise which Brombilian I might include in this book, Annelise suggested Michelle. I had noticed Michelle when I had watched her teach the year before. The precision of her pedagogy had been impressive. Annelise's recommendation confirmed my hunch that Michelle was someone special.

'I'm fascinated by her', says Annelise. 'She was a teaching assistant [TA] for years before she became a teacher. Her story is incredible. She was … *timid* in the classroom when she was a TA. Wouldn't say boo to a goose. But when she began teaching, it was like a switch had been flicked. She changed completely. She just oozed confidence. She came alive. It's been remarkable.'

Shaun chips in, 'She teaches with the door open. I always think that reflects an inner confidence about a teacher. And she just loves maths!'

'So, before we go to watch her teach. What else makes Michelle truly great?' I ask.

Annelise needs no time to think. 'Her relationships with the students are wonderful. She understands children and loves being in their company. And they love her. There's such warmth. It's like that TED talk … what's her name … Rita Pierson … "Kids don't learn from people they don't like". That's what makes Michelle special. And she's no pushover, either! She has the naughty lads just where she wants them!'

The bell for lesson one rings. As we stand up, I mention the decline of the steelworks. Annelise stops. Her voice suddenly softens. 'My great-grandfather, grandfather, father and uncle all worked there. It was a male-dominated workforce. My great-grandfather fought in Passchendaele in World War I, and came back to work in the steelworks. Women worked there too. My grandma was a wages clerk and my mum was a typist. It was such a vibrant town when I was growing up. It was known as *Treasure Island*. There were good jobs for everyone. Well-paid jobs. The place was vibrant, even wealthy. But now it's lost its shine. It's been dimmed.' She grins resignedly.

Annelise feels the responsibility of her role more than ever. Sustaining high-quality teaching matters in all schools, but in the last few years at Ysgol Cwm Brombil it has begun to matter just that little bit more. We head off into the busy corridor to watch a truly great teacher do her stuff.

Teaching Year 7

Annelise and I approach Michelle's room. She is at the door and greets me with a huge grin and an even bigger 'Croeso!'

Michelle explains that she is teaching Year 7 and I enter the room to find *Tasg Tanio* written on the board. I later discover that it means 'ignition task' in English, which sounds so much more exciting than 'do now'.

The desks have been rearranged to make four dining-room tables. Each one has a sign with a different number on it – 10, 20, 30 and 40. When they enter, the students are given an equation to solve on a slip of paper with their name on it. I sit next to Tyler, who is pondering the answer to the expression $9 \times 4 + 4 = ?$ He recalls brackets, orders, division, multiplication, addition, subtraction (BODMAS) and soon comes to the conclusion that he is on table '40'. It turns out that Michelle has established four tables, named 10, 20, 30 and 40; the answer to the equations is one of those four numbers. Michelle has carefully planned at which table each student will sit. All they have to do is match the answer to their individualised equation with the corresponding table.

Michelle tells them that they are doing something a little bit different today. She is unbearably excited by what she has planned. A buzz fills the room. Convincingly, she explains that she had run out of food at home and on the way to school she had breakfasted at McDonald's. There she picked up a whole load of different order slips and their job was to sort out how much each order cost and what change certain customers were due. Someone asks whether she really did go to McDonald's for breakfast and, without missing a beat, Michelle reassures him that she did. The excitement levels rise from 10 to 11.

It is the last day of a long eight-week half-term for these Year 7s. A week off is edging closer. There is a tangible sense of excitement in the room. Michelle does nothing to dampen the holiday vibe! Essentially, they are working in pairs to solve a number of puzzles involving adding and multiplying decimals, based upon a fast-food menu. It is a lesson to embed the students' number fluency, not that they would know that – they are just enjoying themselves, hugely. One boy asks, 'Is this the thing you said you wouldn't be able to sleep about, Miss, because you said you'd be too excited?' And, as it is nearly holiday time, there are prizes to be had …

I am not sure there is a single student who spends even a minute off-task. It is a straightforward activity, gradated in difficulty, table by table. The tasks are appropriately challenging. Every student is in 'the pit' pulling themselves up by their fingertips. If she needs quiet, the signal is 'tri', 'dau' and 'un'. She secures 100% attention 100% of the time. Mini-whiteboard use is sharp and disciplined – there is none of the copying/cheating I usually see. She runs the room effortlessly.

I look across the bowed heads of 30 children at the poster on the wall, which says, 'Mathematicians aren't people who find maths easy, they're people who enjoy how hard it is.' It's an aphorism made real, right in front of my eyes. Students are scratching their heads, consulting with their friends, getting on with the maths. Amidst the busy hubbub is Michelle. She works the room, is helping almost non-stop for 40 minutes. Occasionally, she will ask for, and receive, the students' full attention to work through a problem, or a misconception. But it is a busy room. Maths! Maths! Maths!

I ask a couple of students what it is about Mrs Goodger that makes her a great teacher. 'Well, she makes it really easy to understand. She explains it. She helps you until you get it.' It is a response that is repeated across the room. No wonder … Michelle is in amongst the students. She clearly loves the work.

In the introductory briefing on interview day, I used to say to potential candidates for teaching posts that, 'We have over 1,500 students at this school – if you don't like children, leave now and we can part friends!'

Teaching is largely founded upon good working relationships between teachers and students. That is the starting point for great teaching. It is much harder to cajole students to become serious scholars, if there is teacher–student tension in the air.

The students continue to go hammer and tongs at the maths. To finish the lesson, Michelle awards prizes but also explores a simple misconception. 'OK, if a burger and fries costs £3.20 and the man pays with a £5.00 note, how much change does he get?' She asks Chloe, who says, immediately £2.80. Michelle knew that was where she would find the misconception articulated, and she carefully chooses another student with the correct solution, to explain why the answer is £1.80.

As she dismisses the class, a lad and his mate come up to Michelle, clearly lost in the moment, and says to her, 'The thing is, Miss, the man found a pound coin on the floor, so he did get £2.80 change!' She giggles and hurries him along with a smile.

Teaching Year 11

We walk to another room: Year 11. Michelle only teaches this class once a week, sharing it with the main teacher.

The students enter the room in ones and twos and get on with the *Tasg Tanio*. Last to arrive is a stocky lad called Liam and my bet is he plays rugby. We all need to know Liam has arrived. He doesn't take his seat immediately. He swans around, talking at a girl who is trying to get on with her work. His two mates play audience. Liam is funny. I have taught many a student like him. He is writing-implement free. Michelle provides him with a pen. A minute later, he is finally seated. He sits at the front on his own, but has two mates to his immediate right. He turns his head every few seconds to check people are still paying him attention.

Michelle builds the lesson beautifully. She is teaching them factorising. They have the basics, of course, but during the lesson, through stepped variation of task, she moves them from expanding $4(3x + 7)$ to factorising $4xy^2 + 6xy + 2x^2y$. Every single student, including Liam, completes the most challenging problem.

So, what is it that enables this group of students to make good progress from a range of starting points, on the last day of a long half-term, as the nights begin to draw in and the days get colder? Well, Michelle narrates the lesson so that students are clear about where they are and where they are going. Her explanations are clarity personified. She has more than one way of explaining things. She creates a fail-safe heuristic that the students can follow to factorise any expression. She uses mathematical terms relentlessly. She provides a definition of factorising *after* the students understand what it is (there really is no point in defining something in any subject, until students understand what it is that is being defined). The students' work has a low floor and a high ceiling. The dialogue with the students is permission-based – 'Would you like to move on to more difficult problems now?' Success builds success; the students make progress because their self-concept grows as they complete intelligently sequenced, progressively harder problems.

Then there is, of course, Michelle's handling of Liam. His peacock-esque arrival to the lesson could have been met (quite understandably) with an irritated put down. That would, arguably, have led to limitless disruption of the lesson. Instead, she handles him perfectly, born of her life experience. As the lesson progresses, it is clear Liam knows his stuff. At one point he whispers imperceptibly an answer to help the girl behind him. Due to where I am sitting, I notice. I wink at him and he grins. There is a spell of five minutes near the end of the lesson, and the students are working on the hardest problems, when pure silence falls upon the room. Every single student, including Liam, have their heads down, grappling with their maths. The silence is only broken when Liam asks Michelle if he has got a question right. Of course he has.

Michelle transforms Liam from potential disrupter of the lesson into an ambitious scholar. It is magical to watch. As they pack away, I drift across the room and ask Liam if he's learnt much this lesson. 'Yeah. Loads, Sir', he replies. On the wall across the room is a poster proclaiming the Ysgol Cwm Brombil values: Aspiration; Belonging; Character. What I have just watched could not exemplify those values more perfectly.

What the students think

Annelise sets me up with students from across the age range. I ask them to talk in pairs about what makes Mrs Goodger a truly great teacher. The task immediately animates them. Two minutes later, I feel mean for having to stop the conversations. They talked, to a person, about Michelle's supportive nature. 'She never shouts. If we mess up, she helps.'

One girl says, 'It's exciting to go to her lessons. Every time I see maths on my timetable, I look forward to it!' If they get stuck, they can ask her anything, because she never makes them feel silly.

'She's strict if she needs to be. And she's patient if we don't get it.' What impresses them is her energy in the classroom. They love the fact – as I had seen – that she moves around the room and helps them individually. That would be an element of Michelle's teaching easily criticised – such an approach often creates learned helplessness – but Michelle has high expectations and provides individualised support. In that Year 11 lesson, when the room fell silent, her efforts in the earlier phase of the lesson came to fruition. She didn't need to help them at the end, because they could all complete the most complicated problems.

I ask the students to agree, in their pairs, a single word to describe Mrs Goodger: understanding, understandable, clear (when she explains things), helpful, patient, kind and extraordinary. What I want to add, but I'm not sure the students will understand what I mean, is the word, 'love'.

Just as the students leave, a Year 11 student, who was down on the list but who has been at the doctor's, arrives late. I invite her in. As she sits down, I say, 'Hi, I'm Mr Tomsett. I am writing this book about truly great teachers. I am profiling Mrs Goodger in the book and I wondered what you thought of her.' Without missing a beat, she replies in her inimitable Welsh tones, 'Oh, Mrs Goodger! She's so lush!'

IRL: Michelle Goodger

John Tomsett (JT): Tell me about how you became a teacher.

Michelle Goodger (MG): When I was in school, I always wanted to be a maths teacher. Maths is my thing. But I was one of those people who couldn't be bothered. I didn't work for my exams, and I got a grade B in GCSE maths. It was only a grade B because I didn't work. So, I then went to university, but I did software engineering, because I didn't have the grades to do anything else. Then I just left, so I didn't even finish that. I began working in a nightclub, met my sons' father, had two boys, and was a single parent for quite a while. Then I started working in a school, so that I had school holidays with the children.

I was just a learning support assistant (LSA). Well, not *just* an LSA. I was an LSA. It was enjoyable. I got the summer holidays off, and I didn't really want to take it any further, to be honest, because I thought I was too old. I thought, 'My time is done now. I just need to sort of carry on like this, and that's fine.' But then a job came up as a numeracy officer, and I thought that could be brilliant – involved in maths, but not having to get any other qualifications. So, I applied for that, got the job and did that for several years.

Then there was one time when there were some boys who were being naughty and a bit silly, and Liz, the head of maths, took them out of class, and asked if they could just come into the small room where I worked. They were quite disruptive, but I only had two or three of them at a time, so they weren't disrupting a class. One time, they were given those charity shop bags that you put clothes in. The boy opened it up, cut some holes in it, stuck it on as a dress, and sat there. I just ignored it. After a while, he got fed up, took it off, and stuck it in the bin. Had that been in a class, that would have been really disruptive to everyone. But I could just ignore it. Another time, he drew all over his face with felt pen. I just carried on the lesson with him with his face covered in ink. He ended up feeling quite embarrassed.

JT: So interesting. I want to talk about Liam in a bit, and how you dealt with him, which I think was brilliant.

MG: I really enjoyed working with those naughty lads. Teaching the maths and seeing them do the work. But I still thought I was too old. I didn't even have a degree, let alone a postgraduate diploma in education (PGCE). I do really enjoy maths so I thought I would just do a maths degree. I had to do it part time, through the Open University because I couldn't give up work, and that was a six-year, part-time course. I did the first two years and then realised that, actually, you could do more years in one go. I did the next two years in one year, and then the next two years in one year, so that it only took four years. I got a 2:1, not a first, mainly because I rushed it, but I rushed it because I wanted to begin teaching as soon as I could.

Whilst I was doing my degree, there were more boys who were a trouble in a class, so I formed a little maths intervention group, and put a couple of tables in the room. The boys were never perfect, but they were working, and they were enjoying it. I got to the point where I wanted to do this work with more than just four students in a class. That led to the PGCE, which I also completed through the Open University, and then to here.

I so wish I had done it sooner, but you can't change the past. It is what it is. But I did get to a point where it really bugged me. I just *enjoy it* so much. I wish I had more time, because I'll be 65 at some point, and then, technically, that'll be it! I don't have as much time left now.

JT: **So how many years have you been in school?**

MG: It's 13 years. Part of that included working as an LSA. This is my first year as a qualified teacher.

JT: **Tell me about maths.**

MG: I just love maths.

JT: **Why?**

MG: You know, when you grow up and you have your little junior puzzle books and your crosswords – that's how maths is for me. It's just like doing a puzzle, and I really enjoy getting something wrong because I like to go through it again and find out where I have gone wrong. I find it really sad that some students have, automatically, a negative attitude towards maths.

JT: **Not in your class?**

MG: No. But I took over their class this year, and their confidence was so low. They would just say, 'I can't do anything at all.' I thought, 'Oh my goodness. I've got so much to work with these children.' I've worked so hard for them and they've worked so hard for me this half-term. So . . . I've got a copy of their internal exam results from last year and what they've got now, so they could see how much they've improved already compared to last year. We're talking an average 12% improvement. Do you know what, that's so, so good! They were all amazed. Alice said, 'Miss, you got us these grades.' I said, 'I didn't. No, I didn't get you these grades. You got these grades. I'm just here helping. You did it Alice.' That's my thing. That's what I really like.

JT: **And those naughty boys?**

MG: There's another one who, last year, wouldn't ask questions, so he got into trouble because he didn't understand what was going on. I've got two boys. They are older now, but my youngest boy was the same. You've got to learn how to talk to him to get out of him what he wants and allow him to think he's getting his own way, but actually he's not! It's the same with these boys who are playing up a bit. How do you get them to work and do what you want them to do, with them thinking they've made the choice to do it? I learned that from my son. It's about communicating with them in their own way and getting them to answer maths problems questions almost without them realising you've insisted they do it.

JT: **So, what are your fundamental thoughts when you're planning lessons?**

MG: What do they need to learn in this lesson? What examples and questions to exemplify that learning? Sometimes, that's all you need. But then I think, 'What else can we throw in? What challenges can we add? Do I need a bit of differentiation somewhere? How will I know if they're getting it?' So mini-whiteboards, obviously, are a really good thing. Plus simply different ways of teaching the concepts. Variety of approach is important.

JT: **You use a lot of energy out when you're teaching!**

MG: It's just natural. It's not an effort! I love the teaching. That's just how it is.

JT: **You never, ever tell them anything, do you?! You never let them have an answer for nothing … It's really impressive. Where did you learn that?**

MG: We have had a whole departmental focus on questioning in the past, so it was something to be more aware of in the classroom. It feels like it's just a natural thing. It is a natural thing *now*, but it has developed from watching other teachers – particularly Liz – throw questions back to their students.

I knew that Liz was going to stop teaching additional maths a few years ago and had wanted to take over so I asked if I could sit in with her when she taught it to prepare myself. Not many people get to see Liz teach, so I was lucky. Seeing Liz just respond to questions with questions or hints, rather than give away answers was inspiring and it was really interesting to see how students responded to it and ended up answering their own questions. Liz is such a good teacher and her passion for teaching and maths just comes through in every lesson. I wanted to be just like her – but my own version – since seeing her teach for the first time many years ago when I was an LSA.

JT: She is equally praiseworthy of you, you know! And then there's your real-world examples.

MG: Real-world examples help with convincing them that maths is relevant to their lives. There are so many times in teaching maths, algebra in particular, when the students say, 'When am I ever going to need to know how to do 5x plus 3x equals so-and-so and find the answer?' But as I keep telling them, the skills that you develop in maths lessons are the skills that are useful for life, when you look at something and think, 'Right, how am I going to go about solving this?' We are constantly met with challenges, and we have to work them through.

JT: Let's think about that Year 11 class. Tell me about the way you structured that lesson.

MG: I was trying to get them to figure out first how to factorise without me just telling them. They'll remember it a little bit better if they have to think about it first. Then, obviously, you need some examples, beginning with easier ones and building it up in smaller chunks. Then we move on to the more difficult ones, and, just in case we needed them, some GCSE questions to look at, which we didn't need but will use next lesson. So, breaking it down, lots of examples that get progressively more challenging. Responding to what they understand in order to know where to go next. They worked it out themselves, anyway. I didn't really need to work through an example with them. They told me what goes on the outside of the brackets, and they told me what goes on the inside. So, they processed the whole thing straight away, thinking it through.

JT: **Working through the process, step by step, gradating the difficulty and varying the pattern to help them apply what they have learnt – it's such a good process. You're so good at it. Tell me about your handling of Liam.**

MG: Liam used to be in set 4 years ago, and we wondered what on earth he was doing in set 4? Initially, he didn't want to move up sets. Eventually he went up to set 3, and then he's now in set 2.

JT: **I think he's a proper cheeky chappy?!**

MG: You get him on board at the start, and then he'll end up doing what you want and working, because he is really good. *He is really good.* But, yes, he does like to come in, and announce, 'I'm here. And everyone needs to know I'm here.' Sit down, joke with his mates. But if you then go in hard straight away, he'll just blow up and think, 'Why should I bother doing anything then?' I want him to be working, so we just sort of deal with it in a non-confrontational way, and then he starts working.

JT: **There was a moment, Michelle, in that lesson, about 10 minutes from the end, when there wasn't a sound because they were all really working. It was magical!**

MG: When they were completing that last set of six harder questions for fluency!

JT: What you did was move from that start, with Liam swanning around and potentially disrupting things, to pure silence as they did the work.

MG: Thank you.

JT: So, you could watch your lesson today and say, 'When she takes answers, she's only taking one answer when there are 19 answers in the room.' But because you've been around every table, you know who can do it and who can't do it. Your understanding of who can do the maths doesn't need you necessarily to do mini-whiteboards all the time because you've been out in the classroom speaking to every single student about their work, assessing them and giving feedback live, in the moment. If you sat at the front and didn't engage with them, then you might have to be using mini-whiteboards to assess where they are, but your efforts around the room mean you know that information anyway. I also love the way they ask you questions if they're not sure. One of the girls I spoke to said, 'I'm not scared to ask any questions any more in maths because I've got Mrs Goodger.'

MG: Oh, that's so sweet.

JT: It's brilliant, isn't it? Because you've created a room of psychological safety. Where they feel completely psychologically safe and when they get it wrong, they can ask questions. They feel completely supported. That is absolutely the heart of it, isn't it? That's what you want, especially at maths.

MG: Because like I said, create the supportive, trusting relationships, and they'll let you guide them. Having been an LSA is so helpful ... 'Come on. We've done this. You know this. What is it they're asking?' It's just *patience*, 'Let's go through it again then. Come on. Let's go through it again ...'

JT: You know what? One of the things I ask the students is to give me one word to describe the teacher I am profiling. About you, they chose, 'helpful, understandable, understand*ing*, patient and kind'. So, your analysis of your own teacher-self is absolutely spot on. Did being a TA give you a really good grounding?

MG: Anybody who wants to go into teaching should spend at least six months as a TA. You see all the other subjects beyond your own, and you pick up good and bad bits of practice from here, good bits from there. 'Oh, that was great, but that wasn't so good. I'm not going to do that.' It's a huge benefit. I would sit there sometimes and think, 'Oh, this is going to kick off', and it always did. The teacher explains the way to tackle a maths problem, and somebody says, 'Well, I still don't get it', and then teachers stays where they are at the board and says, 'Right. Let's do it again', in the same way! The student then says, 'I still don't get it!' I used to sit there and think, 'If they haven't got it the first time, you need to come up with another way for them to understand it.'

JT: That's exactly what the students said … 'If we don't get it, she explains it in a different way, and then we get it.' You need to adapt your teaching. If you keep doing something in the same way and you're expecting a different result, that's madness.

MG: I just think you have to give them time, too. Stretch the top end and give the lower attainers more support. There are some students in my class who have been doing really well and normally this would mean moving up to set 2 … but none of them wanted to go and they have all stayed with me. James in particular … all last year he was aware he had the opportunity after every test to move up as he was getting results that matched set 2, but every time he was adamant that he didn't want to leave my class. James was a nightmare in Year 9 and clashed with the teacher. I taught him in Year 10 as well as this year and he has just gone strength to strength. Nancy, who you also saw, did move up but has recently asked to move back. It's nothing to do with ability. She can get quite panicky if she doesn't understand something and needs it explained patiently a few times so that she feels more confident. Evie, who was also there, is doing really well, but the minute she found out her test result she got quite worried and said she didn't want to move up to set 2. She just needs somebody to check in on her and make sure she is on the right path.

JT: **There were people who you saw teach that you revere? Like Liz?**

MG: Liz is just an absolutely fantastic teacher. She's so good. So good. She's very passionate, very animated in the classroom. She makes it fun, and that's my thing too. I am enthusiastic about it all. Students pick up on that as well. They pick up whether you think your own subject is fun, whether you're enjoying doing it. They can just tell. It's better for them if they see that you are enjoying it.

JT: **Your enthusiasm for teaching maths is infectious. They have to be enthusiastic because if they're not, they're letting you down. That human connection thing is key. What other teachers did you learn from?**

MG: Sarah, the current head of department. She's great!

JT: **So, try and tell me why you think you're a great teacher.**

MG: Oh, I probably wouldn't say that I was a great teacher. I just do me.

JT: **What was it, then, that made Annelise recommend you?**

MG: Well, my boys keep saying, 'Oh, I wish I had you as a teacher when I was in school. You just make it interesting and fun.' I make them test things out for me. If I have a new task, I say to them, 'Hey, give it a try. Let me time how long it takes you, and let's see how hard it is.' I think that I do have quite a knack with, like we've said, the slightly naughtier boys who are a bit more challenging but are actually good at maths. I also have confidence and patience, and I just keeping going and don't give up on *anyone*.

JT: **What are you working on at the moment in your in your teaching?**

MG: I have taken over additional maths from Liz this year, so this is a new thing for me, which is quite fun. I am going to be applying to be a WJEC (Wales' largest awarding body) examiner. Pedagogically, I am into flipped learning. I've got a Year 9 top set. There are the basics that they should already know that we are supposed to spend time going over in class, but it's just a bit of a waste of time. So, when we are working on fractions, simplifying fractions is the first step. Year 9, set 1 … they can simplify fractions, so why do I need to waste lesson time doing that? So, flip the learning. I've made videos to help them. You can hear my voice, and you can see my pen moving on the screen talking them through simplifying fractions on YouTube. Their homework is to work through these videos. I can check in their books … if they've just got an answer, then they've just copied my answer. If they've got workings to go with it, then I know they have worked through it. It's just so that we can get those basic bits that they already know done, and we can spend more time challenging them.

JT: **So you just did that off your own back?**

MG: Yeah.

JT: **You really love this stuff, don't you?**

MG: I genuinely do. It's so much fun. School's not for everyone, is it? A lot of people struggle with school, they struggle with lessons and learning. Well, let's make it the best we can for them. People might be surprised to find someone who just thinks this whole thing is a lot of fun. I am so lucky, because I absolutely love coming to work. I still get days where I get up and think, 'Gosh. I'm so tired.' But I get in, and then the minute I step in front of the pupils it's gone, I'm just in the moment, and it's great and I'm alive again.

JT: **The energy you get from working with those children is so tangible. Thank you so much for letting me come to see you teach. It's been a joy.**

Testimonials

'Thanks for helping me in maths – you've made me feel much more confident for the exam.'

'Thank you so much for putting in lots of effort to help me do well in maths.'

'You're the #1 teacher in school!'

'Thank you so much for teaching us maths so well. You have honestly saved our class this year and have helped and taught us so much. I am immensely appreciative. You've not only taught us so much, but you've also made maths fun and entertaining!'

'Thanks for stepping up and being the best maths teacher ever. I finally understand so many more topics than before. Your love for maths (which I will never understand) has made the whole class improve so much!'

'Thank you. Without your support I would never have gotten so far as I have this year. I was fully ready to give up on maths because I just didn't get it. I didn't get any of it but once you started teaching me, I realised I actually did understand, it was just never explained in a way I could understand it. For that, I am very thankful.'

So, what can we learn from Michelle Goodger?

There are three things that strike me about Michelle's teaching. Firstly, her understanding of child psychology is remarkable. Her handling of Liam was truly expert. How she transformed him from potential menace to model scholar was masterful. Her ability to support the students in a way that rebuilds their fragile confidence in a subject that requires the courage to accept failure as an integral element of the learning progress is, as one of her charges said, extraordinary. Student after student commented upon how they had lost their confidence but found it again once Michelle taught them mathematics. Her craft is built upon the firmest of foundations – her mutually respectful relationship with her students.

Then there is her love of mathematics. It is notable to see reference to her passion for the subject in the students' testimonials. It reminded me of Jerome Bruner's comment in his introduction to the 1977 edition of his seminal work, *The Process of Education*, when he wrote, 'A curriculum is more for teachers than it is for students … if [a curriculum] cannot change, move, perturb, inform teachers, it will have no effect on those whom they teach. It must be first and foremost a curriculum for teachers. If it has any effect on pupils, it will have it by virtue of having had an effect on teachers.'[1] Watching her teach, it is possible to see Michelle's effervescent enthusiasm for maths impact tangibly upon her students.

The third learning point I have gained from watching Michelle teach is her ability to support every single child in the room. It is easy to be critical of an approach that might sap a teacher's energy and encourage learned helplessness in their students. But Michelle never loses the room, nor loses track of time; instead, she provides a level of

---

1 J. S. Bruner, *The Process of Education* (Cambridge, MA: Harvard University Press, 1977), p. xv.

individualised support that is measured and challenging. Listening to the students talk about her, it is this aspect of her approach they value above all else.

Michelle Goodger's students' progress and achievement data

Since Michelle is in the very early stages of her career, she has little progress or attainment data to illustrate the impact of her teaching. However, her Year 10 group's first assessment saw them attain an average of 46%. The same students in their end of Year 9 assessment gained 18%. Those data are presented with obvious caveats, but it is hugely promising.

A Truly Great Food Technology Teacher: Garry Littlewood

Garry Littlewood is the subject leader of food and textiles technology at Huntington School, York.

The school leadership's view

I am sitting in the head teacher's office that I inhabited for well over a decade. It is only the second time I've been in this room since I retired several years ago. I am talking to my successor, Matt Smith, who could easily have been featured in this book. Matt is a tremendous teacher. I learnt a lot about mathematics teaching when I worked with him as deputy at Huntington. But we are here to talk about Garry Littlewood.

I have known Garry for 20-something years. He was in charge of the curriculum during the latter part of my tenure as head teacher. I managed to prise him away from leading the food and textiles department and into senior leadership. It was not a huge surprise that on my departure, he stepped down and returned to lead his beloved subject area.

Matt begins … 'Magic dust'. We both chuckle. 'That's what he's got. The thing is, he never lets a child fail. Students don't fail in food. He will ensure they've all got the right ingredients. He'll be in the supermarket at 7 am buying peppers for the PP students if needs be.' I know all this to be true of Garry, but it is great to hear it coming from Matt. 'His expectations of students are sky high. He stretches and challenges them. And they know he wants the best for them, and they love him for that. They want to do him proud.' Matt is right. York's Huntington School may be in one of the wealthiest cities in the UK, but it has a huge number of what Theresa May called the 'JAM' families, that is families who are 'just about managing'. It is largely populated by white British children from low- to middle-income backgrounds. Old-fashioned blue-collar workers. Whilst it is famous for trains and chocolate, beyond the council, Aviva and health care, the fourth largest employer in the city is Shepherd's Group, which owns Portakabin, the school's close neighbour. I know from bittersweet experience that these working-class kids will test out a new teacher, but once they are sure you are on their side, they'll do anything for you.

As head teacher, Matt is still, primarily, a teacher. He goes on, 'Garry has all the facets of a great teacher. His questioning is spot on. His cold calling, his assessment for learning. He is always anticipating their misconceptions. And he is a really clear explainer.' He tells me that Garry's students' P8 score for food GCSE is +1.8 *every year*, without fail. 'He always says to me in March that he's not sure about his Year 11s, but year after year after year the results come in.' It doesn't surprise me one iota when Matt says that Garry cannot really say why he is a great teacher. His practice is so well-ingrained, that he is genuinely unconscious of his supreme competence.

Suddenly Matt rises and says, 'Garry will be in assembly now. I'll go and get him.' In Matt's absence I look around the office at the changes

Matt has made. He is a smart man. It is much more stylish. Interior design was never my bag. Before long, I hear laughter approaching the room. Matt is giggling as he enters with Garry. 'Look, I told you!' Matt says.

Garry is grinning. In his hand is a small Tupperware box with a raw chicken breast crammed into it. 'It's Tommy's. He had it in assembly. His practical is period 5. I told him I'd put it in the fridge until then, or pathogenic bacteria will have a field day. The last thing we need is a salmonella breakout!' We all start laughing. It is, as ever, so good to see him again.

Teaching

As we wait for his Year 8 class, Garry and I chat. School life is more challenging, post-COVID. 'I just thought, "Yeah, Covid, it'll be all right once they're back". But, blimey, it's just not the same. We have an autism unit for students with very specific learning difficulties now. So many varied needs. Idiosyncratic stuff. More students have no stamina or resilience. Ask them to do something challenging and they just give in. It's not the same and I think it will be a long time before we get back to where we were. Independent learning … it's like it was a decade or more ago.' Garry frowns. This isn't a man blaming the students. This is a man properly perplexed by the changed psychological landscape of our schools.

There is a *do now* task on the board. It is to draw a simple two-column, six-row grid on their mini-whiteboards, and write the words Ingredient-Flour-Water-Yeast-Sugar-Salt down the first column, and Purpose in the first cell of the second. The students write the grid and the words on their whiteboards while Garry takes the register. It's a rarity; this is a *do now* task that occupies students, is meaningful, but does not impinge upon the core of the lesson. There is no time in a Garry Littlewood lesson for activities that have no purpose … Every. Minute. Counts.

Garry moves into the small lobby area where the students leave their coats and bags. He encourages them into the room. He asks after Harrison and whether he has recovered the full use of his arm. Peter needs a bit more help than most, but is never chastised. They are all *do nowing* before you know it.

If Garry is one thing, it is enthusiastic. 'We're going to have a really exciting lesson! We are beginning our design and make task today!' He brims with anticipation, and it is genuine. This is an expert at the top of his game. He has probably taught this lesson dozens and dozens of times, yet he knows better than any teacher I have ever known, that this is the first and only time these particular students will watch him demonstrate how to make bread rolls, 'We're going to be making our own flavoured bread!' A boy literally slavers with excitement, 'It's my favourite lesson of the whole year!'

Expert questioning is Garry's forte. He gives nothing away. He deftly retrieves from the far recesses of the students' brains that self-raising flour gives off CO_2 when making scones, the practical from the previous week. He asks another student, 'What, then, causes bread to rise if we are using strong plain flour?'

'Yeast, Sir', comes the reply. It is precision stuff. He talks through all the different possibilities for making their bread unique. Ideas come thick and fast. With an eye on the clock, he seamlessly moves into the demonstration. He declares that he is going to demonstrate how to make six, perfectly shaped, bread rolls, and invites his charges to gather round the front desk. Everything is exactly where he wants it. His support-staff colleagues replicate his precise approach.

One of the boys doesn't quite settle: 'Did you want to ask something?' No answer. 'Well, cut out the chatter and focus.' His control of the room is absolute, and the students are transfixed. He tells them that they are working at GCSE level today. The students' concentration deepens. He uses words such as 'gluten', 'gliadin' and 'glutenin'. The strong flour is going to give our bread structure. He explains how the yeast is a living thing, and that the sugar feeds it and the salt kills it. He tells them to watch closely. He rubs salt into some yeast and the yeast disintegrates into a creamy mess. He is like a magician. You have to be careful how you introduce the salt. Add it to the flour before it gets to the yeast or it's curtains!

One girl, Eva, watches more intently than the others. I get a sense that she has found something that is speaking to her soul. She offers to answer questions and she asks Garry questions without the need for him to invite her. She is mesmerised by the whole experience.

More technical terms are explained, like fermentation. Garry asks whether anyone can remember the process that makes bread turn a lovely golden brown colour when it is baked. He tells them to think back to last year. 'Is it caramelisation?' one boy asks. 'Oh! Nearly. What's the other word?' asks Garry. The boy thinks. Garry waits. 'Is it dextrinisation?' He's loving this. 'Who taught you in Year 7?' The boy answers, 'You did, Sir.' Garry responds, 'I thought so. That's spot on!' Garry smiles and I cannot contain a full guffaw.

He measures the amount of water precisely, crouching down to ensure the jug holds 175 ml. He is the living embodiment of exactitude. It is a joy to watch this man teach.

It's the final part of the demonstration and Garry is in full swing. He explains how he worked in a bakery when he left school as part of his catering course, before he left to train to be a teacher … but not before he perfected the art of kneading. He cuts the dough into six lumps. With the artistry of a master baker, he rolls one under his palm for ten seconds. He takes his hand away with a flourish to reveal a full moon of dough. 'Now, if you're as good as me, you can make two perfectly round balls at once!' Every single student is enthralled. Ten seconds later his hands produce two more examples of spherical perfection. We have a small ripple of applause. It's into the oven next. And he warns them that they will be putting their own attempts into the hot oven next week. He won't do it for them. Watch and learn.

While the bread buns are baking, Garry gives the students a cloze exercise to do, which details the process he has just demonstrated, with key, technical vocabulary missing. They spend 10 minutes completing the exercise and then Garry tests them to see who has remembered what, so he knows who may need help in the ensuing practical lesson. It also helps the students begin embedding the processes he has just demonstrated into their long-term memory, so that next week, when they enact what they have just observed for themselves (they will, crucially, have had time to forget), they will have rehearsed how to bake bread rolls in three different ways – observed, written and enacted. As Graham Nuthall claimed, three times in three different contexts is the magic combination when trying to make a permanent change to the students' long-term memory.[1] Though Garry's pedagogy is founded to some extent upon his sparkling character, his subject knowledge is second to none and his approach to teaching is evidence-informed; he works, after all, in a Research School.

Across the room is a pristine display. In the centre is a statement that says, 'Food Preparation and Nutrition is NEVER "Just cooking"! It's …' and around that proud assertion are 59 different, cross-curricular things that food preparation and nutrition also encompass, ranging from food photography to microbiology to religious festivals to sustainability to well-being to problem solving to calculating ratios. It's impressive and reflects Garry lifelong conviction that his subject is as important as any other on the curriculum.

The cloze exercise has given time for the rolls to bake. They emerge from the oven golden brown, with wisps of steam coming off them. He wastes not the slightest learning opportunity. 'Why the steam?' he asks and he gets the correct answer, along with an explanation of where the water comes from. He lets them cool and carries on with the lesson.

We have five minutes left. He asks them to imagine what flavours they will add to their rolls next week. For a couple of minutes there is complete silence. The autumn sun streams through the windows. I look across the playing fields, over to the huge Portakabin plant that

---

1 G. Nuthall, *The Hidden Lives of Learners* (Wellington: NZCER Press, 2007), p. 63.

dominates the eastern horizon, and reflect upon what I have been privileged to observe. Young people learning the best of life skills, taught by a man who is just utterly brilliant, whose teaching is a love letter to his subject and to these young people thinking hard in front of me. The ideas flow – oregano, chorizo, chicken, garlic, mozzarella – each one greeted with enthusiasm from Garry and a question to extend the students' thinking. The bell rings. Garry looks up at the clock and says, 'Oh, doesn't time fly …' He doesn't need to complete the aphorism; it is clear they are all having fun.

The students are fully primed for next week's practical. As they leave, each one gets a taste of Garry's golden-brown bread rolls, which he has hurriedly cut up. I get a piece too, and while Garry and I eat, ever the perfectionist, he says, 'Mmmm, they could have done with another minute in the oven – they're ever so slightly doughy.'

What the students think

I chat with Lola, who is the first to arrive. She thinks Mr Littlewood is funny, talkative and kind. I don't press her any further, as other students begin to enter the room. I finally have eleven – a mix of Year 10s, 12s and 13s. I ask them to pair up and try to work out why Mr Littlewood is such a great teacher. While they chat, I hear one say, 'He's just a good person, isn't he?'

I begin the feedback with Year 10. 'He encourages our creativity. And when you go wrong, he never makes you feel silly.' As I move across the room, the same themes crop up. 'He's always there to help … He cares about every one of us, individually … Mr Littlewood properly takes time to help us if we are struggling … He's passionate about his job … I never saw him get angry … he is always calm and fun … He *enjoys* his job.' I probe that last comment a little further. We conclude that

Garry's enjoyment of his job is important. It helps *them* enjoy the subject.

I want to know a bit more about the subject stuff. One of the Year 12s is very perceptive. 'Well, the thing is, he teaches us all the nutritional and food science stuff, but then he also links it into recipes. I like the way he does that. The theory doesn't just sit there outside the practical work – it is a crucial part of it. And because he makes those links, it helps us remember the theory.' Nods of agreement around the room, and, of course, from me – that's exactly what I saw in the Year 8 lesson, with talk of fermentation, caramelization and dextrinization.

Another sixth former, Niall, pipes up. He is one of the few students I recognise from years back. 'If you've had a bad day', he says, 'you know Mr Littlewood will understand. I always feel safe when I am in his room. It's reassuring. I have a place I know I can go, if I need to.' The openness with which he speaks is testament to the culture Garry has created in his classroom and, more widely, of the school's approach to supporting students with additional needs.

I ask them whether they can remember a moment with Mr Littlewood that has stuck in their memories. 'He gave me some chocolate when I cut my head open and I had to have stitches in it.' 'My GCSE practical went wrong and he stayed late until I had sorted it.' 'When I dislocated my knee, he made me sit down while the rest of the class cleared up!' 'My chilled flan was amazing!' Finally, the one that made me laugh out loud: 'Mr Littlewood fixed my profiteroles!'

Before I ask them for a single word to describe Garry, a Year 10 pupil says, unsolicited, 'He's a nice person. He cares about everyone individually. He properly takes time to help you if you need it.' This is a refrain I am hearing repeatedly as I move from school to school, teacher to teacher, across the country. Students feeling confident and happy to ask teachers for individual help with their work seems to be an essential feature of truly great teachers. Relationships, relationships, relationships. I say that despite Tom Bennett once tweeting, 'Apparently @johntomsett just said "People are what matters". WHERE'S HIS EVIDENCE? Oh God, I'm having a breakdown ...'

So, here is Garry Littlewood in single words: bubbly (he's not a 1970s Miss World contestant, but I know what they mean ...), enthusiastic, phenomenal, joyful, supportive, hardworking ('If he's not slacking, we won't ...'), knowledgeable and *organised*. I seize upon the last word. 'Tell me more about "organised".' We're in a food room. They urge me to open the drawer to the desk I am perched on. Stuck to the bottom of the drawer is a graphic template to help students replace the essential kitchen implements in the right place so that Garry can check there is a full set at the end of the lesson. I am incredulous. (see page xx).

They laugh and one of them says, with consensus murmured across the room, 'Green knives! He's obsessed with counting how many we return. You can't leave the lesson until he has a full set!' They're all giggling.

I thank them for their contributions, and once they've departed, I sneak open the desk drawer to marvel again at the sheer precision with which the spatula and the pastry brush have been replaced.

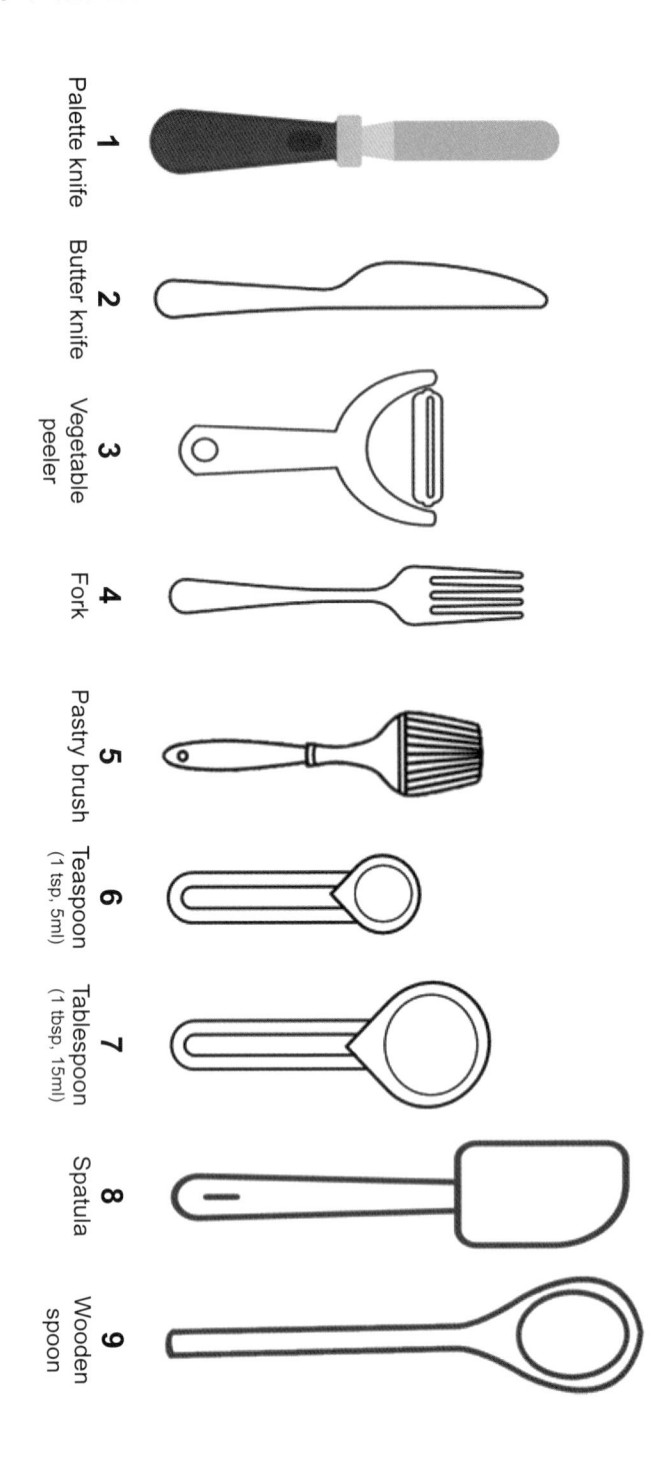

76 | THIS MUCH I KNOW ABOUT TRULY GREAT SECONDARY TEACHERS

1. Palette knife
2. Butter knife
3. Vegetable peeler
4. Fork
5. Pastry brush
6. Teaspoon (1 tsp, 5ml)
7. Tablespoon (1 tbsp, 15ml)
8. Spatula
9. Wooden spoon

IRL: Garry Littlewood

John Tomsett (JT): Why did you go into teaching, Garry?

Garry Littlewood (GL): When I left school, I always wanted to be something to do with food. I wanted to be a chef. I went to college and studied hotel management and catering. I still loved it, but did quite a lot of part-time work in kitchens and I just decided this is not for me, full-time. At college we did a work placement and I did some work with primary children at their school. I thought, 'Yes, I think I could be a teacher of food.' From college I went on to university and did a home economics BEd (Hons) at Sheffield, the traditional degree to follow if you wanted to train to be a teacher. Mum and dad didn't really want me to go to university. Nobody in the family had been before. My sister and brother didn't go to university, so mum and dad were quite concerned about being able to afford to send me, but I was determined to go. I went, loved it, and so I did a BEd and studied to be a food teacher. I started teaching in 1994.

At that time it was still uncertain as to whether food was going to be included in the national curriculum. In those last few years at university, I was unsure whether I was going to have a job at the end of studying. There were quite a few jobs that came up, and one of them was in Cheshire at Winsford, which is between Manchester and Liverpool. I went for the job there not wanting it but ended up being offered the post. I didn't realise you had to accept on the day. I asked for five minutes to think about it. I went and got on the payphone and rang my mum: 'What do I do? What do I do? It's in Cheshire, not my beloved Yorkshire. I don't know. It's a long way.' But the school felt right. It was a brilliant school to start your career. There were a lot of struggling families, probably what would now be referred to as PP. It was, at the time, the overspill council estates for Liverpool and Manchester. I was there for six years.

JT: **Then you came to Huntington.**

I came here because my dad was poorly. He got throat cancer, and I felt I needed to be nearer home to support my parents. That was one of the reasons I left the school. I wouldn't have left at that time because I was working my way up, having started as the food teacher, I then became Key Stage 3 coordinator, then I got head of food. I came as head of food and textiles here in 2000 and been here ever since. I've done different jobs within the school, which I've enjoyed, but my heart, my passion, is teaching food, and I'm happy. I'm back where I think I do my best work and add most value.

JT: **Let's think about teaching, then. I watched you teach that lesson this morning. It was just textbook-ly brilliant. You might have cooked those bread rolls for another minute, but apart from that ...** [*laughs*]

GL: Yes, oh, they were very doughy.

JT: **Someone less experienced wouldn't realise the years and years of effort that have gone into getting to that point of expertise. Tell me a bit about how you've developed your teaching over time.**

GL: I think it all starts with a really good scheme of learning. I'm absolutely focused on having our schemes so that anybody can pick them up and teach the key content. They're really well-sequenced. They're very well planned. I infuriate my departmental colleagues because I change the schemes every year. When you get more experienced, you realise the children change over time. They're very different from what they were five years ago, so you need to alter things accordingly. I do plan everything. I plan meticulously. I think I'm very well-organised; sometimes, perhaps, too organised.

JT: **The students said you were organised when I interviewed them. You can't be *too* organised.**

GL: Well, you can't be a disorganised food teacher. It's probably a little different to some other specialisms because in food you've got to have the ingredients there. You've got to have everything ready, and if you're not organised and you've not planned, you're just going to fail in that lesson. I think it's all about making sure that your planning is as thorough as it possibly could be, and, even now, I still write lesson plans.

JT: **You do?**

GL: I do. Some people, like newer staff in my department, just write in their diaries 'flapjack' or other simple headings like that. I can't do that. I've got to go through that thinking process of how you get the students to learn what you want them to learn.

JT: **Do you rehearse the mental processes?**

GL: I do. *Every* lesson. Because every lesson is different. That lesson you saw today, I've done it three times this week. But it's different every time because you've got different students. They've got different needs. So, the planning is very different for every lesson. The content is the same, but I wouldn't go to some of those higher level questions that I did today with the other group, because it will be overwhelming for a number of them.

JT: **Eva was really interesting in that lesson because she's hungry to learn everything about food, isn't she? She looks like a student who might not be a high prior-attaining student, but she's got something. She's recognised this is her world. This is her subject. She's all over it.**

GL: And she's a SEND [special educational needs and disabilities] student.

JT: **Is she? I thought so. I thought she had additional needs, but she's bewitched by your subject. She loves it.**

GL: Yes, that's interesting you've picked that up, actually, because she absorbs information, doesn't she?

JT: **She concentrating fully, all the time.**

GL: So, I think planning is the key, and, obviously, subject knowledge … I know my subject very well. I know what level to go to at GCSE and at Level 3, and I try and use a lot of the GCSE terminology in lower school.

JT: *Dextrinisation* **was a genius moment, wasn't it?**

GL: We introduce those terms in Year 7. We've just used it now with them making jam tarts. It's just drip-feeding little bits in about the food science because it isn't just about cooking. It's the nutritional basis of cooking, the food science. You need all that to be a successful student at the end of GCSE. If you start in lower school, then you can build it up. I've always said to you, John, that Key Stage 3 is the most important phase in any student's life. You've got to develop the enthusiasm there, and you've got to get some of that key information down into Key Stage 3.

But, however much planning you do, something can always happen … Look at today, we didn't have a smashed bowl. All you need is one smashed bowl, and it just ruins the flow of the lesson.

JT: **There's also those moments of magic. When you destroyed the yeast.**

GL: They'll remember that. Yes, little things like that can just spark their imagination. Matt did ask me in my exams debrief meeting, 'Why do students perform so well in food and textiles?' I think they know that we care about them. I do care about them. I care about every student, as every teacher does, but I think they feel safe in my classroom and our department.

JT: Go on. Tell me a bit more about that.

GL: I think they feel safe. They come in, and they know they're not going to be shouted at. There's a calmness there. I'm not saying that we're soft at all because there's firmness … But I think they've got to feel safe now. There is a small number of students who will not go into a classroom, who refuse to go to their lessons. We can't *make* them go into a lesson. As a teacher, you can't force them in. I think you have to create in your classroom an environment that's safe and where they feel comfortable; they will then be ready to learn.

JT: **To remedy the attendance issue globally, we've got to achieve that in schools as a whole. We need to get back to where they are places that are attractive to attend for every single child.**

GL: Yes, absolutely. I can be a right grump at times, as anybody can. We all have bad days, but creating that calm and safe place, is what makes students enjoy coming up to our department. Obviously, we've got an advantage that they cook, and they do practical work. You've got the buy-in there, but the theory is just as important as the practical.

JT: **Your ability to be enthusiastic is amazing. Baking bread rolls was the most exciting thing they were ever going to do in their lives. That all comes from you. Some of the words that the students used about you – 'joyous', 'enthusiastic' – resonated. In preparation for writing this, I looked up a paper Alex Quigley recommended to me written by Rosenshine et al. in 1971. They did a meta-analysis of all the research about teacher behaviours and characteristics that result in student outcomes improving, and one of them was 'enthusiasm'. Across the school system now, because it's so hard to get hold of a teacher, there's an attitude that says something like, 'as long as you've got a scheme of work that anybody who has passed the DBS**

(disclosure and barring service) checks and has a pulse can pick up and use in a classroom, that will do'. If that's our ambition as a school system, then we're in trouble. It's hard to be enthused about what you're teaching in those circumstances.

GL: Yes, I think when we've seen quite a few trainee teachers over the last few years, I've been really disappointed by their lack of drive to do something exciting, with enthusiasm. They pick up our scheme of learning and just deliver it. No, I don't want that. I want you to put your own stamp on it. I didn't do that when I was learning to teach. I took the scheme of learning and then tried to make it my own. You develop your experience by doing that. I think the evidence-informed approach is important. Absolutely, it's important. Explicit instruction and all that, and we can put that into a lesson, but you've got to have that genuine passion and excitement for the work, and the love of your subject. That's what some new teachers don't seem to have. I don't feel that they're doing it because they love the subject.

I love my subject. I always have done, and it hasn't changed. I fight for the subject in school when things are going to change, because I think it's important. All those skills that you can develop in young people through our subject actually does help them in the future.

JT: **I think the learning process in technology is spot on. You get a brief, you do your research, you enact it and you evaluate it. It's almost a perfect learning model for anything. If I was an employer and I knew someone had that sequence of skills and knew that process, that would impress me.**

GL: Yes, for sure.

JT: What are you working on at the moment in your teaching?

GL: I think it's about rekindling students' independence in the learning process. You'll have seen on the recipes – we've done it for textiles projects too – that they now have a step-by-step method and they've got a tick box for every time they complete a step. After the pandemic, they would come to you in every lesson and ask, 'What do I do next? What do I do next? What do I do next?' I would reply, 'I'm not telling you what you've got to do next. You've got instructions there. I've demonstrated it.'

JT: I noticed in the lesson that you said, 'Next week, I'm not taking your bread rolls out of the oven for you. You're doing it yourself.'

GL: They've got to take some ownership, so I'm working on trying not to intervene too much. I can say, 'I'm not telling you whether yours is cooked or not', and then I go and tell them! You've always got that time constraint in food. They've got to be out by the end of the lesson, and that is just a bind for any practical subject. Yet we've got to get them to start using their thinking skills and their independence. It's exactly the same in textiles. You'll show them something, give instructions, they've got examples in front of them, and then they'll say, 'What do I do now?' So, I say, 'No, I've just spent 20 minutes demonstrating what to do. I'm not doing it for you.' That's something that we're working on – trying not to intervene quite as much.

JT: If we go back to Matt's question, why, then, do your students get such great results?

GL: High expectations.

JT: Yes, tell me about that.

GL: I've always said to you, John, when you were head teacher, and I say to the students, 'I'm really not interested in what your target grade is.' It's about having those high expectations. If we're looking at the GCSE criteria, for instance, I always say, 'Oh, we're not looking at levels 1 or 2. We're not looking at 3 or 4. We're looking at 5 and 6 for starters and then we're looking at 7, 8 and 9.' If you instil that level of unapologetic aspiration in them, they do try harder. They do have higher expectations of themselves. I've always just done that. It's just what I do.

JT: **Every teacher I've interviewed for this project so far has felt the same.**

GL: Yes, you've got to let the kids know that they can get there. You're not going to be successful with every student, but if you get the buy-in from them early on and they know you're on their side, then they will perform for you. They're honest working-class kids here, and I love that … That's what I was. I *get* the vulnerable students – I wasn't a vulnerable student at school, but I can get down to their level. I'm not down-with-the-kids. I'd never say that, but I can get down to their level and see things through their lens. We don't get many high-target-grade students in food. They choose other subjects, which is absolutely fine, but we will get as many 8s and 9s as any other subjects.

JT: **Yes, you're right up there with the very best performing subjects. You always were. So, we've got high expectations. What else?**

GL: I think it's about caring, John. The students know …

JT: **It's the first thing they said when I spoke to them.**

GL: … they know we care about them … that I care about them. I do care about them. Some are really difficult and challenging, but they're kids at the end of the day.

JT: **Do you remember Paula Shanks in the science department?**

GL: Yes.

JT: She used to say to my wife, 'You have to pour love into them when they least deserve it.'

GL: Yes. That's a great way of thinking about it. Some of those cheekiest, most difficult kids need the most care. I've moved a girl from another group. She wasn't getting on at all well. I went to the head of year and said, 'I'm thinking of moving her into my group.' The head of year thought that she wouldn't like it, that she'd want to stay with her friends and just refuse to move. But I thought I would try anyway. I found her and I said, 'Right, Jacinda, I've seen something in you. You need to come into my group. I've seen your practical skills.' I'd been on bus duty, and she brought this cake she'd baked to show me. 'Look at this, Sir, look at what I've done.' I said, 'That's amazing. You should be in my group!' So, I reminded her of that, and I said, 'Right, I've got a space. Somebody's left. I want to move you into my group because I think with your practical skills you can do really well. Would you like that?' She was thrilled, 'Oh, yes Sir.' It was just that taking her to one side … A one-to-one. She could have refused to move but she felt special. She's done really well. She's not going to get an amazing grade, but if she gets a five … my job is done.

JT: I bet it will be the best grade she gets.

GL: It will be amazing. It's just little things like that, that you can do. It's just doing that extra bit sometimes.

JT: I saw in the *TES* editorial earlier this week an article entitled, *What Makes a Great Teacher*. The headline answer is just two things: high expectations and high individual support. Well, *who knew*?

GL: Yes, I mean, when you sent me the email, I just thought, well, I'm not that great. I'm just doing my job.

JT: Yes, but people new to the profession don't always do that now. If you think about your disappointment in the last crop of trainee teachers … I think system wide

> there's probably an issue around workload and where that work/home balance lies.

GL: It's a job that you've got to work hard at. I work as hard now as I did when I first started teaching. I plan thoroughly, and the other thing I do as well – which probably goes against all current thinking – is that I look at every piece of work the students do. I don't mark it all. I put a tick on it, or I'll write little comments. At Key Stage 3, we only see them once a week. It's not like English. It's not like we've got lots and lots of work in, but I do look at everything. I mark it. They know I've seen it, and that makes them work harder because I think they know I'm going to look. I'll just say, 'Oh, I'm not happy with this presentation. You need to improve next time.' I do that all the time, and it takes me a long time, but I think it's worth it. When I had the opportunity to watch other teachers, like Izzy and Jack Bream, they do exactly the same. I do everything against what's on my schemes of learning! We've got targeted pieces of work that you have to mark, you have to give feedback on, but I will look at everything. I do spend more time on things. I haven't got a family at home. I don't have any of that to focus on, so I can do that, but it does make a difference. It does make them value the subject. It just makes them focus on their work more, I think. It's a hard job. We're well paid, John. We get those lovely holidays.

JT: **Lots of professionals work at the weekends and in the evenings. I've got solicitor mates who work all weekend, all Saturday and Sunday, if they've got a case coming up. We're not extraordinary like that. We get well paid, and we're working with young people in a school. What's not to like?**

GL: Absolutely.

JT: **Right, so any specific moments that stand out for you that have been great?**

GL: I think last year when … Did Niall come to see you today?

JT: **Yes. Niall was interesting today.**

GL: Bless Niall. He worked really hard. His target grade was a 4, and I just said, 'No, no, forget your target grade. We're not working to target grade.' He worked really hard. He was really enthusiastic. He's a swimmer. He gets up early mornings. Anyway, he got his result, and he got an 8, John.

JT: **An 8!** [*laughs*]

GL: He got an 8. I was absolutely thrilled for him. On results day he ran across the exam hall. He came up to me and said, 'Look sir, I've got an 8! I've got a grade 8! I can't believe I've got an 8. It's my highest grade.'

I said, 'Brilliant, I told you you'd get there.' Then he said, 'Can I put my arms around you and give you a hug?' And he did. I was nearly in tears. I came up here to my office and I just thought, 'He's a real success story.'

JT: **He said something about that. He said, 'You feel safe with Mr Littlewood.' He used the word 'safe'. I remember him. He must have been in Year 7 or Year 8.**

GL: Niall's now doing level 3. He's a lovely lad. That is probably a career highlight. Somebody's recognised that you've worked really hard with them. It was quite a challenging group that Niall was in, to be fair, and he probably didn't have the attention that I would normally have given him because there were four really difficult boys in there who all did all right, but I was focused on them every lesson. I was just really pleased. I just thought, 'Yes, that's what it's about. We're here to make that student get the grades, and he can move forward, and he's now doing level 3.'

JT: **What would you say then, if you listed the reasons why you're a great teacher?**

GL: I think I have high expectations. I think I've got a sense of humour, which I think is important. I do like to have a bit of fun in the lessons, and I think they quite like it. I'm well-planned. I care about how they do. My classroom discipline is good. They don't get away with anything, but I'm not a shouter. Never have been. I'm consistent. I think they know where they stand.

JT: **You'll always be the same every lesson, relentlessly.**

GL: Yes. I'm pretty relentless as well, I think. Yes, I think they're probably my best features.

JT: **They chime exactly with what the students said. One of them said you are 'talkative'!**

GL: Yes, I can go off on a bit of a tangent. When I'm explaining something, I'll just pick a student's name out. When I was introducing the project briefs yesterday, and I was saying what sorts of things you could make, I said, 'Oh, Imogen, you love a cheesecake, don't you?' I've no idea if she does or not, but it keeps them on their toes.

JT: **They love it. They absolutely loved it today. So did you. You were almost showing off, you were so on top of your game!**

GL: [*Grins*] That Year 8 lesson today, I did that yesterday. It was no different from what I did yesterday. I let my bread rolls cook a bit longer because I probably talked more than I would normally do today, because, obviously, you were there, and I was just a bit more self-conscious.

JT: **It was an absolute joy. Thank you so much.**

Testimonials

I had several testimonials I could have included, but one stood out as representative of them all. Here it is, unabridged.

Dear Mr Littlewood

I can't even write everything I would like to say to you. You truly are my school dad! You have seen me happy, tired, bored, angry, upset, competitive and in disbelief. I will never forget you.

The smile on your face at the gate, your lesson and our class have genuinely been the highlight of two years. All the class love you and your stories. Please remember us!

Even if I see you checking the supermarket fridge temperatures, I'll come and say hi.

I can officially say that you are and have always been my favourite teacher. I will miss your lessons, our laughs, cooking, your carrot love and beautiful music (listen to more One Direction)!

You have been the best teacher, making me constantly laugh, smile and be happy. So, thank you.

I'll always hold James to the time that you said he couldn't have made better quality fruit tarts than me. Your lessons were my favourites too. You never doubt my abilities and always have my back, restoring my confidence. I am so thankful for your efforts which gave me 7s and 8s in every exam – including my 50% coursework grade. I will miss our food technology lessons and our eventful class. Also, thank you through Covid for giving us warm Johnson block over Wilberforce just for us to be able to cook.

Everyone knows but you are the most incredible teacher. I am so grateful for your laughs and your teaching, Sir.

You can't replace me next year either because we were iconic wafflers – I have enjoyed every conversation we've had. I'm sorry for being a constant chatterbox and getting easily distracted and for writing over 20 pages of coursework – which you ended up reducing the font of for moderation. I hope to do you proud on results day. (You never know, if childcare doesn't work out, I might try teaching food like you!)

Thank you Sir. I'll miss you!

So, what can we learn from Garry Littlewood?

Like many good teachers, Garry has a decent sense of himself as a classroom practitioner. At the end of our chat, he listed a number of features of his teaching that were clear from the lesson I witnessed: high expectations, meticulous planning, good behaviour management, relentlessness and consistency. I think they are inter-related. It was interesting that his immediate response to my query as to why he is such a good teacher was 'high expectations'. It's not just his academic expectations of his students – which are, as Matt Smith noted, 'sky-high' and exemplified by Niall's four grades above target GCSE performance – but it's also his expectations of his students' behaviour, and of their commitment to study and to the subject. The way students mirror their teachers' behaviour and attitudes is striking, and we can learn a great deal from Garry in this regard.

Crucially, Garry has high expectations of himself. As he says, he is relentless in his approach to his work, and consistent in his classroom practice. His decision to ignore his own marking policy may well be looked upon dimly by you, dear reader, but he is only being true to his own self when he stays up late reading every page of each and every student's work. And for a man of such expertise, his insistence on writing bespoke lesson plans for every lesson is both surprising and impressive, especially if it results in the quality of teaching and learning I was privy to when I observed him. Like he said, teaching is hard work, and I am not sure standards will rise across the system if we seek shortcuts to what is required to become a truly great teacher.

When I arrived at Huntington as a green deputy head in 1998, the sixth form common room's mural featured Mahatma Gandhi and his aphorism, 'Happiness is when what you think, what you say, and what you do are aligned.' Garry is a funny, happy man. It struck me, editing this chapter, how many times we laughed! In the classroom he is who he is. He doesn't put on an act that makes him fundamentally unaligned. He has earnt the liberty to be himself in a world where teaching to the script is often *de rigueur*. I think his sense of humour is at the root of his enthusiasm for his subject and for teaching. The testimonial is explicit about how much laughter rings around his food room. It would be a foolish head teacher who denied Garry Littlewood the chance to have a bit of fun, just every now and then.

Garry Littlewood's students' progress and achievement data

For the last 10 years at least, the progress score for GCSE food has been above +1.3. Most recently it was +1.8. At Level 3, the advanced level performance system (ALPS) score has never been lower than a grade 2. Every measure of attainment and progress in the subjects led by Garry is way beyond school and national expectations.

A Truly Great Mathematics Teacher: Chris McGrane

Chris McGrane is the principal teacher of mathematics at Holyrood Secondary in Glasgow. He is currently acting depute head teacher at Holyrood.

The school leadership's view

Here is some background on Chris McGrane. He was first recommended to me years ago, when I asked Mark McCourt for the name of the best subject leader of mathematics he knew. When Mary Myatt and I subsequently interviewed Chris for our first book in the *Huh* curriculum series, we swiftly realised he was an expert. So, when I was thinking about truly great teachers, Chris popped into my mind immediately. He works at the biggest school in Scotland, the impressive, 2,200-student-strong, Holyrood Secondary in Glasgow.

Sharon Watson, the head teacher, greets me warmly. Her office is nestled in the very heart of the school. 'He is an expert in teacher-led exposition', she says of Chris, who is her acting depute as well as a great classroom practitioner. Sharon, too, is a mathematician. She goes on, 'He has tremendous subject knowledge. It's second to none. But it is more than that. What marks him out is that he understands how to sequence the teaching of the curriculum content in a way that leads to a deep understanding of mathematical concepts.' She points out how his connection with the students enables him to 'tease' responses out of them. 'Every young person is making progress in his classes. Not just in his Highers (equivalent to A levels in England) and National 5s (equivalent to GCSEs in England), but right across the range of students.'

'Why?' I ask.

'Why? Because the students love him! I have never met anyone he has taught who does not speak highly of him. They work hard because of his investment in them. It's so obvious he wants to be there, in front of them teaching them maths, and they respond to his commitment – which is total – with their commitment. He follows through on every single thing. He marks their homework promptly, every time. He's a challenge-giver and he pushes them.'

'And he's your depute now?'

'Yes, and that has made no difference to his teaching. His expectations are still sky high, even though he has a lot on his plate with such a responsibility. The thing is with Chris,' she says, 'is that he doesn't care where you're from. He doesn't pre-judge and he doesn't see why your background should affect your mathematical skills. He's an intense guy, really strong. Really thorough. He reads people well.'

'When we interviewed him, he seemed as though he wouldn't suffer fools!'

'[*Laughs*] Well, he certainly doesn't sweat the small stuff! He will refuse to argue over trivial things; he says that relationships die once that happens. He can be, how shall I say, "appropriately sarcastic" at times, but with the right people, people he knows well.'

Holyrood is a Roman Catholic school. One of the posters articulating the school's value system ends with a statement that says, 'We are all called to God by serving others in all that we do.' I suggest that what Chris does is merely fulfil the school's religious mission. Sharon agrees.

'While the maths is key with Chris, what stands him apart is his relationship with the students. He treats them like adults, and they respond accordingly. He's never in their face. He's reflective and he is respectful of the young people.'

'What's he like as a subject leader?' I ask.

'Well, I should know, as I'm in his department! At meetings, all the talk is about mathematical pedagogy – the best way to teach this and that. He is always thinking about how we might do things better. He says, "We can control what happens in the maths classroom and that is where we need to focus our efforts." And his favourite line is this: "You're doing your job if every child you teach thinks that maths is all you care about!"' We both laugh. 'I know he's good, because so many of the children discuss him at home … I'm told that by the parents at parents' evenings.'

I ask her if she has anything else about Chris that I ought to include in the book. She grins. 'Look,' she says, 'you've been a head teacher. You'll be as competitive as me, underneath it all. You'll have wanted to have been the best teacher in your department, won't you?' I nod. My first book was originally titled, *Why the head teacher has to be the best teacher in the school*. 'Well, I'll admit that I'm not the best teacher of mathematics in this building …' she grins, '… that's because Chris is …'

Teaching

I slip through a secret door from Sharon's office into Chris'. Sharon is right. He doesn't sweat the small stuff. His office clock is stuck at five past six. Why bother replacing the battery when you have the time in the corner of your laptop screen and on your mobile? Stuffed underneath his capacious desk is his sports kit and all sorts of forgotten paperwork. We are just about to talk when a student knocks. He ushers her in and plugs in a charger for her mobile.

We walk and talk. He's teaching first period. 'Our catchment, the southside of Glasgow, is very diverse. We have students from an incredible variety of backgrounds; we have a lot of students from Asian, African, Roma and eastern European families. We take in pupils from working-class neighbourhoods, pupils from the least affluent parts of the city and pupils from some of the most affluent postcodes.' He teaches Highers.

Chris' teaching room is cavernous. High ceilings and display-free walls. I sit at the back on my own, like a naughty boy. The low-level lighting is a novelty. The main lights are dimmed and there is a lamp on the floor next to me. It feels a bit like a nightclub. The students enter the room in dribs and drabs. Suddenly, there are nearly 30 of them with their books open, working on the starter questions. Chris is as low-key as the lighting. 'There's a starter on the board for you. You haven't done this stuff for a bit. Some spaced practice.' They are the *hardest* starter questions I have ever seen! I don't even know what the second one means (forgive the pun) …

1. For the polynomial $x^3 - 4x^2 + ax + b$, $(x + 2)$ is a factor, and when the polynomial is divided by $(x - 3)$ the remainder is -20. Find the values of a and b.

2. Find the equation of the median from G.

```
           y
           |
           |
  G (−2, 5)|       H (15,4)
    _____|_____/
 ----\-----|-----/---------→ x
      \    |    /
       \   |   /
        \  |  /
         \ | /
          \|/
           J (3, −14)
```

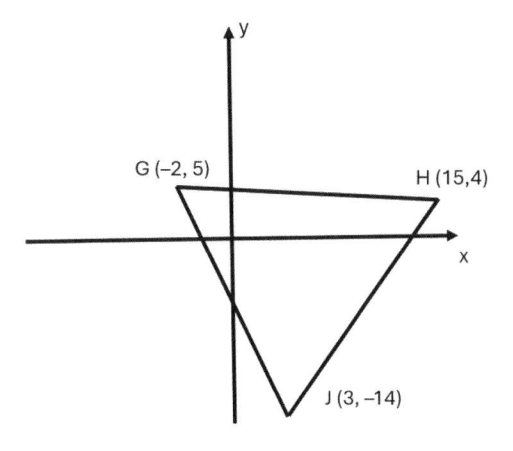

Chris is another truly great teacher who teaches with the door open. He finishes the register and then walks between the desks, looking over the students' shoulders. He stops to tell me that this is an exercise that has a dual aim: to recall the mathematics and to act as a buffer for latecomers. Glasgow policy is to provide a nurturing welcoming environment, so challenging pupils on late arrival to period 1 has to be done sensitively, and not normally in front of the whole class.

He gives the students a tip and, of course, I can suddenly see how the first question unfurls beautifully as a straight-forward simultaneous equation. It's not that hard at all … He works the room, peering at the students' exercise books, while intermittently working out the solution on the board. He doesn't need mini-whiteboards to find out who can do what, because he already knows from his previous knowledge of the students and his over-the-shoulder scrutiny. He completes the answer on the board. It's rapid-fire exposition. High-powered stuff. He is dourly insistent. He is a brilliant mathematician. You have to concentrate like hell and hang on to his mathematical coat-tails! I love it. He then says, 'Look, substituting isn't new. The only higher-level maths is at the beginning. The next four marks are pretty low level. So, $a = -7$ and $b = 10$.' He then does something that leaves me discombobulated … he asks the students to put their hand up if they got that right. If there is a pedagogic crime that I have derided more than any other since I became a consultant, it is teachers asking their students to put their hand up if they've understood something they've been taught. It makes no sense. If I were a student and I was asked that question, I would give a smile and a thumbs up even if I hadn't a flying clue what was going on. So, why does Chris ask for *hands up if you can do it*? The lesson carries on without me, while I'm distracted.

I pick the lesson back up as Chris gives the students a thinking task. 'I'm not going to patronise you, but in your pairs, have a quick discussion about what these three statements mean? You've seen them lots of times, but what do they *mean*? This is just to get you thinking. A quick wee discussion task.'

1 $3x - 15 = 0$
2 $3x - 15 > 0$
3 $3x - 15 \leq 0$

As they discuss the statements, Chris comes over to me. He says, 'In maths everything has a picture. These are all to do with a straight line. They love the abstract at 15 or 16 years old, but they actually begin to hate the tangible, the concrete. They prefer to work in symbols, but this can become detached from meaning.' He carries on round the room, listening. He varies the next set of expressions. He runs the room, diving in, listening and looking. There's no need for mini-whiteboards. He knows who can do what. You have to pay attention or you'd soon be lost. I love this type of teaching of maths! It's unapologetically challenging. But every single student is enjoying the work. They are thinking hard, they discuss the maths. They have their heads down working.

He is building up the mathematics sequentially. He asks them to find the values of x in a relatively easy equation: $x^2 + 10x - 11 = 0$

When he checks for understanding, again he just asks, 'Who was thinking that? Hands up … [*scans the room*] … Right. Cool. Hands down. I could talk to you all day, but the only way you learn is by thinking hard about it. I'll come round and see what you're doing. Six examples for you to do.' He runs the room again. Midway through his tour of every desk, he stops and says to me, 'They get harder. Top hard stuff later. This is foundational. I'm happy to spend a full double on this so that they are good at it.' He teaches between the desks for a few more minutes, then steams through the answers, his brain working at an exhilarating pace.

The student just to my right in the corner of the room, begins eating his breakfast. It's the kind of thing that would have irked me no end. He's chomping on a bagel. Chris notices. I prepare for Armageddon. 'What's on your bagel?' asks Chris.

'Butter.'

'That's a bit boring . . . anyway, who got $x = -11$ and $x = 1$?'

And that was it! He wasn't bothered. He just got on with the maths. This is a man refusing to sweat the small stuff and focusing upon what really matters. A couple of them have coats on, despite it feeling toasty to me (to be fair, I am almost *in* the back wall radiator). On his next tour of the room, he suddenly says, 'Sarah, focus', and that is the sum total of his explicit behaviour management techniques for today. He pops over and whispers, 'This has been pretty easy until now.' You could have fooled me . . . 'This is where it begins to get a wee bit weird.' He returns to the front of the class. 'It's been pretty easy for you up to now. But things are going to get a bit weird from now on. So, you need to concentrate.' He shuts the door. 'You need to be totally focused. If you zone out for two seconds, you'll never understand this. Never. I don't think I ever understood this at school.' We develop the idea of inequalities. Basic stuff to begin with but it ramps up pretty quickly. Chris raises his voice slightly. Concentrate or get left behind forever. He sets them a task and again, he is off round the room, explaining, cajoling and challenging.

We move on to quadratic inequalities. Marvellous stuff! He explains some simple rules about inequalities, and where their respective curves cut the x-axis. The teaching is focused on the sub-skills at this point. Chris says he will join everything together soon. They complete a sheet:

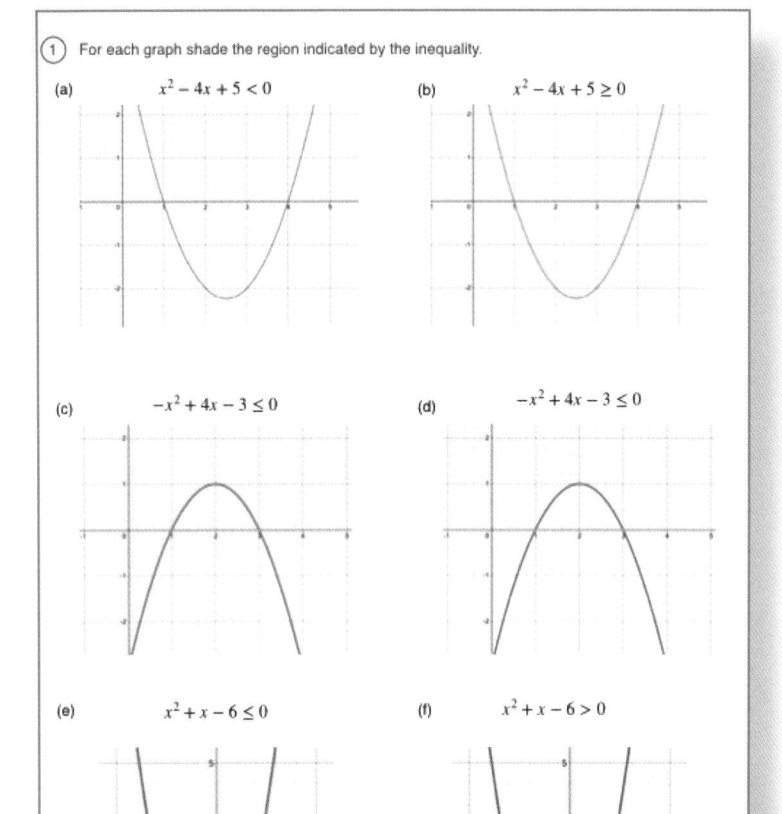

① For each graph shade the region indicated by the inequality.

(a) $x^2 - 4x + 5 < 0$

(b) $x^2 - 4x + 5 \geq 0$

(c) $-x^2 + 4x - 3 \leq 0$

(d) $-x^2 + 4x - 3 \leq 0$

(e) $x^2 + x - 6 \leq 0$

(f) $x^2 + x - 6 > 0$

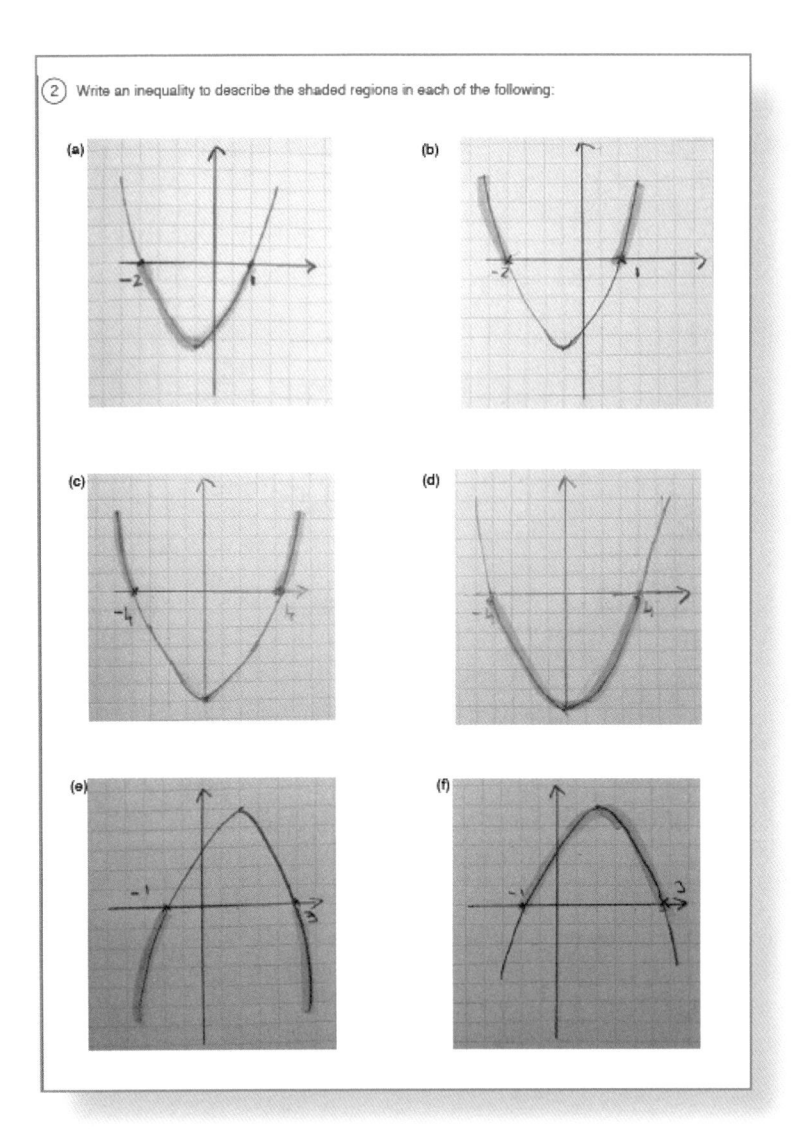

2. Write an inequality to describe the shaded regions in each of the following:

(a)

(b)

(c)

(d)

(e)

(f)

It gets more complex as everything is brought together. It takes utterly clear thinking to plot your way through a question. Chris models an answer:

Example 1

> OK. Solve $x^2 - 4x \geq 0$.
>
> What does x^2 tell us?
>
> Yes, it's a curve. Is it a smiley curve or a sad curve? OK, it's smiley. Why? Yes, because the x^2 term is positive. If it was negative it would be the other way up. Good.
>
> Right, Step #1: Solve = 0
>
> $x^2 - 4x = 0$
>
> $x(x - 4) = 0$
>
> So, $x = 0$ and $x = 4$. What does that tell us about the smiley curve? Yes. It cuts the x-axis at 0 and 4.
>
> So ... Step #2: Draw the curve.

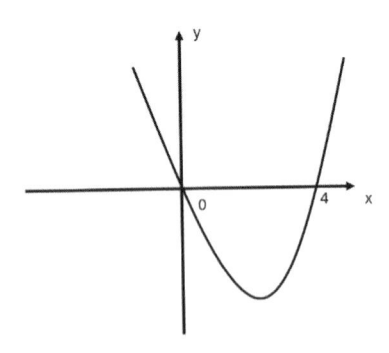

[A graph showing a smiley (upward-opening) parabola crossing the x-axis at 0 and 4, with the y-axis and x-axis labelled.]

> So, it cuts the x-axis at $x = 0$ and $x = 4$.
>
> Step #3, then, is to decide where to shade. Where is the curve greater than or equal to 0? If there are two values for x, how many

sections of the curve do we shade in? Yes, correct, two. At this stage in the question >0 means above the x-axis.

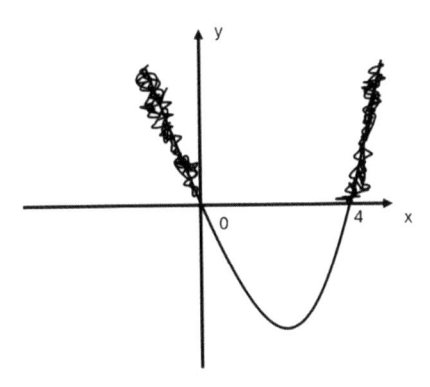

Finally, Step #4. Give the answer. Remember, how we think about the inequality symbols changes at this point … left-right and in-between …

$x \leq 0$ and $x \geq 4$

So absorbing is Chris' modelling, I get fascinated by the maths and forget to type my commentary notes for example 2! This is mathematics teaching at its finest. I am in my element. He does the next example with them, and then the students are on their own, facing this question:

$$-x^2 + 6x - 5 \geq 0$$

As he roams the room, observing but not intervening, he stops at my desk and I tell him how much I am loving watching him teach. He tells me that in the four years he has led the department, the students now almost attain more A grades than they used to get *A–C passes*. There is a bit about Chris that puts him in his own world. But he is in touch with all the students. The chatty girls don't affect him. They can do the work and they are largely talking about the maths, anyway. It is fascinating. Behaviour tsars would be having a nervous breakdown!

The final stage of the lesson sees Chris hand out a worksheet, 'a Susan Whitehouse resource – fantastic task designer.'

QUADRATIC INEQUALITIES

Original inequality	Solution of quadratic equation	Graph showing inequality region	Solution of inequality
$x^2 - 1 > 0$			
$x^2 + 8x + 12 \leq 0$			
$6 + x - x^2 \geq 0$			
$25 - x^2 < 0$			
$x^2 + 3x \leq 0$			
$3x - x^2 \leq 0$			

One student is in a dream manipulating his pen like a drum stick, thinking about the lesson. They all just get on with the work. I think Chris is slightly scary in his intensity about the subject, but in a good way. I'm not sure the students would dare to dawdle. The only break in their concentration is Sharon's intervention over the tannoy with the daily prayer. He moves around the room. He clearly knows them all, with mathematical humanity. He pays his last visit to speak to me. I mention the student eating his breakfast. Chris says, 'I don't care. If you've done the work and you're on your phone, I don't really care. I don't sweat the small stuff.'

The 100-minute lesson has flown by. It's Chris' ability to make them think hard that is at the heart of his success. The whole approach is a challenge. But he gives them a simple heuristic, underpinned by some foolproof rules, which allow every student to tackle the hardest problems. '*All 4 steps!*' he hollers, as he finishes up the lesson. 'Your homework's due in tomorrow, so please remember that …' With that polite reminder, we're done. Almost. There's just the $64 million question to resolve … *why does Chris ask for hands up if you can do it?* The answer lies, surely, in his *between-the-tables* pedagogy. He knows who can do the maths and who cannot, *anyway*. If I were one of his students, I would know that I couldn't afford to mislead him because he would discover the truth the next time he toured the class. The show of hands gives him a big picture number of class-wide understanding, which helps him decide whether to crack on or reteach. This man has been adapting his teaching for years.

What his colleagues think

Across from Chris' office is the Holyrood Diner, a kiosk where students can buy refreshments. Its frontage is pure 1950s art deco America. It looks very cool. Over a cup of tea, I am chatting briefly with Nino and Emily, two of Chris' colleagues in Holyrood's mathematics department. They begin, straight away, talking about curriculum development. 'We spend so much time planning', says Nino.

'And we see him physically teach', adds Emily. 'We consider everything about the curriculum, so that the kids are learning. Hinge questions especially. We have to ensure everyone can progress and use the hinge questions to help know whether they understand or not.'

'So, what are his underlying characteristics?' I ask.

'He is so consistent and . . . measured', replies Nino. 'He's relatable. He gets it. And he gets what's required for the kids.'

Emily smiles and says, 'He builds *amazing* relationships with the students. He really does care.'

Nino is running the department since Chris has moved up to acting depute. 'He is consistent. He develops a bond built on mutual trust. You want to do the work for him. He says to students, "If you match my effort you'll be successful." And personality in the classroom is not enough. Chris really knows his stuff. We talk about maths. A lot!'

Emily finishes off this short session. She laughs. 'He can be wickedly sarcastic! He is a very funny man. What I like is that he gives us liberty to teach in different ways. As long as the results stack up, it doesn't matter. He often says that we're not dealing with robots. We've all got to be the adult in the room, all the time.'

I look round and there are students at the door. Emily and Nino exit, with my sincere thanks, and four smartly dressed students enter.

What the students think

I talk to some of the students Chris has previously taught and some he is still teaching. Once the two minutes I give them to confer about Chris' truly great teacher credentials is over, the response is overwhelming. I have two sessions with the students, and the second is similarly effusive. The key feature of Chris' teaching is, essentially, his commitment to supporting them, individually. 'It's the extra time Mr McGrane gives you. He'll do anything to help. We have supported study, and he will be there until 6 pm if you need him to help, and he doesn't have to be. It was the highlight of my week! It was! And it's the same at break and lunchtime.' They replicate the sentiment, student by student. 'He would email us solutions if we were stuck with something. Late at night he was still up, working.'

Then one of them says, 'If he puts the effort in, then we have to. I didn't want to let him down.' This is an emerging theme in my research. It's something I knew from my own experience, but I didn't realise that it was such a powerful phenomenon in terms of student motivation. There is also evidence they understand Chris' teach-between-the-desks strategy.

'He knows when we might struggle. It's like he can read our minds. If you're reluctant to ask questions because you're stuck, it doesn't matter. He can tell by the look on your face that you're struggling and he will come over to you to help.' But, it doesn't stop there. They also know about his judicious streamlining of the curriculum.

'There were things that we didn't have to know. Mr McGrane would tell us that he had taken the non-important things away from the curriculum. He taught us what matters, what we need to know and left out what we didn't need to know.' I tell them that I have never met students who are so knowledgeable about the curriculum. It is pretty amazing.

Another aspect of truly great teachers that is emerging, manifests itself here too: 'He genuinely wanted to be in the classroom teaching us. It's true. Sometimes you get teachers who are passionate about their subject but not about teaching. We can tell. Mr McGrane is passionate about both. It's like it really matters to him. And we weren't just another number to him. He really cared. He truly loves to see us do well.' I asked them what all this did for their understanding of mathematics.

'He motivated us. I suddenly felt I could do maths. Sometimes we would go over things five times until we actually got it. And we love the booklets and worksheets he produced. They really worked. All the stuff was there in one place. It made it really easy. We could see how it all built up.'

The tsunami of praise for Chris is nowhere near abating. 'He is such a good person. That's part of it. I don't do maths any more, but we still come to see how he's getting on and he always has time for us. And he does lots of joking around. He is actually funny!' They laugh. 'You could make jabs at him – we felt comfortable enough to do that. We would always have a joke.'

'And he made maths so much more interesting,' says another, 'and I'll never forget when he had paternity leave. It was the worst week of the year for us, exam-wise, but he delayed his leave by a couple of days so that we were fully prepared.'

I gather in their single-word descriptors. It feels like it will be an infinite list: generous, dedicated, passionate, patient, understanding, empathetic, selfless, real, unique, talented, entertaining, inspiring and caring.

I bid them farewell and good luck. They really are a testimony to the quality of Chris' teaching, but also to the school. Just damned fine young people. I make myself a cup of tea and reflect upon Chris McGrane. I knew he was good, but, blimey! It all adds up. All the threads of evidence support each other. I am gazing out the window at the *Holyrood Diner*, thinking, when the office door opens. It's two of the students who left here 30 minutes ago. They just want to say a bit more about Mr McGrane and why he is such a brilliant teacher. It's a duologue of praise for our man ... 'Look, we know he has four kids. We were doing our prelim exams. He only took a week for paternity leave when he had his fourth. We were stunned at how he got everything done. When he came back, we were always in his room asking him for help, and he still got everything done. We knew we were a class who hadn't done well the previous year, but he differentiated his teaching methods for everybody. It was incredible. You just wanted to be there. He made us feel comfortable. We had cakes and stuff. We never felt judged by him, no matter our mathematical ability. We never felt disrespected. And when we came to thank him for all his help, when we got those unbelievable grades, all he said was, "It's you who did the hard work – it's you who got those grades, not me."'

IRL: Chris McGrane

John Tomsett (JT): Tell me about why you decided to teach.

Chris McGrane (CM): I did a degree in computer science and maths. I'll be honest, computer science was where I was more talented. I did want to teach, but around about that time, early 2000s, computers were the big thing. Lots of opportunities. I found myself with a part-time job in computing. This was fourth year of university. I'm sitting there two days before Christmas thinking this is mentally stimulating, but emotionally dead. So rather than going into teaching at age 40, I'm going to do it at 21. I emailed Glasgow University and said, 'Am I too late?' They said, 'For maths and computing, you're never too late.' So, I got in off the back of my computing credentials, and immediately changed to maths because I always knew I wanted to teach maths. I found maths hard at school. I enjoyed it a lot, but I had to work at it to be able to cope with it at university level. I felt I could do something with that in teaching, whereas computing, as much as I loved it, from a teaching point of view it wasn't attractive.

JT: **Where was your first job?**

CM: At a school called St Kentigern's Academy. Then I went to Linlithgow Academy, where my world changed, because I went into a department, me and one other person who was at the same stage as me, with eight other folk who'd all been teaching for a minimum of 20 years. It was an incredible learning place because the guidance, the support, the encouragement, the criticism, were all really, really useful. There were some real zany characters, but they all brought personality to it. Great mathematicians, but also great people. By the end of my time there, I was involved in decisions about curriculum design. It was middle-class, very leafy with high levels of privilege. It made it realy easy to learn to teach maths, though.

Then I came to Glasgow in 2015. Head of maths at Hillhead. The thing that shocked me was just how marked the impact of poverty was on the Hillhead community, despite it not being amongst the *poorest* areas in Glasgow. It had significant levels of deprivation. I had been relatively insulated from the effects of poverty on attainment at Linlithgow. That was an eye opener for me.

About three-and-a-half years in, after some significant gains in attainment, I got the opportunity to step out and work with Mark McCourt. I ended up being the maths lead for Scotland. The whole time I was out, I missed teaching, but it was a fantastic opportunity to stop, to reflect and to read. I read a lot – the key stuff in the canon of literature on mathematics education, as Mark would say. I also wrote a book in that time about task design in maths called, *Mathematical Tasks: The Bridge Between Teaching and Learning*, and I got to travel all over Scotland. I met so many amazing maths teachers, and got to see lots of lessons in primary and secondary education. I joined up my thinking across the phases. I got into primary mathematics.

It rounded my understanding of maths teaching. I was able to add theoretical frameworks to underpin those personal theories of teaching that I developed, because so much of the time was spent reading research. But I always wanted to come back to school.

The job I always wanted was the head of maths at Holyrood. When I got that job, I was ready for it, because I had earned my stripes, and I'd been a head of department. I wanted a job in maths where you could make the biggest difference to the most number of kids. Where better than the largest school in Scotland?

JT: So you arrived here in 2019?

CM: April 2020. Lockdown had just started. I did start, but at home, so I was having meetings with department members who I didn't know, to decide exam results for students I didn't know, based on preliminary assessments that I hadn't seen. It was chaos, but we got through it. But I knew what I wanted to do, deep down, so, despite it being a tough time for curriculum reform, we got started in the August of 2020 with a first-year cohort who are now the fifth year. It's been quite successful.

JT: Tell me how you measure the success of it.

CM: I've got a big department with a wide variety of staff. To be truthful, how they teach is their business, I'm going to be honest about that.

JT: How they teach is their business?

CM: That is their business, because as long as they deliver results, I'm not going to tell anyone how to teach. We will talk about learning and teaching at every department meeting, and I will offer this idea or this evidence. I'll say, 'I would like you to go and try it once, so I don't want you to just hear it and then ignore it; I want you to try it and bring me back evidence.' So, we will try it and discuss how we all tried it. Some people will keep it going and some people won't, and that's up to them. You can't be who you're not. I know that sounds absurd, but I believe there's got to be some sort of professional autonomy. I go around and observe, and I can't say I have any concerns. Some of them teach differently to me, but, you know what, it seems to be working. The results are good. So, there's a professional respect there. There has to be. We've got internal data measures we look at, but the main ones are our fourth, fifth and sixth year exam results. Two things that stand out. Every single year since I came here, the fifth year Higher results I've set have beaten the previous year. In each of those years, it's a new record. So that's where we're at.

JT: **Why are the results so stonkingly good?**

CM: The curriculum is the key. The progression pathway and the tasks that make up that curriculum. Teach it how you want (as long as the kids learn it) but I want you to teach the right stuff. That has involved a streamlined curriculum, particularly in early secondary. Maths is vast; we could do tonnes of stuff, but I have to be honest, we have narrowed the focus somewhat. Cut to the chase. What do we need to know in order to make the next step? There might be something that seems inconsequential when they're 12, but if I don't teach that, it's got ramifications for the next five years. Then there might be something else I could teach that has no ramifications, and it's just a nice bit of maths, but there's no need to teach that – we might, but it's not the priority. A lot of our kids arrive here a year behind the kids in the most affluent schools. You don't have time to do the nice maths. It's a moral obligation to maximise their life chances by getting the best attainment for them. By doing that, you're going to have to narrow down the focus. That's not me advocating the pedagogic drill and kill; but teaching less stuff better, doing it deeper and richer, enjoying the subject, finding enthusiasm and creativity, all of that is important. But you've got to create the space to do that with a narrower focus on what matters for progression.

JT: Mary Myatt and I interviewed Dylan Wiliam a couple of years ago, and he called it having the 'need to know' and the 'neat to know'. It'd be *neat* if they knew that, but not essential, but this stuff they *need* to know.

CM: That is exactly it. That is the case at every level, all the way up through the secondary journey. That's not a popular perspective, sometimes. You've got the idea that kids have got an entitlement to the whole curriculum. They've got an entitlement to this; they've got an entitlement to that.

JT: Your entitlement's success, and that's the way to get it.

CM: Yes. To me, I would rather they walked out with the National 5 or the Higher maths, which is going to get them into nursing, or into primary teaching, or into an apprenticeship, or whatever they need it for. The majority of young people are not going to become mathematicians. The majority are not even going to become engineers or scientists. For those that do, we have a really good journey for them, and lots of the kids leave here inspired by and enjoying maths, and want to pursue it, but it's not a failure of a maths department that not everybody wants to be a mathematician. Much the same, it's not the failure of a music department if not every kid in the school wants to be a musician. It's like, when you leave here, have you got the capital you need from the subject? Yes. Are you a bit more aware of what the subject is and what it means?

JT: You seem relentless about what matters and what doesn't matter, and you ignore the stuff that doesn't really matter.

CM: Yes.

JT: [*Laughs*] **I saw your clock earlier. I thought, he doesn't give a damn that that clock's not right because it doesn't really matter! It's a great metaphor for your approach!**

CM: Yes. I'm sure my colleagues would say the same. Some of them sweat the small stuff, and I don't. I can just block it all out and just focus on what matters, and that's the kids.

JT: **The children know that.**

CM: That's nice. Yesterday summed it up for me. The rest of senior management were in teasing me, 'You'll be all stressed out with these vaccinations happening next week. The nurses are always grumpy.' I said, 'I'm not too bothered. It's inconsequential to me whether the nurses are grumpy or not.' Then I heard the student teacher in maths had asked, 'How many times does 48 divide into 4, as opposed to 4 into 48?' I felt my heart rate go up about ten beats. That upset me.

JT: ***That* really matters!** [*Laughs*] **I love that. Pedagogically, what were you thinking today about the way you structured the lesson?**

CM: Right. So, today's lesson, procedurally, was not that difficult, but notationally and conceptually, it's at the tough end. It's something kids don't grasp intuitively. There's got to be some explicit instruction there, but I don't think you can tell kids understanding.

JT: **You can't tell kids understanding?**

CM: You can't tell kids understanding, no. Now, there is a lot of debate about this stuff on Twitter. I don't give a hoot about these pedantic arguments. It's whatever you want to think, whatever the evidence says. Basically, I could tell them procedures and get them doing procedures. That's fine. I can do, 'I do, you do; I do, you do'. I'll do that lots, because that's what needs to be done. Today, I needed them to understand. Now, how am

I going to get them to understand? By saying it again and saying it again? Well, I might try that, but I wanted them to engage very quickly with what I'd said, which was what that prerequisite sheet was about. 'I've said this, but are you understanding what I'm saying? Are you using what I've said in there at all?' That's why the prerequisite sheet was important. I needed them to think the same way I was thinking before we could do the maths that we were there to do. I suppose it was a very scaffolded lesson, in that sense. I'd say most of my lessons, particularly at that level, are very scaffolded.

Even the task I gave them to do, the final task, we scaffolded with support. The independent practice comes. It's like, 'I've said my bit; I'm not going to say more than I need to say. Now get going'. I'm really, really keen to talk to every kid in the lesson every day, as many times as possible, particularly on hard stuff. Those are the conversations that matter. Okay, with the younger kids I am more inclined to get the mini-whiteboards out, because it's not as taxing stuff, but today, to have conversations about the shading and all that . . . I wanted to see what they had thought, and fix the misconceptions.

JT: There and then, in the moment.

CM: Yes, because I knew those misconceptions were going to arise. I needed to give them opportunities to arise so we could correct them. That is part of the plan. You know what the misconceptions are going to be, so you need to air them and tackle them. Even though you've said it, just because you've said it, doesn't mean they understand what you said, so they need to do something with what you've said. They think they understand, but they don't know if they understand. You've got to make sure they understand what's going on and then build it up from there.

JT: **What I found really interesting, and slightly triggering, is you saying, 'Hands up if you got that.'**

CM: People hate that.

JT: **People hate that?**

CM: I know they do, on Twitter. They hate that.

JT: [*Laughs*] **I was thinking, 'Oh, my goodness!' I guessed that the students are not going to lie to you.**

CM: They don't. They never do. I go around and check their work all the time. I'd seen enough of it that I knew. I've got my four key students. I know I need to see everything that they do.

JT: **So, you have your bellwether people?**

CM: Yes, but also, if Martha's got a problem, for instance, she's going to put her hand up, or she'll tell me, because she is confident and trusts me. Again, this all comes back to relationships, and the environment; the mathematical classroom community you build. It all comes back to that.

JT: **Exactly. You didn't need a mini-whiteboard exercise, because you knew who knew it and who didn't know it, anyway.**

CM: I knew who was going to struggle. I knew who to check in on, and that's basically it. It's a deeply interpersonal endeavour. The kids know they're not going to be able to sit and do nothing. I'm going to be in amongst them all the time.

JT: **Are you always like that?**

CM: Yes. 'Teaching between the desks', is my mantra, and we often change seating. When we're doing a mastery cycle with first- and second-year classes I'll say, 'You guys come with me now up to the back.' I'll leave a couple of tables clear at the back, and up certain kids will come. We'll do that sort of stuff. Very fluid.

JT: They had no choice but to concentrate.

CM: Yes, but I think I'm adept at identifying when they're not, and I will slow down if I feel like they're struggling, and I will go round, and I'll challenge them, and I'll talk to them, and I'll catch up with them if I feel as if they're struggling. Get in amongst them.

JT: Your pitch is perfect. You know the whole class.

CM: Yes. So, the class you saw today is mixed ability at that level. Last year, there were two classes and one was more able, but the other class, that Nicola and Ginny you spoke to were in …

JT: They knew they were different.

CM: I was upfront with that class. I said, 'I'm going to be honest with you. When I look around the room, only one in five of you gets to pass if we go with the national statistics.' I told them that at the beginning, but I said, 'That will not happen in here. I'm not going to let it happen. We're trying something different with you guys.' So, we did, and over 70% of those with a grade C on entry passed, versus 23% with a grade C on entry nationally. It was just basically what you saw today, but with lots of clever curriculum design underneath it, and mastery cycle type stuff.

JT: Sequencing the right order?

CM: Yes.

JT: They were interesting. They said, 'We did this random stuff. We didn't know why we were doing it in this order, but Sir said, "Just trust me to do it like we're doing it", and then at the end of the year we thought, "blimey, there's all those links between those bits".'

CM: Yes, that was basically it with those guys. We had it all planned. We sat and planned it during May and June the year before. We spent hours and hours planning it out, and we designed all these booklets and these units of work and the resources. It's incredible those kids achieved what they did. Definitely the best moment in teaching was seeing those guys' results this year. It was so satisfying, because we'd worked hard, but so had they. It's about building. I just think maths teaching is a confidence game. You need to give kids a taste of success, and you need to hold them in continual positive regard. You need to be nice to the kids. You need to like working with them. The maths is second to that. It's about your relationship with the them first and foremost, that you care about that, and you're going to work super hard for them, and you expect them to work super hard, but you also need to be realistic. I had kids in that class last year who told me they did one hour of maths a week outside of class, and they would do no more because their lives were hugely challenging. So, what happened in the 300 minutes in class a week was designed in a way that assumed they wouldn't study at home. So, we designed a curriculum that helps kids that don't study. We planned the studying for them by spacing, interleaving, and building it up in a narrative or journey where you're revisiting stuff every now and again because they're going to need it.

JT: **Is there anything else you want to tell me about the way you design the curriculum, and the way you think about maths teaching?**

CM: It's always planning for the long term. I'm always thinking, 'Well, what's come before this? What are the potential issues?' So, take today's lesson, what prerequisite knowledge do we need to have here? There are certain things that I need to assume they can do, like factorising and solving. I saw that recently in other tasks that they could do that, so I knew I didn't need to address that, but there were graphical skills that I knew we would need, so we worked on it.

Before I even started today, I had to make a decision: 'Is this lesson worth it or not?' With the borderline class last year, I did not teach that lesson to them. They didn't see that lesson. With those kids I'd be filling in gaps at National 5 to enable access to Higher level. So that means I had to scrub some of the Higher. So, that top-end stuff, like today, we didn't do, but still quite a lot of them got an A. So, there's that. Then the task design, that's a big bit of it.

JT: **Tell me about that.**

CM: I suppose that's one of my passions. It's not just how you teach, it's not just the curriculum; it's what you're getting them to do with what you've taught them.

JT: **How they apply what they understand?**

CM: Yes. It's this idea that the task is a vehicle for cognition in mathematics. It's a tool for them to engage with the mathematics. So, the task, it's the centre of it all. The teacher is here. The mathematics is here. The pupil is here. You'll meet in the task, if you see what I mean. That's where we discuss stuff; it's where we work on stuff. I love this quote from John Mason: 'The purpose of a task is to initiate mathematically fruitful activity that leads to a transformation in what learners are sensitised to notice and competent to carry out.'[1] The tasks have got to be quite deliberate in terms of channelling attention to the right things. A random textbook page isn't going to cut it 90% of the time. You've got to draw attention to the right things. So, even the examples I did on the board, I didn't change the quadratic I was using; I just changed the inequality because that was the thing that mattered, so greater than this x^2 term, you could then do less than. So that *variation*, rather than variety, because it's the inequality that mattered. It wasn't what the quadratic was that mattered, it's what these symbols mean.

JT: **The implications of those symbols were massive.**

CM: Yes, that's exactly it. So, in the task design today, it was a scaffolded sheet, and some other tasks. I'd never seen tasks like that

---

1 J. Mason and S. Johnston-Wilder, *Designing and Using Mathematical Tasks* (St Albans: Tarquin, 2006).

in any of the textbooks, but I knew those were the tasks my class needed because that's what I wanted them to think about. So, I need to put stuff in front of them that gets them thinking about that. That's the key. Sometimes as well, with tasks, it's not just what you see them write. That's the outer task. It's the idea of the inner task: it's what they think about that matters. Sometimes, kids get stuff wrong, so that's what you see, but what did you think to get there?

JT: **That's where you're going to find out, isn't it?**

CM: The task gives you an opportunity, then, to discuss, and that gives you the opportunity, then, to fix and move on.

JT: **To shape that thinking in a different way.**

CM: Yes. Don't get me wrong, with some tasks in some lessons, what you're trying to do is develop a sense of kids as a mathematician. Last week, we were a bit of the way through a topic, and we still had six lessons to go … but I did the full six lessons in one lesson. 'What about this question now? You know how to get started, but we've come to this wee crossroads; what could we do?' They told me. 'Well, I don't need to spend the lesson on that.' I said, 'Here's another wee twist. Here's another twist.' So, I spoon feed and support when needed, but when the kids have got it … I take the reins off and really accelerate with a bit of pace. What you want to do in maths is build up what's called the example space.

JT: **What's that?**

CM: The example space is the range of all the examples they've ever encountered, and the bigger the example space you have encountered, then the more you've got to draw upon. You can think, 'I've seen one like that before.' Kids doing Advanced Higher will say to me, 'How did you know how to do that?' I'll say, 'I'm sure I've seen one like this before. That's how I knew how to do it. I wouldn't know how to do this particular one, but I've seen one similar before. That's how I know.'

JT: I don't know if you remember EdExcel's *Hannah's Sweets* question in 2015. It was simple maths but tricky application. But the question was an easier variation of *Heather's Buttons* in 2002. It would have been easy to have done the *Heather's Sweets* question if you'd encountered *Hannah's Buttons*.

CM: Yes, that's exactly it. Again, it comes back to problem solving. It's a bit of a red herring. I'm going to admit: … we all have different aptitudes; we all have different IQs. Some people are capable of making bigger leaps, so they need an example that is maybe three steps removed from the problem they're solving. I might not be as gifted as them; I might need to see an example that is two steps removed from the problem I'm trying to solve. How analogous is this problem to a previous problem you've seen? How many leaps can you make? Sometimes in class, you're trying to reduce the number of jumps they've got to make to one, and you might be able to open it up to two, but when you're getting to three and four leaps, kids are going to struggle. So, you need to build that up. They can sometimes get through these different examples on their own. They don't need to be shown every different example to get them there, but unless they've encountered examples and they've thought about it, then they're not going to be able to complete problems. Kids don't solve unseen problems, in general.

JT: If they've not seen something like it before, they've rarely got the ability to marshal their mathematical knowledge and apply that to something they've not seen before, is that what you're saying?

CM: Yes. The likes of Hugh Burkhardt, Malcolm Swan, these guys at Nottingham University, they always spoke about maturation. Mark McCourt talks about this too. Kids can only problem-solve with stuff they've known and have been competent with for about two years. So, the UK Mathematics Trust have this challenge. There's a junior one we would give the first and second year. The intermediate one you give the third and fourth year. Then the senior one. If we give the seniors the junior problem, they can do it, but if we had given them it in their junior years, they wouldn't have been able to do that much, even though it would have been on the work they were doing, because it requires time to mature their understanding. Later, they will have built the connections.

I keep it simple. I don't have notes, I don't have PowerPoints, I don't have anything. I accumulate tasks that might have worked well, but the way of talking about it has evolved over time. It's probably on my … [*A girl appears at the door*]

JT: **Go on. It's all right.**

CM: Sorry. It's going to be about picking up her phone I've been charging [*quickly unplugs and hands over the phone*].

JT: **Is there anything you want to say that you've not had a chance to say, that's important?**

CM: I find it easier to be nice to kids than I do to adults.

JT: **Sorry?**

CM: I find it easier to be nice to kids than I do to adults.

JT: **Do you?**

CM: Yes. I can be quite a dour Glaswegian in the staff room in the morning, but you come into a class … Some of my colleagues sometimes think, 'Why do they like him?' They perceive me as surviving on coffee … sleep deprived, tired, fed up, but when you go in that classroom, it's a different thing. It's taken time for people to see that.

JT: **That you love being with the kids, don't you?**

CM: Yes, I really do. That is it. Relaxed, but purposeful. That's what I would want to be with the kids. I just want them to know I care, because I really do.

JT: They know that in spades, Chris.

CM: If being a good teacher was as easy as following a checklist of what good teachers do, then everybody would be awesome, but it's not like that.

JT: That's where this book comes from. I had a child say a couple of days ago, 'We love Miss so-and-so because it's really fun, it's really interesting, they really care about it, and some teachers are just like robots and read out slides.'

CM: Yes, I think that's it. I work almost every problem out along with the kids. Like today, I worked the problem out while they were doing it and then went around and checked their work. I get lots of people emailing me about my website. 'Have you got the solutions for that?' My answer's always the same: 'No, because you will not understand the purpose of the task, and the design features of the task, unless you do the task yourself.' If I'm putting something up on there for people to access, it's not because it's just a worksheet on solving equations; there's something else underneath that, which will only become apparent when you do it.

JT: It's been extraordinary. Thanks so much. It's been brilliant.

CM: Cheers. Thank you.

Testimonials

'Maths has always been my worst and most dreaded class, but this is the first year I've not only been good at it, but enjoyed it!!! I hope I can make you proud in the exam after all the work you did with me!'

'You have been an amazing teacher and have helped me to have more confidence in myself. Thank you for your encouragement and support and for always being there for me. You believed in me even when I thought I couldn't do it. You have truly gone above and beyond for each one of us this year. You have pushed me to do things I didn't think I was capable of and never gave up on me. I can't thank you enough for being such a great teacher.'

'You are an inspiring teacher. I remember before I came to the Academy, the only piece of advice I took in was "Mr McGrane is the best teacher on the planet" and to hope that I got you as my mentor. Well, I did! I hope you always enjoy teaching because the world will continue to improve if you stay teaching maths.'

'Both my children are lucky enough to have been taught by you. Their confidence and ability levels have soared during their time with you and they have gone on to achieve fantastic results in maths. It's rare to find a teacher who can not only teach but who can relate to his pupils in such a genuine and special way.'

So, what can we learn from Chris McGrane?

A caveat. I could have written many thousands of words on what we can learn from Chris McGrane, but there just isn't the word count available.

It is clear in the extraordinary interview with Chris that his knowledge of the school mathematics curriculum is both broad and deep. He cites the curriculum as the key to his students' success; even they remarked upon how the *sequencing* of the mathematics enabled them to tackle problems that had previously appeared intimidatingly impossible. Crucially, Chris worked with Mark McCourt, an equally impressive mathematician. In his book, *Teaching for Mastery,* Mark says this:

'The curriculum is the single most important tool we have at our disposal. A carefully planned route through our subject – which is not linear, but complex and takes into account forgetting and unlearning as well as learning – is vital if we are to know when and how to reveal the canon of our discipline … There is no point in trying to lay another brick unless the brick underneath is secure. Those bricks have to be ordered extremely carefully.'[2]

It's clear how Chris' approach to teaching mathematics exemplifies Mark's reflections upon the curriculum. In the moment, live formative assessment is central to Chris' pedagogy. He calls it *teaching between the desks*. The approach is apparent in my account of the lesson I watched and is referenced several times in the interview. A couple of days after I was in Glasgow with Chris, he copied me into this Tweet that he had posted back in 2022:

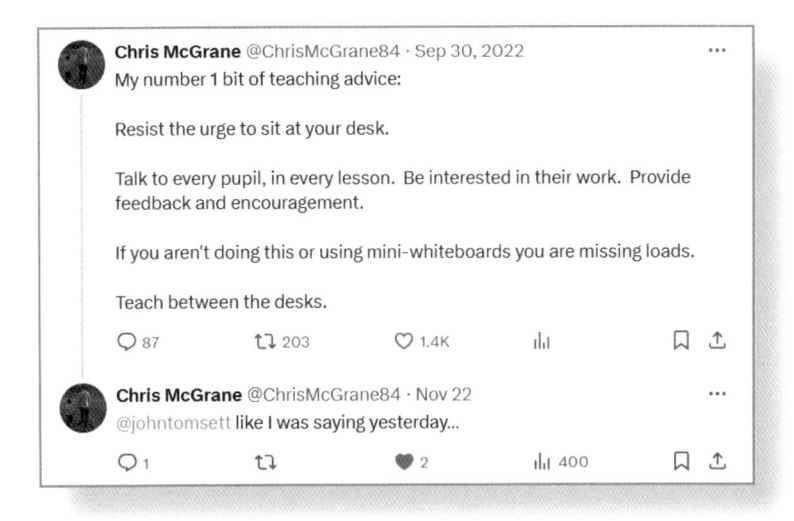

> **Chris McGrane** @ChrisMcGrane84 · Sep 30, 2022
> My number 1 bit of teaching advice:
>
> Resist the urge to sit at your desk.
>
> Talk to every pupil, in every lesson. Be interested in their work. Provide feedback and encouragement.
>
> If you aren't doing this or using mini-whiteboards you are missing loads.
>
> Teach between the desks.
>
> 87   203   1.4K
>
> **Chris McGrane** @ChrisMcGrane84 · Nov 22
> @johntomsett like I was saying yesterday...
>
> 1   　 2   400

What strikes me is just how simple Chris makes it all look. Nothing flash – just deeply thought-through teaching, his assessment radar is switched on permanently; he has genuine ambition for his students, and a profound understanding of his subject.

---

2 M. McCourt, *Teaching for Mastery* (Woodbridge: John Catt Educational, 2019).

Just days before Chris posted that Tweet, I was in Ireland. On 24 September 2022, I spoke at the researchED Dublin conference. The keynote speaker was the American, Professor Barbara Oakley. She is an utterly impressive woman. Her CV is extraordinary. She explained how her parents had peripatetic jobs, which meant she had to move school numerous times during her childhood. There are 15,000 educational jurisdictions in the USA and she gave up 'math' at the age of 12 as each time she moved the mathematics curriculum changed. But at 14 she realised she needed mathematics and so she learnt it herself. She became pretty good at it and is now an Emeritus Professor of Engineering. In her talk, she said that there is no such thing as maths anxiety, just badly taught maths: maths that is taught in the wrong sequence, maths that is taught without the accompanying guidance on how to apply it to new problems, maths that is taught by teachers who do not understand maths conceptually themselves. Taught well, mathematics can be learnt by anyone. The trouble is, instead of focusing our efforts on encouraging truly great teachers like Chris McGrane into the profession, we tend to foster the anxiety that exists around maths. Incredibly, we have a 'Maths Anxiety Trust' in this country. On the first page of its website, it cites data from *its own research* that claims that, 'between 20% and 30% of secondary maths teachers report that during lessons they sometimes suffer from maths anxiety ("a negative emotional reaction leading to varying degrees of helplessness, panic and mental disorganisation when faced with a maths problem").' If you read all the testimonials from Chris' students – I just selected a few for inclusion here – what strikes you is how many students say that they realised they could do maths, that they found they even 'liked' maths after being taught by Chris. Forget the learned helplessness engendered by self-diagnosed maths anxiety … just *Be More Chris*!

There is a postscript to the Barbara Oakley story. I remember the exact date that I heard her speak because that evening, as I drove home from Manchester Airport across the Pennines to York, I listened to an episode of 'Bringing Up Britain' on Radio 4. Each episode explores one of the modern-day challenges of bringing up children in our country.

The title of that episode was, remarkably, 'Why Does Maths Make Me Anxious?'

Chris McGrane's students' progress and achievement data

Chris' strength is in teaching SQA Higher maths. Last year was his greatest achievement. He had a class of students who all had a grade C at National 5 maths. It is difficult to progress to Higher maths with this grade. Nationally, the pass rate for students entering Highers from a grade C is 23%. In Chris' class, 74% of the students passed the final exam, and 32% of the class achieved a grade A versus the typical 1%, achieved nationally. This gave him much greater satisfaction than the year where he had 29 grade As and 1 grade B. Those students were expected to do well, and did, whereas the class with a 74% pass-rate wildly exceeded expectations.

A Truly Great English Teacher: Tom Fraser

Tom Fraser teaches English at Malet Lambert School in Hull. He is currently acting director of English.

The school leadership's view

Malet Lambert High School in Hull is part of The Education Alliance (TEAL) Academy Trust, led by my old friend and co-conspirator, Jonny Uttley. His colleague, Hayley Nickolay-Walker, recommended the school's Tom Fraser for this book, so here I am! Hayley greets me and, a cappuccino later, I am sitting with her colleagues Pamela Tarbet and Paul Fortune, members of Malet's senior team, to talk about what makes Tom truly great.

'Tom trained with the Trust', says Pamela. TEAL has a wonderful training arm led by the redoubtable Alison Fletcher. It is a smart outfit. It's why I trusted Hayley's recommendation of Tom. 'He was a teaching assistant with us and then he returned here when we appointed him as an [early career teacher] ECT.'

'So what makes him a truly great teacher?' I ask.

'He is incredibly knowledgeable about English', says Paul. 'His teaching style is very gentle. There is nothing intimidating about him, whatsoever. He forges great relationships with some of the trickiest students. He tunes in to their interests. He chats with them at the gate at the end of the day.' The 'gentle' attribute is interesting. Tom is the ninth teacher I have met as a part of this project; *geniality* is emerging as a strong characteristic of these truly great teachers.

Pamela continues to paint the picture for me. 'He's relaxed, but industrious. There's no crossing lines in his classroom. One of the key things is how he has built up his subject knowledge from his days as a TA to being the acting director of English. He plans his department meetings like a lesson! He helps everyone extend their subject knowledge. He is great at developing leadership across his team. He's only 32, but his colleagues have really warmed to him.' If you're good enough, etc., etc.

This is a school focused intently upon improving the quality of teaching and learning. The main aim of the Trust's School Improvement Strategy is to have a great teacher in every classroom. I ask them, 'What is the focus of your school's CPD [continuing professional development] this year?'

Paul replies, 'Checking for understanding and effective questioning, with the aim of tackling students' passivity in lessons.' It's something I hear a great deal as I work from school to school as a consultant.

'And what is it that Tom is particularly good at?'

Pamela takes over. 'His explanations are so clear. He extends their subject-specific vocabulary, without inundating the students. He is an inspiring teacher – I know that sounds a bit vague – but he is brilliant at getting disengaged boys on board. He's sporty and a bit of a role model for them.' The ability to connect with boys is another common thread.

Then they make some interesting general points about how truly great teachers develop. 'There's an element of being a great teacher that is unteachable. You obviously need a core of training, but ITT [initial teacher training] can be mechanical. Someone who has been a TA, like Tom, sees lots of teachers teach. They notice what works and what doesn't. And then you need relentless energy. The students need to know you care. Ring home. Send postcards home about good work. Go the extra mile. Tom does all that.' The warning bell sounds for first period. They bid farewell and depart.

I sit for a few seconds, while I wait for Hayley to take me to find Tom. I am in one of the school's conference rooms. It is impressive. It feels like a highly purposeful, professional environment. I am struck by one of the quotations on the wall by Dwayne Johnson: 'Success isn't always about greatness. It's about consistency. Consistent hard work leads to success. Greatness will follow.' As I reflect that 'consistent hard work' is another essential element of being a truly great teacher, Hayley beckons me to follow her to Tom's classroom.

Teaching

We walk through the narrow corridors to Tom's room. Elgar's *Nimrod* is playing over the tannoy system. The door is wide open and Tom is finishing off a Year 11 revision session. They have mocks coming up. The 11s leave as the Year 8s appear. Tom greets the students at the door, chatting away, directing them to the mini-whiteboard starter. This is a white working-class demographic, one of the worst-performing demographics nationally, similar to Huntington where I was head teacher. It's not an easy gig.

'Hello Year 8, it's lovely to see you. Apologies for my absence last Friday.' Geniality. Immediately. They are answering the starter questions on mini-whiteboards. Tom reminds them to avoid copying. 'Turn your whiteboards over when you have your answers and don't let your neighbour see what you've written.' As he takes the register, I notice Ivan, sitting beneath the whiteboard, with his head on his desk.

Tom narrates the lesson. Date and title on the board. 'Goodness, we're whizzing through November', he remarks.

'It's 34 days til Christmas, Sir!' says one boy.

'And I haven't bought a single present yet!' is Tom's reply. Geniality. An exemplary '3-2-1, show me!' follows. He walks the room, between the desks, interacting as he goes. 'Just imagine', he whispers, animated. 'Just imagine the children in this book. They're a year older than you and they're already working in a factory.' Young minds are whirring. 'You've been working brilliantly these past 8 weeks, and now we're going to do some creative writing.' He embarks upon an exercise to ensure that every student is familiar with some basic language features of creative writing. He shows a definition, they have to name the feature: *When I say something* is *something else*. '3-2-1, show me!' and 95% metaphor, but one student has written 'simile', which he unpicks with such sensitivity that the student knows the correct answer but hardly feels she has made an error. Tom praises, endlessly.

Next up: *When an item, object or colour represents something else.* Suddenly, Ivan pipes up. 'Sir, a cannon symbolises Arsenal football club on their badge – they're the Gunners!' It turns out Tom and Ivan are fellow Arsenal fans. Ivan is delighted he has made such an illuminating contribution.

Tom pursues the theme. 'Which football team is symbolised by a Ram?' Lost in the moment, I put my hand up. But Ivan beats me to it.

'Derby County, Sir', he cries.

'Amazing', says Tom. 'If I did a lesson on football, only Ivan would get full marks!'

Ivan beams. It's clear he wants to please Tom. In this class, boys are volunteering answers, unsolicited. They are fully engaged with this teacher. Behaviour is exemplary, and this feels like it could be a tricky class. Attention is the currency of learning, and Tom's raking it in.

The next task, in preparation for some recreative writing (where Tom takes a paragraph from the text and the students rewrite it to improve it) is to determine the top five features of an effective piece of descriptive writing. Once that is done – lightly, but thoroughly – Tom models the recreative process. As he is writing and thinking to and fro with the students, deciding which word would be best instead of this one or that one, something suddenly strikes me, and I think it is at the heart of Tom's success …

He tells the class he wants to use zoomorphism. He says to a girl, 'Can you help me out a little bit here?'

The girl thinks, then replies, 'The machine roared into life …' Tom expresses his delight. Deep enthusiasm.

He moves onto the next line. He is searching for a synonym. 'James, help me out with this …' There! Again! It's as if he and the students are learning this together. He is collaborative and invitational. It's as if he doesn't know either, and he is asking the students to help him. He uses that frame for 90% of his interactions with the students. I make a note to ask the students and Tom about it when I meet with them later.

He gives them a short time limit to complete their recreative writing. It reminded me of Ted Hughes in his book on creative writing, where he extols the virtues of working to time, even when it's creative writing you're teaching: '12 minutes in silence, until 9:57.'

Silence descends upon the room. But a boy has a leaky pen and his hands are covered in ink. It's the type of thing that would have irritated the hell out of most teachers – 'I've just got the bloody kids writing and his mucking about with his pen has ruined everything!' But Tom makes no fuss. He is *so* lovely with the boy and agrees that pens like that can be a pain. 'Go and get your hands sorted out in the toilets. There, off you go.' What could have disrupted the lesson, Tom turns into another small win.

I notice a boy who isn't writing much. So does Tom. Obviously. He kneels down with him and, like the best coach, is hugely encouraging. 'I know it's not your favourite thing but you can just let your mind go wild when you write like this.' The boy doubles down and puts pen to paper. He moves around the room, reading as he goes. He says, 'I really like that simile . . .' and the girl smiles. 'I really like' is a refrain that whispers around the room.

This was the original paragraph upon which the recreative task was based. It's taken from Fabio Geda's *In the Sea there are Crocodiles*:[1]

> 'Whenever rocks arrived in the factory, they were cut using huge machines, some as big as my house in Nava. The noise was incredible, and there was water everywhere. These machines broke up stones like terracotta and sliced through them like butter.'

At the end of the lesson he showcases some of the work. He asks every child their permission to showcase their efforts. None refuses. He knows where he will end up. To finish the lesson, Ivan reads out his rewritten paragraph:

> 'in the terrifying factory, I stood smelling the materials of the rocks i was amazed the traumatizing machines as brutal as a wild cat soon as the heavy rocks broke the you could here BANG CRASH BASH of the rocks hitting the floor this was like the end of the rocks life it was like a grave yard for them suddenly it all went silent quickly it had never been so quiet in the factory'

Tom says, 'I think the way you've rewritten it, is the best way of saying it, Ivan. I really do. I love the fact that you're thinking about cyclical structure, and beginning and ending with the factory, and the graveyard simile is fantastic!' Ivan beams. From head on the desk to

---

1 G. Fabio, translated by H. Curtis, *In the Sea there are Crocodiles* (New York: Doubleday, 2011).

recreative writing maestro, in one short lesson! To be fair, a bit of heavy-duty editing would sort out Ivan's paragraph. 'As a class, you've taken the work of a published author, and elevated it. You have just improved a published author's writing!' An air of celebration fills the room as Tom bids them farewell.

Next it's Year 11. They are revising *A Christmas Carol*. Tom's pedagogic nuances are in evidence throughout. The permission-based and invitational nature of the teacher–student relationship is so distinctive. Again, he asks them for help, and they want to help him. It is manifested in the language he uses. 'Jess, please could you help me here, with this … Liam, help me … Who can help with this question?' I resolve to ask the students and Tom himself whether they notice it.

His knowledge of the text and the text's context is deep. I spot some further intentional things he does. When he helps individuals, he sits or kneels next to them, at their level. There is a tangible level of mutual respect in the room. When there *is* minor silliness, his tone modulates slightly and becomes marginally more insistent.

Great teaching takes energy. Tom runs the room with relentless enthusiasm. There is a gentle industry about him. He is a *gentle* man. It doesn't look like work from where I'm sitting. Watching Tom makes me want to go back 36 years to start my career anew.

At the end of the lesson, they conclude that through the character of Fezziwig, Dickens suggests that when it comes to being rich or moral, it isn't a binary choice – you can be both. You don't have to choose. Surely a valuable lesson for life.

The bell goes and Elgar's *Nimrod* fills the corridors; I have just witnessed a similar work of genius – Tom Fraser is like the loveliest quiz show host whose show only has winners.

What the students think

As the students leave the Year 11 lesson, four of them volunteer to give up their break and sit round the table with me. I begin by saying that I have made an observation about Mr Fraser when he teaches that I want to test out with them, just in case I have imagined it, but that I will ask them about it at the end. It takes all my powers of self-regulation not to spill the beans immediately.

I ask them about Mr Fraser's teaching. One of the boys leads off. 'Well, some teachers are a bit robotic and they are programmed to say certain things. Mr Fraser's not like that. He relates what we talk about in English to our lives. He's a normal man. He does the same type of things we do, and he shows us how the things writers have written about life are important to the way we live.' I think of Dickens' Fezziwig … 'That's true', says another. 'He knows his stuff and he shares it with us. Others just read off the board.'

All of them agree that Tom's subject knowledge is impressive. 'We know that he spends so much of his own time finding out about the texts we are studying. Weekends and evenings. He loves studying and that makes us want to study too.' It has begun to emerge just how important teacher attitudes and behaviours are to students' attitudes and behaviours. It is obvious, really, but again and again students talk about how much they imitate their teachers and how teacher commitment to the work engenders pupil commitment. 'He genuinely cares,' the student continues, 'he cares so we care.'

It seems Tom has taken a leaf out of many primary teachers' books: 'When we study a play, we act it out. It's fun and he does all the different voices and all sorts of things to bring the text … alive!' He's also incredibly personable. 'He's a really nice person. He wants the best for us, for us to do well.' They talk about his passion for the work. He treats them as equals. They feel like adults in his English lessons. 'With Mr Fraser we feel we're maturing, rather than being treated like a 5-year-old. And sometimes he marks all night to get all 30 exam papers back to us, because he actually cares.'

When I ask them for a single word to describe this truly great teacher, they begin with the fact that he 'cares'. He is also: accomplished, engaging, kind, passionate, enthusiastic, thoughtful and improving. I want to pursue the last one, but I am running out of time and I want to enquire about Tom's pleas for help.

'So, before you go', I say, 'I think I have noticed something about Mr Fraser that I have never seen before, and I want to see if you have detected it too. When he is demonstrating or explaining things, he doesn't ask you direct questions ... he asks you for help. "Jake help me here ... what's another word you'd use to describe Fezziwig?"' All four of them are nodding. I go on, 'It's as if he is finding out about this stuff too and you're working on it together.'

'Yes,' says one of the girls, 'that's just how it feels. It's not him and us. We do the work for each other. He's learning as we're learning.'

I say, 'But sir knows it all, doesn't he, but he kids you into helping him? It's almost like not for you, it's for him too and you're all working it, together.' They nod again, in unison. I sit back, but before I can ask a follow up question, time is up and they are off to their next lesson.

IRL: Tom Fraser

John Tomsett (JT): How did you get into teaching, Tom?

Tom Fraser (TF): I come from a family of educationalists. My mum was a primary deputy head teacher and my dad worked at Hull college, so I was exposed to education from a young age. I was unsure about what I wanted to do with my life after university. I kept choosing courses at college and university that I enjoyed as opposed to ones that might give me a good career. So, I started to think about how I might use this English degree.

After a frank chat with my mum, she said, 'Why don't you go and be a TA for a bit? Get into a school and see what life is like as a TA.' There was a job here at Malet as an English TA. I applied, got the job and it was the best decision I ever made because I got to see what happens in the classroom from a different point of view, from the students' perspective, listening to these brilliant teachers and how they got across complex information … I learnt what worked well and what I might have done differently. I was able to cherry-pick some of my favourite moments, and it was the best year I ever spent. I loved working with the members of staff, and decided to sign up to train as a teacher. I was attached to Malet, but via the University of Hull. So, it's my first and only school. I've gone from being a TA to, now, director of English. It's surreal working with these people. I'll be honest with you; I couldn't really imagine being anywhere else because I just absolutely love the team. I love the pupils that we get, I like the personalities in the English team. I just love working here.

Early on, I learnt a lot from Sarah Beadle and Pam Tarbet.

JT: What, specifically?

TF: It was their demeanour with the pupils. The way that they spoke to them … how, at once, you felt completely welcome in their classroom. They'd be stood at the door, and would say, 'How are you doing? Are you all right? Nice to see you.' It would be a bit of a whirlwind of a lesson, in a sense, considering the content that they covered in that time, but it never felt laborious. You were swept away by their teaching style, by their enthusiasm and their passion. I've really tried to embody that because I'm convinced that passion is very difficult to fake. You've either got it, or you haven't, and I think kids know which it is. Pupils can detect when you're not passionate about what you're teaching and what you're doing. I think it does rub off on them. I think that's what Pam and Sarah did so well, in the sense that the children in the class were engaged, and they loved what they were doing because they were *so* engaged.

Look, you can give, and you can take away. If anybody's coming into my classroom, I want them to feel like they are valued, they're being recognised and seen, and also, I want them to see the effort that I'm putting in for them, so that they feel valued and feel respected by me.

JT: **I talked to those four. They know exactly how hard you work, and they're impressed by it.**

TF: Well, that was very sweet of them to say. I think relationships are – I know it sounds silly to say, as it's the most obvious thing – but I think they are integral to everything. If you want great results, if you are looking for good experiences in school, relationships are everything. If you don't have positive working relationships with the students, then it can feel like a bit of a chore.

JT: **I think you're right, but there's a certain type of relationship, isn't there? How would you define those relationships?**

TF: Do you know what, I was thinking about this last night because I was looking at your email with the interview prompts. I thought to myself, 'Dare I use a football analogy?' in that in any walk of sporting life, you can win a dressing room as a manager, and you can lose a dressing room as a manager. Great managers will get people to run through brick walls for them … players will do anything for that manager. They'll all be running in the same direction. Equally, you've seen the stories of a once great manager who does something wrong or loses his or her love for the job, and all of a sudden, that dressing room is lost, heads turn, they've gone. I genuinely think teaching is like that. Early on with a class, you have to try to lay the foundations of being that good manager, so to speak, showing that you have a genuine, vested interest in them, not just as a pupil, but as a person. I don't think it's about, 'How can I help develop a great *pupil*?' Ultimately, it's about taking an interest in what they did at the weekend, about their football match or concert or charity event or even their visit to grandma's. They can tell that you're listening. They can see that you're laying those foundations, that you genuinely care … 'He cares about me, because he's not just telling me to get on with that work, he's actually thinking about me as a person and not only as a pupil.' I think that's one of the first things I always try to create every year. I'm convinced that if you can show them that you're willing to go the extra mile, or even the extra inch, for them, they'll go that extra mile too, for you and, ultimately, for themselves.

JT: **There's something important about mimicking teacher behaviours, isn't there? If you're bored by this stuff, why should they be interested?**

TF: Yes, exactly. I completely agree. If I walked in and said, 'Right then, guys, you know what you're doing? Get on with that work, now!' it just rubs off on them. Obviously, it's about high expectations. You have high expectations for yourself. You have high expectations for them, and, therefore, those high expectations are established with that class. Mutually high expectations of each other.

JT: **You're young, Tom – half my age – but you get how hard you have to work.**

TF: Yes. It is a bit of a balancing act. There needs to be that autonomy. I know on the weekend … on a Sunday, sometimes I'll hit pinch points where I mark some books on a Sunday morning from 8:00 til 11:00. I'll listen to some music maybe, and I'm marking, and that is my own time, but that's my choice. The important thing is to have a choice, but I choose to do that because I want to give them that feedback.

JT: **It impresses them. They appreciate it. 'We get our work back marked really quickly.'**

TF: Well, that's what I always want to do. I know it sounds very cheesy, but in my mind, if I am asking them to do 25 minutes of extended writing or getting them to write an *Inspector Calls* essay, I want to make sure that they know that the effort's reciprocated. 'I understand how hard you've just worked for me, and how you've got another four lessons to go to as well. I want to make sure that you get feedback promptly, and really precise diagnostic feedback as well, to, ultimately, improve.' So, if it takes me three hours on a Sunday morning to give them that kind of feedback, I think, personally, it's important to get it done.

At the same time, you must look after yourself as well. At the minute, I don't have children. I live with my partner and she's also a teacher. It's one of those things where we know how things work, and we know that we need that time, but I also appreciate that people's lives are very busy, and it's their life as well.

JT: **I always think the most important asset in the room is you, the teacher.**

TF: I had an ECT last year who works in the department now. I said to him, 'You're an actor. You're not just a teacher. You need to be like an actor to carry that wave of enthusiasm across the lesson.' The number of teachers I see when they're tired and they've had a really long week, can still, all of a sudden, just switch it on, and go into that classroom and perform. It's amazing! You wouldn't think they were tired at all because they've preserved something of themselves just for those pupils. You're giving a lot of yourself away, aren't you, when you teach?

JT: **Yes, you are. I've loved watching you teach today. Tell me how you structure a lesson.**

TF: It's not anything groundbreaking, but, obviously, I begin by retrieving key information for that lesson. I always like to bring in a bit of debate or discussion into the room, and I'm there to facilitate it when needed. I hate lessons where they're sat in silence, and it's just purely teacher-led. I despise it because that's where you lose classes. Then, perhaps, we move on to a new key piece of information. Then we find out if they can assimilate the new knowledge with the old. Not every single lesson has all these stages exclusively. I always like to have a line of enquiry or an argument that they must either prove or disprove, or something that they must argue for. I always like to give them a new piece of information, so our key argument in this Year 11 lesson was, 'Fezziwig is the antithesis of Scrooge, prove it.' That's why they got that sheet where we were bandying back and forth. I keep it rooted all the time in the literary text. Again, it's all about knowledge. Fundamentally, it's around your assessment objectives of knowledge, your ability to analyse quotes, and to link it back to that authorial intent. I try and thread that through all the way through my Key Stage 4 lessons, so without them knowing it, they're always hitting those examiners' expectations.

JT: **It didn't feel like a regimented assessment objective-centric lesson.**

TF: Yes, so it's hidden beneath the surface. You've got your evidence, you've got your subject knowledge, AO1. You've got your analysis, AO2. Dickens' intentions and contextual factors, AO3, and before they know it, they're bringing all those ingredients together ready to answer examination questions.

JT: **But you're not just teaching to the exam.**

TF: Exactly. That's the thing. At the start of the lesson, I always ask myself, 'What am I teaching them? What do I want them to know when they walk out of my door at the end of the lesson?' If I don't have an idea of what I want them to know, then the lesson is an immediate failure because it's just hoping they leave with something, and hope is not a plan. Today with Year 11, I wanted them to know that Fezziwig is the antithesis of Scrooge and how Dickens isn't criticising every single member in society, but perhaps a small cohort. Fezziwig can be moral and also generous. That's my key argument, and then throughout, it's that journey of discovery via class discussion, via independent learning, via modelling

I think modelling is a key teaching and learning process for every single year group. It's so easy to catch yourself thinking, 'Oh, well, I know what I'm talking about, so why don't you know what I'm talking about?' It's not as easy as that. It could be modelling of sentence stems, and then, ultimately, taking that scaffolding away. It's worked a treat this year.

I don't want to regimentally follow my lesson plan all the time. Sometimes I'll think, 'You know what? They clearly don't get this.' I remember the first lesson we looked at comparing texts. They were really struggling to grasp the concept of analysis and were summarising the texts. So, we just took a step back, I did some whole class modelling where they were compiling the response with me, but I was facilitating and typing it up on the board. We were stopping. We were debating. 'Is there anything else we could add here?' That worked wonders because the next time we attempted comparative analysis, they weren't asking the same questions. I gave them about 35–40 minutes. Then after that, they were down to 20–25 minutes. Taking that time away from them is removing yet another scaffold. If I hadn't stopped that original lesson, if I had ploughed on anyway because I'm following my lesson plan, the learning would have fallen apart. I think lesson planning is really important, but so is never being scared to adapt your plan when your students aren't understanding what you're teaching them.

JT: You wanted to find out if they knew the definitions, and the most effective way of finding that out is if you use mini-whiteboards. The one 'simile' answer that you got instead of a 'metaphor', meant you could then help that pupil.

TF: Exactly. It's ironing out those misconceptions, isn't it? I would never have noticed that Year 8 pupil had simile and metaphor confused without the mini-whiteboards. But you have to act on what you find out. I remember once observing a teacher on interview where they were doing whiteboard tasks and they looked across the room at the boards and said, 'Good, good. Well done, everybody. Put your boards down', and that was it. You could see from where I was sitting at the front observing, that several pupils had got the answer wrong.

JT: Dylan Wiliam says, 'It's wrong to do too much assessment. It's a crime to do nothing with the assessment data you do collect.' You collected all those whiteboards with this assessment data, and you helped the one student with a misconception.

TF: Yes, and straight away I said, 'You've written "simile", but don't worry ...'

JT: 'Don't worry' was lovely.

TF: I get it. Pupils really fear getting something wrong. One thing I always try and do in class is that if you get a question wrong ...

JT: It didn't matter in your class. It doesn't matter in your class because it's completely psychologically safe in your class.

TF: Like I say to them, 'If you get it wrong, it's on a whiteboard, and we can rub it out, forget about it, it's over and done with.' I was able to say to that student, 'Why have you put simile? What's the key phrase that determines as a simile?' She got it. Like or as. Straight away, she was able to iron out her own misconception and get on with the lesson.

JT: **Thinking about that Year 8 lesson, tell me about the Arsenal fan.**

TF: Do you know what, Ivan is really interesting, but he's been a bit of a battle.

JT: **Well, he had his head on the desk at the beginning of the lesson.**

TF: He has a few problems behaviourally. At the beginning of the year, in one of the first lessons we had, he said, 'Sir, I hate English. I hate it. I hate the subject. I hate doing it', and I get it because not every single person is going to love your subject. I'm not going to be offended by that. I know what he likes. Last year, I met him when he would pop into my room to grab a Chromebook every English lesson, and he always asked me if I'd seen the Arsenal game or the Arsenal result, establishing those relationships. I'd reply something like, 'I did. I was furious! How was that not a penalty?' and so on, just as he's walking out of the room. He's come in this year, and he had some really negative misconceptions about the subject, that it's just about writing. You're right, he came in, and he had that head on the desk attitude, but it's about knowing your pupil. I know that I can get him involved in this lesson. I *know* I *can*. I know that through the whiteboards, through the questioning, and, before you know it, by the end of the lesson he's working as hard as anyone.

JT: **He's all over it.**

TF: I read that piece of work out. As he was writing it, he was turning around and saying, 'Sir, sir, what do you think to this?' He was pretty much saying, 'Sir, can you read this out to everyone?!' [*Laughs*].

JT: It was a masterpiece of manipulation.

TF: Yes, and I just thought, no way will that happen to somebody who hates something with such a passion. You're getting nothing from them, but I'm trying to … Again, it's a slow process because I don't know what kind of experience he's had in Year 7 with English, but I'm trying to slowly change and foster that love of the subject that I want every pupil to feel when they come in that room. Ultimately, that's what it's all about. If I can get somebody leaving a room where they feel like they've done something new, they've learned something new, and, equally, they've *loved* what they've done in that lesson. Even when he was walking out – he was the last to leave the room there – granted, he was still talking about Arsenal, but again, I'd hooked him in. That symbolism thing. Do you know what? I was blown away by him being able to link the Gunners' cannon to Arsenal and symbolism. For a pupil who is a relatively low attainer like Ivan, if that works, that's brilliant.

JT: He's learnt loads today. Does he have additional needs?

TF: He does, yes, so on his pupil profile, it says he has to use a laptop. His handwriting is rather poor. His resilience for writing is quite low. I'm just really pleased to see how he took that re-creative writing, that piece of work from an author, and in his eyes, he improved it. That's all I was asking for that lesson for him.

JT: What I thought was extraordinary … was, firstly, how permission-based your dialogue is with the students. You asked them permission all the time. 'Is it okay if we move on to this now?' It was also invitational. 'Ivan, I need you to help with this.' How deliberate is that phraseology?

TF: It is intentional. It goes back to stuff that we spoke about previously, in the sense of the analogy of the manager and winning over the team and being a single unit, so that we're all going in one direction together. It also goes back to the principles of relationship building. Yes, I do it intentionally.

JT: **You do.**

TF: I'll say, 'Can you help me out?' as if I'm struggling, and you're the person, you're the provider of the information for me.

JT: **It's amazing.**

TF: It has a really strange impact in the sense that they want to help you out. It's like they think, 'Well, I do know the answer to this and I will help him', rather than me saying, 'Let me help *you* out.' It's interesting phraseology. When I'm saying, 'Can you help me out', it suggests, 'Come on, help me on this journey. Help me what we're doing here', and they're seemingly more willing to contribute.

JT: **You're unconsciously competent at it. It's hardwired into your brain. When you open your mouth, that's the phraseology that comes out.**

TF: The only caveat is that it depends on the class. I'll have certain students who I have some concerns about behaviourally. I change my questioning a little bit. I begin with cold-calling and adopt quite an imperative-based kind of question. Then, as that relationship builds throughout the year – and the Year 8s have got there already in the first 13–14 weeks, it feels like we're all rowing in that direction – so it gently changes.

JT: **As you stood in the Year 11 class, in the centre at the back, you had your most off-task students. You focused nearly all your attention there. You came back to them three times, and I wrote that your tone modulates slightly, becoming marginally more insistent. You weren't asking for permission then.**

JT: Yes, I'm glad you picked up on that. I have a principle of – and it's my own principle – I never shout. Never shout. Once you shout, you've lost the class. It's gone. It goes back to the loss of the dressing room, isn't it? It's all about tone. It's about proxemics for me. It's about where I am in the classroom. It's about how I deliver commands and instructions. They knew straight away, when I came over – and it was the same old characters who perhaps get a little bit carried away by what's happening – I said, 'But we're getting on with it now, aren't we?' They'll say, 'Yes, yes', heads back down. That's all they need. That's how those reciprocal relationships are built, where there's that understanding between the two of you. I've seen it time and time again where shouting and screaming doesn't get you anywhere. What happens is, ultimately, that relationship is out the window. It's gone and it's very difficult to build back up again once you've broken the collaborative bond, the unspoken contract between you and them to work together.

JT: **You've lost everything, then. But what you did with those students in the middle at the back was so expert, and your tone just modulated slightly.**

TF: Oh, thank you for that.

JT: **I wrote, 'Tom teaches with relentless enthusiasm. It doesn't look like work from where I'm sitting. Watching Tom makes me want to go back 36 years and start my career anew.'**

TF: That's really sweet, thank you.

JT: **It's really impressive.**

TF: Thank you. I absolutely love this job. My time flies by when I'm in a classroom. I'm a head of department, but when people ask me how the job's going, I'll say, 'I'll be honest with you. If I can hunker down for five hours in a classroom, I'll take it.' I just love it. Your day flies. No lesson is the same. You get different challenges every single day. What a joy it is, ultimately, at the end of the lesson when they file out and they just go, 'Thank you very much, Sir.' Just a thank you. That's everything.

JT: It's all you need, isn't it?

Just seeing those Year 11s leave with the grades that they need. They'll probably forget about us. Maybe not. They'll go to college, and to them, school will be unimportant because they're on the next stepping stone of their career, but we've helped them get there. That means a lot because you're making such a fundamental difference to other people's lives. I can't imagine doing anything else.

JT: Not sure whether to say this, but … what did I write down … please don't be insulted by this …

TF: No, no.

JT: I wrote, 'He's like the loveliest quiz show host whose show only has winners.'

TF: I'm going to have that on my tombstone, I think!

JT: You are all just having a good time, but the pupils are being challenged, and they have to think hard about things.

TF: That's a perfect description there. I want it to feel like they're coming into this lesson and they're not leaving with a puff of their cheeks thinking, 'Good God, what an awful hour that was.' I want to make them feel like they're coming in for a bit of fun and to enjoy English, but it just depends how you pitch it and, how you phrase it, and how you deliver it as well. Thank you for that. I like that.

JT: Well, thank you *so* much.

TF: No, thank you.

JT: It's been a pleasure.

TF: It's been amazing. Thank you so much for your time.

Testimonials

'The most striking attribute of Tom is his ability to make every pupil in his presence feel "seen". Each pupil feels valued and heard due to his kind, compassionate and caring nature. He spends time with individual pupils and reflects continuously on what makes them "tick" in order to be the very best for them. He understands that knowing a pupil entirely fosters growth and that academic success is a symptom of this overall care for each pupil.'

'He isn't afraid to take risks in the classroom and implement research that he has taken time to explore in relation to his own teaching. He will always reflect on this and share his reflections with others to either gain further feedback or offer advice to others.'

'As a leader Tom strives for the very best and is excited by new challenges. He listens and fully analyses new obstacles before acting. This is what separates him from others, but what really separates him is that he doesn't truly know how exceptional he is.'

'As someone who had the pleasure of being taught by Mr Fraser for two years, I know that he has an extraordinary ability to create an organised and welcoming classroom for his pupils to learn and thrive in. I remember how Mr Fraser was just one of those teachers that everyone you knew adored! His aptitude for building strong pupil–teacher relationships, combined with a keen attitude, means he helps pupils every day to not only succeed but enjoy English. I can't express how grateful I am to Mr Fraser for helping me grow in confidence, skill and passion for learning.'

So, what can we learn from Tom Fraser?

One of the features of truly great teachers, IMHO (in my humble opinion), is the way they develop their ability to assess the situation in the room and act upon it. Such teachers have their radar on *all* the time, as though they are somehow meta-physical, and are watching themselves teach – analysing both what's going on in the room and their own teaching – and making deliberate changes to ensure all the physical and metaphorical corners of the classroom are with them. I call it, 'building situational assessment', a term I borrowed from my colleague Matt Stone. Tom Fraser has some of the best powers of situational assessment I have ever seen: the Year 11s who weren't quite on it; Ivan with his head on the desk; the *simile not metaphor* girl. It's about being intentional about your practice. It's about choosing the right pedagogic tool at the right moment. It's about having your radar on every minute of every lesson.

Tom's keeps his radar switched on for the whole lesson because he cares for the students. Now, when I say something like that, I give the behaviour expert Tom Bennett a nervous breakdown! You'll have seen in our conversation, that I pushed Tom Fraser on this issue. He talked about how having positive relationships with the students was the foundation of his success. But our Tom has learnt from truly great teachers before him, that affording students unconditional positive regard works, but only works when coupled with high academic expectations, of both the students and himself. Tom loves the academic work he does to prepare for challenging lessons and the students admire him for it. Whilst he cares about the students unreservedly, he cares about his subject too and he cares that the students are academically challenged by it. Caring about the students *alone*, is not enough.

It would be impossible to finish this section without referencing Tom's permission-based, invitational style of communicating with the students. It really was remarkable. His pedagogic approach would be a great model for new teachers. The whole classroom is filled with learners, and, even if it is a piece of psychological trickery, it damned well works! In 2022, Michael Young exhorted teachers to encourage 'pupils to engage in the process of acquiring knowledge'. Tom's students don't realise how they are being drawn into acquiring knowledge by his collaborative, invitational approach. Both lessons were crammed full of students enjoying themselves and working hard. It is, of course, completely deliberate, emphasising just how truly great teachers think about what and how they are doing during the lesson … and often outside the lessons, when they're driving home, doing the weekly supermarket shop and when they're cooking the tea …

Tom Fraser's students' progress and achievement data

In 2023 and 2024 Tom's Year 11 classes averaged a P8 score of +1 grade above expectations.

A Truly Great History Teacher: Louise Booth

Louise Booth is a history and politics teacher at Fulford School, York.

The school leadership's view

I'm driving into Fulford and things feel very familiar. Both our sons attended the school and received a tremendous education. I've known Andy Rosie, the deputy, for over 20 years and we greet each other as old friends. We settle in his office, I set up my microphone and after a quick sound check, we're off, discussing Louise Booth, teacher of history.

'So, in terms of *teaching*, what would you say about Louise?'

'Well', says Andy, 'Louise knows the students really well. It's those relationships she fosters, the compassion she shows, the empathy ... she understands how to break down the barriers that students face. She's good at finding out what they understand and what they don't through her rigorous questioning.' He talks about her teaching sixth formers and the lessons sound, in effect, like preparation for seminars at university. 'When you go to one of her A level classes, they'll be sat in a group around a big table, and the whole lesson will be delivered purely through her questions. They become self-generated discussions with really powerful contributions from all the students, based on the prompting and the probing of Louise's expert questioning. The way she bounces responses onto other students, the way she requests them to clarify what they say, all structured in a way that involves everyone.' Non-participation is clearly not an option in a Louise Booth lesson.

'I think Louise understands what students value about a teacher', Andy continues. 'Basic things like the consistency of the quality of the lessons ... students come in, they know what they're going to get, they know how they're going to be treated, and *they know that they're going to come out knowing more than they did when they went in*. And I think that consistency is something that drives her success, because her teaching is always of the standard that you'd hope to see when we are taking visitors around school!' As an erstwhile head teacher, I know that is a huge compliment.

Andy goes on to discuss Louise's expertise. 'Coupled with the love she's got for teaching is the fact that she's very knowledgeable about her subject, but also knowledgeable about the wider field of pedagogy. Her wealth of experience is a vital contributor to our success as a school. If there was one thing that marks her out, it would be how she's got the confidence and expertise to be selective about changing things that make things better for her and her classes in the moment, in the lesson. And that comes with deep experience. No student in her lessons gets an easy time because her questions will be targeted, differentiated, and adaptive.' Her expertise also goes across the age ranges. 'I think traditionally people would think Louise is a teacher who is really strong with the older students, especially considering her experience in the sixth form, but you see her doing exactly the same things with Year 7.'

One of the strategic roles of senior leaders is to make sure that your best teachers influence the quality of what goes on in classrooms across the school. I ask Andy about that with Louise: 'We were delighted when she stepped forward to be one of the ECT mentors, because of the experience she's got and the support and challenge she provides. She loves being a form tutor, and her tutees love her. She's got so much understanding of human emotions, and so her empathy is massive. She was a great union rep – really fair-minded – and, of course, she runs the staff socials!'

Andy reminds me that, on top of all this, Louise's students' results are amongst the best in the school, and this is a truly great school, academically. His final comment is telling: 'In my days as a form tutor, when you used to give out timetables and students saw the teachers they had for the coming year, there was often a kind of murmur one way or the other, but with Louise it was always a, "Yes" and a fist pump!'

Teaching

Andy takes me over to the history office. It is full of stuff. Old school filing cabinets labelled 'Year 8 Suffrage and Russian Revolution', 'Year 10 Cold War, East and West'. On the main tables in the middle of the room are boxes and boxes of resources, topic by topic. I can hear teaching going on … 'Take a look at the fact sheet in front of you …' A student is catching up on an assessment to my left; a trainee is planning his lessons to my right. There's a noticeboard entitled *History Student of the Month*, the lettering in Suffragette colours – purple, white and green. A picture of Frederick Douglass looking statesmanlike is on the far wall. Boxes of marking, stacked at the far end of the room, remind me that schools are about the rhythm of the calendar, year-in, year-out: 'USA Nov 2024 mocks', 'Cold War Nov 2024 mocks'. There are orders on the whiteboard behind me, presumably from the subject leader to her troops:

- Get to know your students!
- Survive!
- Eat chocolate (see tin!)

The student has finished her test, the trainee is packing up, and the classes begin to empty into the corridors. Seconds later Louise Booth strides in and greets me.

As we walk to her room, she tells me that the Year 7s I'm watching her teach next have been nicked back off the student teacher, just as a one-off. She tells me she's taught this lesson every year for the last 20 years. We laugh. She also says they are a little lively at times.

I sit back left. She goes to the door to await her charges, which leaves me the luxury of taking in the view. Her teaching room is stunning. It would make a fully paid-up member of Sweller's Cognitive Load Theory: bare walls painted pastel green brigade have a nervous breakdown. It is the eighth Wonder of the World. The walls are covered in elaborate, colourful, fascinating displays related to history and politics, both subjects Louise teaches to A level. One poster features 15 members of the new Keir Starmer cabinet. Beneath the photographs of each politician are details of their higher education degrees. The poster's slogan reads: *Study Humanities. Run the Country.* That's not such a silly aspiration. Fulford is a highly academic school. In 2020 it was named Comprehensive School of the Year by *The Sunday Times*, and a matter of days after I watch Louise teach, the same paper confirms Fulford is the top Comprehensive School in the north of England for 2024. The GCSE and A level progress data, for students who are already high achievers on entry, is relentlessly good. York is a small city with two thriving universities, and all the benefits such academia brings with it. The Fulford school site is a stone's throw from the University of York. The school is unapologetically aspirational.

Beyond the Starmer poster, there's Hockney, Muhammed Ali, Olaudah Equiano and a whole host of feminists. Rosa Luxemburg proclaims: 'Freedom is always the freedom of the dissenter.' Next to Louise's desk is a purple, green and white display (I mean, *what other colours were they likely to be?*) called, HERSTORY. The history department was, indeed, 100% female until very recently. As the young male lead inspector of their recent OFSTED visit was told, in no uncertain terms, 'the department does well because it's a sisterhood – intelligent women who know what they're doing'. What catches my eye is a dressing up rail. It is stacked full of clothes and looks like it is an active learning resource.

The Year 7s file in and Louise greets them with some lovely chatter. She is witty and animated. The students clearly like her. 'What's this teacher like?' I ask the boy who sits in front of me.

'She's a good teacher. She's funny', he replies.

Suddenly Louise says, exaggeratedly, 'Year 7! Ridiculous noise! I'll wait.' Then to a student slurping on their water bottle, 'You've just had break time, why are you drinking? Ridiculous.' She waits and waits until she has complete attention. Silence. 'Have your books out ready, please … Stop faffing. There's a lot of faffing going on … Right! Challenge number 1: You will close your eyes, while I am taking the register. Challenge number 2: I will say a word and you have to be ready to tell me the first thing you think about. Halfway down the register, I will change the word you have to think about. Can we do that?' asks Louise.

'At least we can try', says Emily.

'OK. 3-2-1- eyes closed, the first word is "Hell".'

'Here Miss', repeated at speed until we arrive at Heather, where we get the new word 'Heaven'.

Standing front and centre of the room – she has incredible presence – she says, 'Open your eyes, but do not talk.' She takes hands up. The hellish answers come thick and fast: 'lava', 'fire', 'volcanoes', 'Satan', 'darkness', 'death', 'colour red', 'horns', 'hades', 'blood', 'knife', 'torture' and 'crusty, and the ground was all cracked'.

The heavenly responses are equally copious: 'golden gates', 'wings', 'paradise' – 'No one has mentioned history lessons yet', quips Louise – 'people on clouds having foot massages', 'walls that are white', 'angels', 'death (to get there)' and 'white angels bouncing on clouds.'

I scan the room. She has 100% attention. 'Why do you think I am asking you about heaven and hell?' She takes hands up.

'They link to churches', says one student.

'Because we've been studying feudal systems and the church is part of that?' posits another.

'Good. So, why are we talking about the church now?'

'Churches are powerful, and lots of people were religious', says a girl called Kim. I check my seating plan. She is on the SEND register. ADHD. She is certainly a live wire.

'Good. They were incredibly powerful. The problem we have is that people are not so religious now. And the reason why that is a problem is because we can't get a sense of just how much the church, and religion in general, dominated normal life in medieval times.'

She checks they are all paying attention. She holds the room. 'Who visited a place of worship this weekend?' Just two hands go up. 'There you are. Six hundred years ago, all of you would have been to Church on Sunday.'

'The last time I went to Church I was at primary school', blurts out a girl to my left.

'I took my dog to church once', says another.

Louise segues into some tried and tested old school questioning. 'Who do you know who goes to church?' There are numerous students bursting to contribute.

'Older people … My Granny. Grandad George – he's Greek and he knows all about the Greek gods … he has statues all over his house.'

Louise says, 'I quite like the sound of him.' I stifle a guffaw.

The lively Kim then says, with being asked, 'When I went into a church I started crying.'

Louise follows up this gold dust moment. 'Why do you think you cried, Kim?'

'Because I was scared, Miss.'

'There you go', declares Louise, 'That's what I'm on about. The power of the Church. What happened to you, Kim, is connected to what we are doing today.' She turns to the whole class. 'Right. This is a big challenge. I'm thinking you can do this … because you have already done a challenge today. Can you do this?' Nods and mumblings of assurance around the room. 'OK, pages 54 and 55 in the textbook please.' This is the first time on my travels I have come across a textbook in use. I've seen thousands on bookshelves, but none in use.

'Thank you people. Here's your title: "Why was the church so important in the Middle Ages?" Use capital letters, or it makes no sense at all.' She clicks to an image of the *Chaldon Church Purgatorial Ladder Doom Painting*.[1]

---

1 A. Marshall, Chaldon, Surrey c.1200, The Purgatorial Ladder, or Ladder of Souls, with the Seven Deadly Sins (2018). Available at: https://reeddesign.co.uk/paintedchurch/chaldon-seven-deadly-sins.htm.

'This is a Doom Painting.' She checks they know what the word 'doom' means. 'They were meant to scare people. Why would they be *paintings*? Turn to your partners. Ten seconds to decide why they would be *paintings*?'

'The thing is, Miss, not many people could read or write, so they had to look at images.' She is cracking on at a pace.

'Good. Now, there are a number of things to spot in this image. Here's the list. This is how I want you to write them down in your books, next to the handout of the image. I'll give you 3 minutes.'

She works the room along with the TA and the trainee too. There is 100% student engagement. She narrates what is going on. Her commentary keeps them working. It's like she creates a team effort, where everyone is working for the class as a whole; that's certainly how I feel being in the room. 'Some people have done this superbly. Some people are still working on it. Come on, keep going.'

She goes through the answers swiftly, matching each aspect of the Doom Painting to the description. Johanne says, 'Miss, what's a pilgrim?' She offers the question up to the room and an answer soon comes back.

'Someone who goes on a religious journey.'

'Right, pens down. Focus on me.' She addresses one boy who isn't quite sitting up straight. He has also drawn his knee up and has his foot on the seat. He is directly in front of me. 'Fraser, put your foot down.' I think she's slightly scary. In a good way. The foot goes down without a murmur. 'Here is your question for homework. We're going to explore this further during the rest of the lesson: "Why was religion so important in medieval life?"'

They look at a chapter from the textbook, sharing the reading around the room. A forest of hands goes up to volunteer to read. They all read fluently. She is working hard, keeping them focused. 'If you're looking at me you're looking in the wrong place.' For the next 10 minutes they read two pages of the textbook and she questions them back and forth, back and forth. The engagement is tangible, and all they're doing is reading from the textbook.

Louise is intent that they remember what they're doing. The amount she wants them to learn in this lesson doesn't appear to be huge, but what they are learning, they are learning, understanding and committing to memory. She gets them to test each other on what they can remember of the *Doom Picture* and then what they can recall of the text that's been read out. She then asks them to draw a cross in the centre of their page, like the one she is drawing on the board. 'Looking round, the standard of drawing in this class is really, to be honest, quite poor.' She looks over someone's shoulder and says, 'Oh no, that's awful . . .' It's all affected and ironic.

The boy laughs and says, 'It's better than yours, Miss.'

'Now, around your cross I want you to write notes about the six aspects of religious life that we read about. Not every word, just a little summary of what we've read. Peter, why do I want you to do that?'

'To help us remember it Miss.'

'Correct. Five minutes. We will come round and judge the quality of your work . . .' She breaks off into mock horror mode as she stops in front of one boy.

'What's wrong, Miss?'

'It's the quality of drawing . . . it's really not good!' They argue. It's funny. People laugh for a second and then get on. 'Beautiful! I can see some *quite* good ones . . .' Kim gets giddy and Louise calms her down gently and expertly. They are all note-making. There is emerging evidence that physically writing notes with a pen helps with embedding new learning in the long-term memory.[2] Suddenly, complete calm descends upon the room. For two minutes there is not a sound. I look across the room. William Wilberforce stares back at me, saying, 'You

---

[2] P. A. Mueller and D. M. Oppenheimer, The pen is mightier than the keyboard: advantages of longhand over laptop note taking, *Psychological Science*, 25(6) (2014): 1159–1168. Available at: https://doi.org/10.1177/0956797614524581.

can choose to look the other way but you can never say again that you didn't know.'

'You'll need the information for the "explain" question for homework.' Louise works the room. I glance at the seating plan. Her support is equitably allocated. She is a stickler for pens down. 'Close your books and close your textbooks. How many of you could tell me the six reasons why the church was really powerful in medieval times, without looking at their books? Jarrod?'

Jarrod's hand was only tentatively up. 'Maybe', he says. 'Errr … you had to give 10% of your wealth to the church … you were worried about whether you would go to Heaven or Hell … God controlled everything that happened … Holy days are our holidays and they shaped the year … the church was there when you were born, baptisms, weddings and deaths … and, umm … priests were powerful figures.' A massive round of spontaneous applause breaks out.

'Think of your own learning, could you have done that?' This is 'less but better' teaching. No rushing through the syllabus.

The lesson is nearly done. They are given a sheet to complete, and a diagram to fill in, which is the last step in embedding the learning about the power of the medieval church. 'See if you can you answer the questions without the notes', says Louise. They do a final recap about the importance of the church, with Louise cold calling around the class.

For the last 10 minutes of the lesson they play the old Indian game of 'Heaven and Hell' (Jnana Bagi) adapted for medieval times. Known to us as 'Snakes and Ladders', I hadn't realised it was originally a vehicle for teaching ethics. Each square has not only a number but text, which comprises the names of various crimes and virtues, turned medieval. When she says that is how the lesson is going to finish, she declares, with some authority, that it 'only works if people are sensible. If not, we stop and get on with the homework. Right, into pairs, and threes if necessary.' Her threat of not continuing are real, and they know it. She is great on the instructions. She checks and double checks. They can't wait to get started. She makes me think of Michael Young's quote about engaging young people into *wanting to become scholars*. She is drawing them in. They want to turn up to these lessons. They want to get involved. They want to *learn*.

Off they go. They spend the last few minutes playing the game, intently. The crimes and virtues are relevant and interesting. I hear one boy near me exclaim his frustration. He sounds truly gutted. When I ask him what the problem is, he says, as if method acting the role of a 13th century English villager, 'I'd tricked the bailiff by putting bricks in the bottom of my bag of corn to make it weigh heavier so I could sell it for more money, but I got caught.' He records his misdemeanour on a crimes/virtues tally chart. They don't realise that, by doing so, they are committing more information to memory.

'Remember, if you have more virtues than crimes, you're off to Heaven, but the other way round you're off to Hell! It'll bring home to you what life's like in this game of chance!' There is 100% engagement and perfect self-regulation. They are genuinely disappointed at having to stop. 'So, did you make it to Heaven or Hell? Stand up if you are going to Heaven … 50% roughly … Hell? Mmmm … about 40% … and equal crimes and virtues? Just you two! Well, you're both in purgatory. You'd stay there for a *very long* time.' A quick check on who knows what 'purgatory' is and Louise asks them, once they've packed up, what the game taught them about medieval times.

'I think it shows what a game of chance it was about whether you went to Heaven or Hell, Miss.'

'Excellent. And, finally, who can tell me the six reasons why the church was so powerful in the Middle Ages?' This time a girl volunteers to answer. She gets there, just! Louise is great at holding the silence and letting the students struggle for an answer. She never puts words in their mouths.

Then they are dismissed, row by row. She stands at the door and sees them off into the corridor, *every single one of them* significantly more educated in the power of the medieval church than they were 60 minutes earlier.

What the students think

Louise parks me back in the department office and marshals six students into seats around the table where I'm sitting. Once she has departed, I explain why I'm here and what I want to find out about Ms Booth. Lesley is a Year 11. According to my notes from Louise, she is destined for Oxbridge. She is straight in. 'I just love the dressing up! The lesson I remember more than any other lesson in Key Stage 3 is re-enacting the Battle of Hastings!' All five others nod furiously. There is complete consensus. I had thought the dressing up rail looked well-used.

'Who were you?'

'Oh, I was the Pope', replies Lizzy. 'The interactive prancing around was such fun. The lessons were a good mix of academic stuff and fun. It just makes you want to do the work.'

Terry likes the challenges. 'She sets these challenges and if you win, you get no homework for a fortnight!' She clearly breaks the rules, and I'm not sure anyone is going to tell her to do anything other than get on with what she does. As Andy said, her students' results are amongst the best in the school, and this is a truly great school, academically.

There are a few sixth formers. 'We just get on so well with her. When she is explaining things in class, we're just so engaged with what's she's saying. You never know what you're going to do in her lessons. When we were revising for our GCSE, she ran Ms Booth's Café. Five tables around the room and she had given each one a different topic, and we moved round – ten minutes on each table – and revised in teams of five. We had coffee and biscuits. It was amazing!' The other sixth former takes over. 'It's not just the extraordinary things,' he says, 'like with the Cold War unit in Year 10. As soon as she started talking, I immediately enjoyed it. I remember everything about those lessons.'

More associative memory model, perhaps? Or just teaching that deliberately embeds learning?

Year 11 Lesley says, 'She's also really approachable as a teacher, not everyone is like that. She is an expert. I trust that she knows what she's doing and we'll get good grades if we do what she says.'

'She goes through each test paper with you individually', Mark, the third sixth former adds. 'I went up five grades from the mock to the real thing. From a 2 to a 7. She's marked for the exam board. She really knows what she's doing. I trusted her completely.'

Lesley continues. 'There's a really good balance between course content and exam technique. She integrates how to answer exam questions into the lesson. And although there is an incredible amount to get through in GCSE history, we never feel overwhelmed. We just get on.'

These six are bright-eyed, brilliant young people. It's invigorating being in their presence. 'It's about her personality. The stories she tells. They keep everyone in good spirits. Her love for history is inspiring. It's things like her vacuum cleaner! I think it was her grandma's. It's a 1930s model from America. We were talking about how women's role in the home has changed over time. And she tells us about all the places she's been.'

They are gaining in confidence. I don't really have to orchestrate things or provide prompts. 'She's full-hearted', says Terry. 'When you get in her lessons she's always ready to go, really well-organised. All sorted.' Being well-organised is emerging as a highly valued feature of the truly great teacher.

Year 8 Bob hasn't said much, but even he starts talking without me needing to give him an 'in': 'She is joyful and happy all the time. But she was scary at the start. Her passion for the subject is intimidating. She whacks you with these facts.'

'She's so hard working', says a sixth former. 'She's fun, for sure, but she knows how to get us to do the work. You'd feel guilty if you hadn't done the work by the end of the lesson. She only raised her voice if you hadn't done the work. You never left the lesson without finishing.'

Time is against us. I ask them to give me a single word to describe Ms Booth, quickly, before the bell for break. I get a fascinating list: passionate, intelligent, iconic, diverse (in the way she goes about the lessons), thoughtful (in terms of being well-planned and how she cares about us), approachable and exciting (I always look forward to the lesson if it's history). That final comment came from Year 8 Bob. I like how he has the confidence to say such a thing, to be unashamedly enthused by academic learning. It's culturally unusual in a country like ours that's suspicious of academia.

We didn't have time to do the interview, so we postponed it until the evening; *I happen to be Louise Booth's husband* and it's heartening to have heard the students talk about her so positively.

IRL: Louise Booth

John Tomsett (JT): So why did you start teaching?

Louise Booth (LB): I was always going to be a teacher. It's vocational; it's in my DNA. I played games as a teacher in my bedroom with my toys, and I became a teacher despite everybody trying to put me off being a teacher. I did all that graduate milk-round stuff, and went home and said to my mum and dad, 'I'm not doing any of that'. Even the Durham careers people tried to put me off teaching, it was very disappointing to them. That's why I went and did my Master's in the USA. Then I came back because I was always going to teach.

JT: Did your Master's change you at all?

LB: Only in that it confirmed for me that I'd like to be a teacher, because I'd been inspired by one of the professors! Professor

Leila Rupp. She was brilliant. She was extremely knowledgeable. She was very inclusive. She was charismatic. She was teaching me something I really didn't know anything about. My life changed after learning women's history. It was a whole different prism through which to look at your academic study. It was mind-blowing because I'd just been taught all that white-men history before, and then it was like, 'Oh, you can see it from different points of view', and I absolutely loved it. Truly loved it. *The Majority Finds Its Past* by Gerda Lerner is the book that changed it all for me, but it was written back in the 1970s.[3] It was foreseeing what was to come. Nowadays, there's women's studies departments.

Then I came back, and I did the Sussex PGCE. Which was OK. I can't remember being taught to teach or taught to plan a lesson on that course. I learnt most from Dave Bradley, my tutor in school. He was very old school. He loved kids, and his best advice was, 'If it's going wrong, don't blame them. Look at yourself.' I did. He was kind, he was supportive, he was funny. I learnt more from watching Dave teach than I ever did at the university.

I knew, from the first moment I stood up in front of that first class – I was the most nervous I'd been probably in my life – as soon as I started [*clicks tongue*] I was in my element. From that first lesson on ancient Greece I knew I was born to do this. I wasn't nervous once I began. I knew I'd come home; *this* is what I was going to do. I can remember that distinctly, that feeling. I let them in, they sat down, bang! My first job was at Longhill School.

JT: **Tell us about that.**

LB: I loved it! It was fun; it was challenging. I was supported by the best head teacher I've ever worked for: Denis Mulkerrin. I was part of something. Nobody took anything too seriously. I

---

3 G. Lerner, *The Majority Finds Its Past: Placing Women in History* (Chapel Hill, NC: University of North Carolina Press, 2014 [1979]).

worked with Annette Buttifant, who became my best friend! She was the head of department who taught me, 'If you're going to do something, do it really well. If you're going to do a display, do it brilliantly. If you're going to go on a school trip, plan it to the nth degree.' I learned from her about the importance of the detail.

JT: **What did you learn about pedagogy and teaching history?**

LB: Freedom. I had the freedom to do a lot of things. That's what I learnt. Denis and Annette would say, 'Have a go at it, and we'll be there to support you. If it goes wrong, we're there.' So I did the group work and we did the dressing up. We were doing all of that, and with tough kids. You'd have an afternoon when it looked sunny, and Annette and I would say, 'I think we'll pop them down to see Rottingdean Church', and no one died. I can't remember being scared.

JT: **So what do you say to people who say they'll just remember the drama, not the history?**

LB: They do both. It's not a dichotomy. They learn *through* the methods. It's not just about the knowledge. They're going to recall it because they're going to remember, 'Oh, I was dressing up in that outfit because we were learning about Henry VIII.'

JT: **So, you use what would be called an associative memory model?**

LB: Yes, always. Maybe that's because it works for me. Well, I tell them to revise by lying in the bath in their clothes. Because it'll be such an odd experience, and your brain is disconnected. So, you say, 'Right, okay, there's something you really can't get hold of, like the Korean War, go and take your book, fully clothed, sit in the bath, read the book, or read that bit. When you're in the exam, you will think, "Oh, yes, the Korean War, I was sitting in the bath, and I remember that bit".' They all come back and say,

'I love that tip. It works for me.' Do anything, just displace yourself.

Longhill was the best 10 years of my career because I didn't have children, I had no responsibility, and I was backed by a head who was saying, 'I'll support you.' He liberated me. Really believed in me. Said to me at the end of my first year, 'You'll be a head teacher', but he took none of my dramatic nonsense either. I can't remember why I'd flounced into his office, but he'd cancelled something or other, and I was cross with him, and he said, 'Come back in the room. Stand there.' He said, 'Louise, you're just the head of history in a comprehensive school. Let's get it in perspective.' He was right to say that. I wasn't the *Duchess of Fulford* then. I felt he really believed in me, and I felt lots of people did.

JT: **What are the hallmarks of your teaching?**

LB: Everything is based on the relationships I have with the kids. Forget how clever I might be about history. I could be teaching anything. I could be teaching geography, RE. The main thing is the mutual respect. I'm never going to humiliate you; I'm never going to bully you, but I'm going to be firm and you're going to feel safe in my classroom.

JT: **What did they have to do? What was their part of the deal?**

LB: They had to respect me, they had to respect each other, they had to behave. I said at one point about a boy who needed to sit up, 'Body language is very important to me. Yes, sit up straight. Get you backside in your chair. No slouching. I can't have slouching. I think slouching's disrespectful.'

JT: **Anything about working hard?**

LB: No. I'll tell you what I did do. This was from Denis, thinking about it now. I just expected them to work hard. His thing was all about expectations. The school took in a tough element from a disadvantaged part of Brighton, but Denis treated it like

Longhill *Grammar*. Nothing was too good for those kids. We were going to have strict uniform, we were going to have homework, they were going to behave. So, at the time, he got mocked for it.

JT: **What do you mean, *he got mocked for it*?**

LB: Delusions of grandeur, I suppose; but his line was, 'Expect, expect, expect.' That's what I inherited. I still do it. I'm not going to think, 'I've got all these SEND pen portraits, so they're not going to behave.' I just expect them to behave, and I expect them to do really well, and I expect them to work hard, and I expect them to listen to me, and I expect … because the alternative to that is playing down to the lowest common denominator. I won't do it. So that's what I got from Longhill. If you think about it, it ties in with what I'm saying about Annette. Her expectations were, 'that display will be beautiful'. The expectations are that the books will be marked, and all of that. If sometimes you didn't meet those expectations, that would be dealt with as well, but *expect, expect, expect* – and that is right, actually. That is what sticks with me.

JT: **So, if I was a pupil in your lesson then, what could I expect?**

LB: You'd expect the lessons to be planned, you'd expect the lessons to be fun, you'd expect them to be relatable. So, I've always done that. I say to classes sometimes, 'I'm going to see you twice a week, so I want you to value the time we're spending together. I want you to sit there and think, "What's this all about? Why am I here?"' Like today, why are we learning about medieval church? What's that got to do with anything? Ultimately, they'll see why it matters. It helps form your world view, and we need to respect people. So, it's all about making it relatable. Especially history.

JT: **Where after Longhill?**

LB: So, I was head of history within a couple of years. Then I was a head of year. Then I was the acting deputy head. I went briefly back to head of year, and then left. So, by the time I was 27, I was an acting deputy.

JT: **Then you had a career break.**

LB: Then I came up to York and started teaching part-time at Fulford. I ended up with the full-time job at Fulford. It took me a while to adjust because I'd had the career break. Technology had moved on, and I didn't feel part of it. I felt anonymous. Felt the kids were not what I was used to. They were much more middle-class, much smarter than I was used to, and there was a sixth form, too. So, it took me a while to get used to Fulford, but eventually I did. The same teaching style, really. It's very clichéd: firm, funny, fair … and fierce! I do get that. 'I thought you were scary, but I know you're not.'

JT: **One of the lads, Bob, said he was intimidated by your passion for the subject.**

LB: It's a funny thing to be scared of … He was in the enslavement lesson, period 1. They enjoy the lessons, because they are built on relationships and relationships are timeless. I'm going to expect you to come in my room and sit down, and I'm expecting you to engage with me in a civilised way. I'm expecting you to learn. That's what I'm here for, for an hour, and we're going to get the absolute best out of it.

JT: **What was really interesting today was that you didn't cover very much. You insisted on them covering the content in two or three different ways. So, you got them thinking. Then you got them doing the match up with the picture and the words and the description. Then you got them to make notes on the same stuff, on the six reasons that the church was influential.**

Then you got them to recount it, and you got them to play the game.

LB: I'd set up the homework, though, as well. They could see why they were doing it because they needed this for their homework. In another lesson, in another group, I would have done that homework instead of the game. That game could only be done with certain groups. You make the decision. You think, 'Right, are we on board? OK, we'll do the game, or no we won't.' But that's experience, isn't it? You know they potentially could muck about with the game. You say I didn't cover a lot, but they don't *get* religion, so you really have to hammer it home to them. It's not in their lives. The reason I spend a whole lesson on that single topic is because it is important for the next six lessons; in fact, it's important for the whole of Key Stage 3. Religion influences the course of history in so many ways. So, you've really got to get that lesson right for the following lessons to work. If you don't get that lesson right today, they haven't got a clue what they're doing because they say, 'Why are we talking about the church?' Tomorrow, they will say, 'Oh, yes. They believed in Heaven and Hell, and if you didn't do as the church says, you went to Hell.'

JT: **I just want to talk about the lesson today because I was really interested in how you gave up your time when they were on tasks. I had the seating plan in front of me and you targeted need all the time.**

LB: It's a big group there, with differentiated needs. I went around, and asked, 'Do you want this support?' Some said, 'Yes'; some said, 'No'. I'm also aware that you can't overdo that because you've got a TA in the room. Otherwise, you've got adults swarming, and they hate it. I don't always go around. I can sit at my desk, and I will announce, 'I'm doing my work, and you will do yours', and I will model that behaviour. I worked the room today, because there was a lot going on.

JT: I was impressed by how you insisted you did stuff to help them remember it. They'll have remembered a lot more than I see in many lessons because you embedded it.

LB: I think that's experience, isn't it? Student teachers have got their plan, 'I've got to do this, I've got to do that, and I've got to do the other.' My sense of security means that, if they hadn't played the game today, it would have been fine. We'd have done something else. I'm not tied to a lesson plan anymore, whereas when you're learning to teach, you think 'I've got to get through this', whereas as an older, mature teacher, you think, 'If I don't get through this today, I'll get through it tomorrow.' So, you have that ability, but I think I've always done that.

A level is my favourite thing to do. It's just, intellectually, the most interesting thing to do. You don't get bored with it. The A level I teach in Russian history is really interesting. Young people of that age are fascinating. It's creative and it's stimulating. It's just the best thing to do.

JT: Do you enjoy researching some new material and finding out about stuff?

LB: Yes, and you're doing that with the kids. So, you might go to a lecture series, or I've just done a History Association activity online. All of that is intellectually satisfying. It's nourishing for me and them. A level politics is the same. If you are smart, it is satisfying, that bit.

JT: How many trips do you think you've been on over the years?

LB: Loads. I can't imagine. Hundreds. Berlin, Washington, London, Dunkirk, Manchester, museums, theatre trips, the House of Commons.

JT: **How many battlefields trips?**

LB: Oh, so many! I led a battlefields trip in probably the third year I taught. Starting from Brighton at midnight and coming back at midnight the following night. Taking them on a ferry. I was in charge of that trip. A coach load. It'd be 50 kids. I would have been, what, 20 something. Now, I don't see that in school as much anymore, and I don't blame colleagues, because there wouldn't have been the paperwork back then, and there wouldn't have been the threat that somebody might sue you!

JT: **So, you teach A level politics, too?**

LB: I'd done that as part of my degree. It's an equal love. A level politics groups are slightly different. You've got to nurture an atmosphere where they really contribute all the time. Lots and lots of discussion. My A level style is very seminar based. You do the work, you come to the lesson and you talk. A lot of it is about thinking and talking about what you think. So, I will always set work to read, and then you will come to the room and discuss it. Then that might be followed up by a written piece of work. I very rarely say to an A level student, 'Right, shall we sit and make notes now?' We need to articulate what we're thinking. Many of them will go to university and come back and say, 'It was just like being in one of your lessons.' Early on, you have to be quite firm … I don't take any prisoners. They need to know that they will be asked questions, but in a safe environment, and they will *have* to contribute. If you don't do the reading, you can't contribute. I will say, 'You will be leaving the lesson immediately if you haven't done the reading.' Why would the student be allowed to stay? You only need to send someone out once, and then they all do the reading. My job is to make sure that you're not nervously sitting there thinking, 'Oh, God, she's going to ask me something.' You know what I mean? I can't have that. They have to feel safe, but challenged.

JT: **High expectations …**

LB: It's their expectations too. So, I'm expecting you to have done the work, and you're expecting me to ask you about it. Everybody will be asked.

JT: **Andy said, 'There are no hiding places in Louise's classes.'**

LB: Did you hear me today? I said, 'Oh, Trinny, I've not heard from you today.' I'll have the seating plan there, and I'm ticking names off in my head. 'Right, I've spoken to Tim and now I need to speak to Alfie, and blah, blah, blah.' Especially at A level. Today, the lesson after the Year 7 was Year 12, and they'd done some reading about the American Civil War. So, they knew that, in that lesson, I'm going to say, 'OK, so what have you brought to the lesson?' Sometimes, they're very broad questions I ask at A level. Much bigger questions. Less precise.

JT: **Lizzy was great on the balance that you have. You're teaching her GCSE. She said, 'The course is potentially overwhelming, but it doesn't feel overwhelming to me. She doesn't make it feel overwhelming.' The older ones said, 'It feels like you're studying history. Then you're taught how to answer the questions. You're not *just* being taught how to answer the questions.'**

LB: That's nice to hear, because I don't feel like that sometimes. This is the history … and this is the hoop to jump through.

JT: **They admire your expertise at hoop jumping. They say, 'We learn all this stuff. Then we just go, "Oh, I know what to do now. Bang, bang, bang, bang, bang".' They all feel they are learning history, above prepping for exams …**

LB: Their history's not getting lost?

JT: Far from it. It's the central bit. They mentioned you'd been an examiner. Tell us what the benefits are of being an examiner, for you.

LB: Oh, massive. I only did it once, but head of department's an examiner. Second-in-department's an examiner. Every year they bring new stuff to the table on examining – nuanced changes to what the examiner board want. You share that with the class. You say, 'Miss Jones is an examiner. Miss Smith is one. I am.' They trust you that you know what you're doing, and you do because you're getting it from the horse's mouth. I'm very open about that. I'll say, 'I've been an examiner, duh-duh-duh-duh-duh.' They buy into it because they need to feel confidence in you. Then they'll do as they're told!

JT: Is there anything that you're working on at the moment?

LB: It's all to do with special needs. It's all to do with trying to meet the needs of the kids in the class, definitely. More than I've ever done, because that's the biggest challenge going on at the moment.

JT: What kind of things are you finding yourself doing?

LB: Just in your planning. Little differences can make it easier – like having a worksheet ready that just will make it easier to do those low-level tasks. Like today, a couple of the boys wouldn't have been able to do that drawing from the board. I had a little scaffold for them. My aim is to get them all up here; they're all aiming for the same target. So, you go around and offer support. Doing that five times a day is exhausting. If you think, in that class, 10 kids out of 28 had specific needs, and one of them wasn't there, which would have made quite a difference today, to my TA help and to what I would have done today. That's the massive difference, compared to when I began teaching. To be fair, in those old classes in Longhill, I just thought there were some naughty boys, if the truth be known. You just thought,

'Oh, he's got some issues!' Children with additional needs get a much better deal now, *if those needs are met*. But they weren't even identified, back when I started teaching. You probably could look back with rose-coloured spectacles thinking, 'Oh, yes, I had it all sorted.' I'm not sure I did, though …

JT: **Those pedagogic threads that have remained through 37 years … they still work. Handing the baton on then, what advice would you give to teachers entering the profession now? What reflections would you have for them?**

LB: Firstly, most of the time, it's not personal, so be the grown up in the room. Remind yourself every time you're the grown up. If a kid's having a go at you, they're not really having a go at you.

Secondly, every pupil is someone's child, aren't they? In 99% of cases, someone at home is worried about that child. They can't be anonymous in your classroom. Every single one of them is important, so you do have to speak to all of them, and you do have to care about them, and you have to make sure that you don't have your favourites. Do you know what I mean? The kid at the back, make sure you've engaged with them.

JT: ***Don't have your favourites*** **is a great tip.**

LB: Then what else would I say? I say it all the time, just have *fun*. You've really got to have fun because, otherwise, they won't learn anything, and you'll go mad! They're human beings. All that stuff today about, 'I think you're rubbish at drawing.' They bought into that!

JT: **They love dressing up. Tell us finally about the dressing up.**

LB: The dressing up rail was in the department, but I moved it into my classroom because it's so big! We've always had dressing up. Year 13s love it. That particular group you were talking to, we did do a lot of dressing up last year. The dressing up is freedom, isn't it? The dressing up is about not sitting Victorian style at a desk, and, again, it's that idea that if you take your brain away, you'll remember, 'Oh, we dressed up as a monk', or 'We dressed up as the Pope or William the Conqueror.' It's all that bit about remembering. You'll notice, as well, I like movement in the classroom. Like I said, 'Stand up if you went to Heaven or Hell.' Particularly those boys need to, by that point, stand up a bit. You've got to have the movement.

JT: **I couldn't believe how quickly the hour went by.**

LB: I do get that comment. The kids will say, 'Is it over?' You go, 'Yes'.

JT: **Anything else you want to add?**

LB: No, I've just had a fantastic career, all this time.

JT: **You have, haven't you?**

LB: Yes. What else would I have done? Not because I couldn't think of anything else to do!

JT: **You weren't born to do anything else.**

LB: I know! But I'm done now.

JT: **That was really great. Thank you.**

Testimonials

'Thank for being an excellent teacher. You have really helped me increase my confidence through your encouragement of me to realise my ability, as well as taking my enjoyment of history to another level. I know that you're going to carry on inspiring people like me for generations of students to come.'

'You make learning so much fun!'

'In and out of the classroom you are helpful, supportive and just the kind of teacher everyone would wish for. Michelle Obama would love you just as much as you love her!'

'I hope you don't mind me contacting you out of the blue, I am busy organising a 21st birthday party for our daughter, and wondered, since you were so inspirational in her education, whether you would be able to join us?'

'Thanks so much for the last two years. The history lessons have been wonderful. I'm going to Cheetham's music school next year and it has the oldest public library in the English-speaking world! Thanks again!'

'I honestly don't think I would be here with an Oxford offer and having completed my EPQ [extended project qualification] without your advice! I hope I can do you proud on results day!'

'You were the first teacher to see the potential in our son when he moved up from primary and you have been an absolute inspiration to him since Year 8.'

'It gives me great pleasure as Fulford's head teacher to congratulate you formally following on from feedback we were given by OFSTED that the history lesson you taught on Thursday that was observed by the lead inspector was graded as "outstanding".'

'I actually can't thank you enough. Without your teaching, encouragement and guidance, I wouldn't be where I am today, emotionally or academically! I'll always appreciate the time you set aside for me, your insight and your ability to make me smile!'

'Thank you for being the most amazing teacher ever! You were the one who showed me how to love history and I'm so glad I'm taking it for A level. You made every lesson so enjoyable (even if it was the Normans!). You also inspired me to want to become the best version of myself. You are 100% my favourite teacher and always will be, and I will always remember the stories you told us.'

So, what can we learn from Louise Booth?

I took some time to think about what Louise does …

Louise breaks rules. She has a dressing up rail, *for goodness' sake!* But she ensures they *remember* what they have been taught, so that it's been *learnt*. Socrates said that, 'there is no learning without memory'. She helps them remember through using many of the cognitive science strategies that Daniel Willingham et al. espouse. She insists on 100% attention 100% of the time and then makes sure they think hard. More than that, however, she also employs associative memory strategies. They associate her lessons with learning and fun, derived from the memorable moments when they play a game or role play a moment in history. Consequently, they *want* to turn up to Ms Booth's lessons. Why wouldn't you?

I meet lots of schools who claim that they have the highest expectations of their pupils, only to find pupils completing low level administration tasks as they fill in their commercially produced, downloaded handouts. This extraordinary teacher – who has no behaviour difficulties, whose curiosity underpins her forensic questioning skills, whose subject knowledge is extensive, who is not easily impressed, who works tirelessly, and who, *crucially*, has some fun now and then amidst the academic culture that distinguishes Fulford School, *never* compromises her high standards. Louise Booth is high expectations *personified*.

Yet she confounds the zeitgeist. In an education world beset by binary arguments between the traditionalists and progressives, she is neither. For all her strictness, her students are given the licence to *play* in her classes, and that's what brings them back to learn, lesson after lesson after lesson.

Louise Booth's students' progress and achievement data

Louise works in a department whose P8 score has not dipped below +0.5 since the P8 score measure was introduced a decade ago. Their best performance was +1.6. At A level, ALPS scores have never been below 3, and in 2024 the average was +0.6 of a grade above expectations.

A Truly Great English/History/Media/EPQ Teacher: Jack Bream

Jacqueline (Jack) Bream teaches English, history, media studies and the extended project qualification (EPQ), at Huntington School, York.

The school leadership's view

I have only ever nominated one teacher for the national teachers' awards *thingy*, and that is Jack Bream. When the idea for this book emerged, she was the first name on my list of prospective truly great teachers. So, it feels a bit odd to be back in my old office talking to Matt Smith, my successor, about someone I know so well. But Matt has had three years to get to know his colleagues and it is important to get other views of Jack, because any head teacher's single viewpoint is just that – a single viewpoint – and is always going to be subjective and biased.

'Jack's such a lovely human being', says Matt. I nod in agreement. 'Lots of what makes her a great teacher is her personality and her approach to her students. It's summed up in that no one fails in her classes. The statistics tell the story. Her media results have been a 1 or 2 on the ALPS forever. At Huntington, media studies has been the best performing A level in terms of value added over the last decade, and Jack's GCSE class had a P8 score last summer of +0.8. You can't argue with that.' I nod. A lot. I think of Rob Coe. He would love this.

Matt continues, 'When you see Jack, she lifts your spirits!' I know what he means. Headship is often a very lonely place, and it is always good to have someone on your staff team who asks after *your* well-being, just like Jack always did for me. 'She has the emotional intelligence to see people. The unremarkable and the potentially invisible students. The quiet girl in the corner. She sees them all, and that is worth everything.' Matt is beaming. 'What makes Jack so great is the hidden stuff about her. She is super bright and has taken on so many subjects, all to A level. She is not afraid of hard work. She's principled, and her teaching is really clever. Gentle. She teases learning out of her students. It's an art.'

Matt has a lot on. We part at the reception door, and I sit waiting for Jack to pick me up, while he goes off to walk the corridors, to ensure that everyone is where they should be after lunch break. She arrives spot on time, and we nip into a nearby maths room. We catch up with stuff, nothing to do with this book, and then I realise that this is the time allocated for interviewing Jack for the book. She's been happy to keep me talking, because she doesn't really want to do this thing! The best teachers are often the most modest.

IRL: Jack Bream

John Tomsett (JT): So what made you teach?

Jack Bream (JB): I left Warwick University with no idea what I wanted to do. I was determined I was never going to be a teacher. That was definitely off the list. Then I got a job for a summer on a tennis exchange camp where French students came to the UK to learn tennis and English, and, somehow, I ended up with a job teaching French kids English, even though I was not good at either of those things. No skills in either French or English teaching – or tennis, for that matter! I can literally say from the first day, from the first morning when I took a class teaching these French kids English, that was it.

JT: What, you loved it?

JB: From the very first day. I'm so lucky I had that. It was a proper road to Damascus moment. This is it, yes, and 28 years on I still feel the same.

JT: What did you love about it?

JB: Well, just being in the room. It wasn't about standing at the front and it still isn't. It wasn't about the subject. I teach four subjects – I do love teaching them English, history, media studies, EPQ – but it's not about the subjects. It's about the energy in the room, and I can't really say what that is; it's sort of inexplicable. The relationships I suppose. Every day, every encounter being different. Yes, just the energy. When it was lockdown and we were teaching remotely, it was just awful. I hated it. And when we were stuck behind a line at the front and I couldn't circulate around the room, it was just not the same.

JT: **I've just seen a brilliant teacher, Chris McGrane, teach. His main thing is to *teach between the desks*.**

JB: Yes. I never sit down. That's the best advice anyone ever gave me in teaching.

JT: **Keep standing on your feet?**

JB: Never sit down. I know not everybody's able to do that, and that's fine, but for me I'll take the register sitting down and then that's it, I walk and walk and walk because that's the only thing I've got, that vigilance. Is every kid doing every task? If not, I've failed, haven't I?

JT: **Every kid doing every task?**

JB: In every lesson, that's the goal. They need to know they're not leaving the room until I'm happy with what they've done. Probably, that's control freakery on my part, but I am moving around the room all the time, and it's about … I suppose it's the micro-engagements isn't it, the micro-interactions.

JT: **Tell us about your micro-interactions.**

JB: A trainee teacher watched me about five years ago and they'd been sent to me as somebody to watch who had good behaviour-management skills, because they were having behaviour issues. They watched me for an hour, and the trainee teacher said, 'Well, I can't learn anything about behaviour management from you because you don't do anything.' I thought, 'You have so missed the point!' I had done 300 tiny things – clearly very quiet interventions – and felt I had been working really hard to manage the classroom. It was just a look or a glance: 'Put your chair down', 'Put your gum in the bin', 'Pick your pen up', 'Do you need a ruler?' I felt like I'd been spinning all the plates. I'd walked that room, and I'd looked at every kid's book, but the trainee teacher thought, because they weren't misbehaving, that I hadn't done anything. It was a fundamental misunderstanding. So, for me it's about the little things. It's not the big stuff. It's not about standing at the front and giving out the wisdom, it's about the chats as they come in. 'How's your sister?' 'Oh yes, I've heard …' Greeting them at the door, connecting with them. But there are so many variables in that room, I think. Whether they've eaten breakfast? Have they fallen out with their best friend at lunchtime? How's their family situation? How do they feel about my subject? How do they feel about the people in the room?

JT: **Do you make yourself, then, a non-variable?**

JB: Yes. I try to be consistent, positive and upbeat, and have high expectations of them, I suppose. I try to be the same for them every lesson, and if they've really crossed a line the lesson before, I'll reach out again and start with a clean slate, all of those things.

JT: **Tell me about your range of subjects then, because you're an historian by trade.**

JB: Yes, well, I did a joint honours degree, history and English literature, and couldn't decide which to do, so I did a joint PGCE back in the day when you could do joint PGCE. I was trained in both. Then in my first job, I taught mostly history and bits of English. Then I moved to a new city and ended up doing just bits of maternity covers here and there because I only wanted to work a couple of days a week when I'd become a mum. Then I got a job here with you, and it was English and media, which I'd never taught, so that was really hard. I was teaching A level English language for the first time too, and I'd only ever done English literature at university. That was really tough; learning new A levels ... boy, that was a steep learning curve for a couple of years, hitting the specs hard and doing the research hard. It's a long process. I would say that once I've taught a specification three, four, five times I would start to feel comfortable with it, and now I'm very happy to pick up lessons on the timetable where I'm needed. So, if they're short in history, I'll do history; if they're short in English, I'll do English. That's given me longevity in my career, because I did one thing for a very long time then I did something totally different, then I did something different again, and that's really given me an injection of energy and expertise every time, I think.

JT: **You said you taught *four* subjects, media, history, English …**

JB: Well, I teach EPQ as well, which is great, because I'm doing subatomic physics. Why do humans hate other humans? Why did America win the space race? So, you're not an expert and that's the most stretching subject for me academically.

JT: **That's nourishing.**

JB: Really nourishing. Hard. We have a phrase in my family that I've coined, 'Harder but better'. So, we say, shall we go on holiday? What shall we do? Shall we go on a nice quiet beach holiday or shall we go interrailing? And we go interrailing because it's harder but better, and it really is harder. You put your backpack on, and you slog from place to place, and it's fantastic. So, yes, it's been harder but better doing the various subjects, I think. It's kept my bounce over the years. I have taught English literature, English language, history, media studies and EPQ, but over a long career. I've been teaching for 28 years and not all at the same time.

JT: **It's pretty impressive.**

JB: No, it's not impressive, it's just how your life twists and turns isn't it? I feel really lucky about that. It's been great.

JT: **When you're planning a lesson, what are your thoughts?**

Well, first of all, it's a team sport, so you look at the central planning. I think people don't realise how much teaching *is* a team sport. We've all got each other's backs. Some of it is joint planned, so for English or for history, there are schemes of learning already in the system, and then I adapt for myself. If it's my own stuff for media it starts with the specification and I think like everybody else, how many lessons have I got for a topic, how am I going to break that down, and then there'll be medium-term planning and each lesson gets shaped by the previous lesson. Not rocket science.

JT: **Tell me about challenging them to think academically.**

JB: I like it when students get things wrong. I want to create a climate where they say, 'Oh, I'm not sure if this is right but …', and they have a go anyway.

JT: **How do you create that climate?**

JB: By praising wrong answers, by saying, 'Yes, I couldn't disagree with you more but I'm so glad you've said that.'

JT: **Right, that's a nice phrase.**

JB: And if you feel like they're getting somewhere close, rather than shutting it down, saying, 'Can I bounce that back to you? Can you put another layer on that?' I sometimes say, 'Can you go any deeper on that? Can you build on what so and so said?' Yes, I like it when they get things wrong and are prepared to do that. Hopefully, I create quite a tolerant environment where people know that it's a safe space for getting things wrong. I think if I've created that, I'd feel good. I often tell them, and you'll see this in the lesson you're going to watch, they'll interpret things in ways I've never thought of, and I often say, 'You've taught me absolutely heaps today, because I haven't thought about this, this, this.' I think I'm saying that I'm learning all the time, and that they're learning all the time. I've said it four, five times already in lessons this morning: 'I'm going to ask you a question, but I don't know the answer.'

JT: **Do you?**

JB: Oh, all the time, yes, because who does?

JT: **How often do you go off-piste?**

JB: Well, I'm not particularly a *down with the kids* kind of person. I'm not their friend. I'm very much the adult in the room, and I don't particularly share a great deal about my own life. I'm quite closed about that, because it's a professional mask isn't it, when you come into school? They don't know me; they know the Ms Bream that I'm sharing.

JT: **That you project?**

JB: Yes, but inevitably you go off-piste. You talk about your own life experiences sometimes. I go most off-piste when I do register questions.

JT: **Register questions?**

JB: If you ask 100 kids I've taught in 10 years' time, what do you remember most about Ms Bream, they'll say *register questions*.

JT: **Tell me about register questions.**

JB: If I've got a tricky class, I wouldn't do this at all, but if I've got a class I'm comfortable with … it's when I read their name out, they have to respond with an answer to a pre-agreed question. So, sometimes it's, 'Complete the following quote.' Sometimes it's, 'Here's an image that we studied last time. Give me an adjective to describe it.' Sometimes it's just random and I'll ask the students, 'Do you want to propose a register question?' This morning we had, 'What's *your spirit animal*?' So, I began with, 'Right, register question today is, "What's your spirit animal?"' Then I called out, 'James?' and he said, 'mole'. Somebody said, 'narwhal' then someone else says, 'What's a narwhal?' So, then they're all on their computers and they go, 'Oh, that's not a real animal. Oh, it's a narwhal, Yes, it's like a unicorn but it's a whale, oh yes, that's cool …' Yes, so that's when I go most off-piste: register questions – 'Annoying habits of family members', those kinds of things. So, I'd like to tell you that it's always about the syllabus, but it's not, and that's where you learn most about the kids. The other piece of really good advice I got from you, on my very first day in this school. Kat Wood stood up in the staff meeting and said, 'Say something to every student in every class you teach, every lesson', and that changed me … I thought, 'Wow! I want to work in this school.' It wasn't just about exam results, and that register question is a conversation with every kid in the class, because that's so hard to do every lesson, every day. There's 30 children come in, the bell rings, 30 children go out, and the next lot come in, and the next lot come in. Parents, I don't think understand that, that their kid could go through five lessons and an adult's never spoken to them. That's nobody's fault, it's just really difficult to do. Five lessons a day, 30 kids a time, it's so hard, and so a register question is my little chat with people.

JT: What are you working on at the moment in your teaching?

JB: I'm not brilliant with the visualiser yet, because I don't like sitting … I feel quite vulnerable sitting at the front and not watching the class, because, like I said, that vigilance is important. I wouldn't feel very comfortable just standing annotating at the front, because I'd worry about what's going on at the back, etc. That said, I'm getting better … I like the visualiser. I use it a lot for showcasing student work, 'Here's an answer … what's good about it? … but I could do …' I need to get better on that. The thing I've never done satisfactorily yet is giving back an exam paper, so I guess I am working on DIRT – dedicated improvement and reflection time. How do you give back a mock exam paper, and not turn it into, 'Here's what you should've done. Here's one absolute cock-up you made of that, that and that. Yes, you're an idiot, do better.' How do you make your response meaningful?

JT: How do you give feedback about things they could've improved without them feeling stupid?

JB: Without them switching off, or so that it lands, because they look at the number on the top of the paper and then they feel, great, dreadful, or somewhere in-between, and then by the time you're going over question 3.3 (a), or whatever, you've lost them. How does that change next time they sit an exam? I've never done that well. I hate going over tests, it's my least favourite thing to do with a class. I don't feel like it's meaningful. I have never found a way to make it feel meaningful.

JT: **Do you think teaching out of subject where you haven't maybe got the depth of reference, has been a disadvantage? Has it grown over time?**

JB: Some of the best results I ever got were the first year I taught English language A level, because I didn't have anything extraneous to give. So, counterintuitively, I was checking everything on the specification. I wasn't teaching them it if it wasn't on the spec. I was a few pages ahead of them myself, and it almost kept me lean and mean. That's not always been the case.

JT: **So, you taught them just the 'need to know'?**

JB: Yes, and I read everything that the examiners had said about what might come up, what the AO1s and AO2s were, and I think the longer I teach things the more I probably do go off-piste, and it's not quite so distilled. Something like history has a huge number of facts. When I got the job at Fulford I was teaching 19th century British political history to students who were going to go to Oxbridge, and I had never studied it myself. All that really in-depth period of Gladstone and Disraeli, and the events in Ireland, etc. That was hitting the books big style. That was really, really hard. Every new specification I've taught in history means huge, huge amounts of work, whereas for something like, for example, GCSE English, although there's still a lot of preparation to do, a lot of it is much more thematic and skills-based. People think English and history are exactly the same. They couldn't be more different. Lessons are so different. They come into a history lesson and they might know nothing about Olaudah Equiano at the start of the lesson, but when they leave they know tonnes. In English, you're teaching them a skill over six, seven, eight lessons. Sometimes, when and how the students pick things up is imperceptible. It's not the same thing at all, so I think in some cases starting a new subject and specification has been a disadvantage and in other cases it's been something I could overcome more easily. But there's been a lot of discomfort and a lot of slog to prepare over the years. I don't want to make it sound like I'm a martyr. I've enjoyed the preparation, but yes, sometimes I haven't had any reserves to rely on and dip into.

JT: But the work you've had to do, it's nourishing? [*JB nods*]. Would you teach again if you had your time again?

JB: Oh yes. I don't want to do anything else. I've never done anything else even within teaching … Since I became a teacher, I've not been head of anything, never had a promoted post out of the classroom.

JT: Have you never wanted to?

JB: Nothing, no, never applied for anything. I just want to do teaching, that's all, that's it. Yes, I'd do it again a heartbeat. I've done 28 years and I still love my job. How many people can say that? Oh yes, it's great, harder but better.

JT: What is it though that makes it so great?

JB: I don't know. I guess it's just a good fit for me, and I've been really lucky. I've worked in schools with fair leadership and ace heads of department. I've been a member of great teams, and I mean *teams*, where everyone is working for the common good, sharing resources, and celebrating the good times and looking out for you in the bad. I hear stories about the working conditions of many teachers, and I just don't know how they do it. I've been lucky, I've been trusted, and I've worked for and with people who've got my best interests at heart. That's massive.

JT: That's such an interesting perspective. I went to see a drama teacher in Cambridge [Suzanne Marston]. Her P8 score for drama was +2.8 in 2024, nearly three grades above predicted on average, for every student. I was talking to my very perceptive cousin about the book – she was Direct Commerce Manager at Adobe Systems, so she knows what she's on about – and I mentioned the drama teacher and my cousin said, 'So you've got a head teacher there who allows that teacher to do what she does best, without constraining her.'

JB: Mm, that's interesting, but you need the systems in place to support them, but systems that don't constrain what makes them great.

JT: Exactly. I think that is a real lesson that's coming out through the book.

JB: Yes, because sometimes if you work in a place that's at odds with your value system, that's really hard, and I've come to realise, having worked for several heads, that schools come to resemble their heads.

JT: Too much, I think, way too much. Heads have way too much influence.

JB: Yes, and you really can feel the difference in a school and a lot of it comes from the head, and so I've been fortunate that I've worked in schools where I was, I wouldn't say left alone, but I think I was trusted to do the work well … and I'm not saying just leave me alone, close the door and never come in!

JT: I know you're not. But no one's directing you to do X or Y where you wouldn't normally do X or Y?

JB: True. I've worked in positive environments, and I'm also only working four days a week, which is a massive privilege as well. It's still a lot. It's a lot after 28 years, but I think I wouldn't be bouncing to school if I was doing five days a week.

JT: Are you still bouncing into school?

JB: Yes, usually. Not today, because I've been absolutely terrified by the thought of you coming in.

JT: [*Laughs*] **Yes, but less terrified now. It's been fun! Is there any advice you'd give for newbies?**

JB: Don't teach them to ignore you.

JT: **Don't teach them to ignore you. That's a great line.**

JB: If you tell them you're doing a test next Tuesday, you do a test next Tuesday. If you tell them to do homework, you check the homework. If you tell them, 'If you talk again I will give you a sanction', whatever it is in your school, and then they talk again and you don't follow through, you're just teaching them to ignore you. You're teaching them that, 'She says one thing and means another.' To be fair, we all do it to some extent. We all have the classic *teacher five minutes*, 'You've got five minutes to complete that …' and then give them ten! Don't sit down. Expect good behaviour. Have high expectations, as long as you follow them through, and *don't teach them to ignore you.*

JT: **That's a great line. Well, Jack, thank you so much. You've been great.**

Teaching

I pick up my laptop and microphone. Jack says, 'I've not picked a class where you're gonna see perfect anything …' and I reassure her that's not a problem. We walk down the corridor to the new media studies base. I taught economics in this room for years. If I tot up the hours, I must have spent several weeks of my life within these four walls. Karl Elwell, the subject lead and another person I could just as easily have included in this book, is finishing up. Karl and I set up media studies at Huntington in 1999, a quarter of a century ago. We embrace, and then we chat animatedly about media and what he's been up to. He shows me some amazing work on the walls from a visit to *The Guardian* offices. The students had lunch in the canteen with the journalists. There are displays of Boris Johnson partygate front pages from *The Times* and *The Mirror*. 'A man with no shame.' It is exciting to be in Karl's presence. I felt 35 again, not 60. To a student, his class thank him as they leave the room. He is a truly great teacher.

With Karl and his charges having exited, Jack's Year 11 GCSE class enter. They settle quickly and there is a retrieval task on the board, requiring them to set up a spider diagram and to try to recall everything they discussed about the representation of women in the Lizzo video, *Good as Hell*, from last lesson. Oh, and they need to get ready to submit their homework. A girl at the back catches Jack as Jack shuts the door and whispers about not having her homework, how she's done it but not brought it in. I don't catch Jack's reply, but it is fuss-free and she proceeds to take the register.

Today's register question is, 'What's been your biggest improvement, or best memory so far, in media studies?' The students respond to their name call. 'Doing Finn's photos for his magazine.' 'When I was editing the coursework with Eddie.' 'Watching a scene in *The Inbetweeners* – and Sir was standing behind me, watching and I didn't know.' 'Doing my coursework … in a glider.' When she gets to the left-my-home-work-at-home girl, Jack cannot cajole her to answer the register question. The girl doesn't even look up. Jack is kind. She makes no fuss, and the lesson begins.

The students have been making notes on their whiteboards. Jack says, 'OK. Hold up your boards … Shaun's looks interesting. There's a sense of community. Girls help girls to build confidence – to be the best version of themselves. That's good Shaun. Nominate and then empty your mouth.' Shaun names the next contributor and then, dutifully, goes to the back of the class and puts his gum in the waste bin. I hadn't noticed him chewing. It was a beautifully understated piece of behaviour management, one of those 300 micro things a lesson Jack does that she talked about minutes earlier, which the trainee teacher hadn't realised was behaviour management.

There are some speedy reactions, full of specialist vocabulary: 'stereotype', 'sorority', 'mise-en-scene' and 'non-verbal communication'. Jack says, 'We're stimulating those memory synapses … Why is the lettering gold on GQ magazine?' They recall a Vogue front cover of Malala. I look it up on my phone and then spot it on the far wall. Malala is staring at the camera, dressed in deep red, with a deep red background to match. She looks Mona Lisa-esque. Her hands are held in front of her, with the fingers of her right hand softly touching the bottom of her palm on her left hand. There is a great discussion of the connotations of the image, the students giving some wonderful responses: 'Delicate … Gentle … Vulnerability … The delicacy contrasts with the vividness of the deep red colour.' Jack's running of the room and the engendering of discussion is seemingly effortless. She manages a quiet chat with the left-my-homework-at-home girl, who is still distressed. Jack is warm but insistent. 'Do you want to go to head of year, lovie?' The girl remains. Jack is fulfilling her mantra. Don't teach them to ignore you. Homework deadlines matter and there are consequences.

They watch the Lizzo video again. This time they are looking at the representation of men and thinking about it in relation to the representation of women. 'Make sure you jot stuff down. I will be asking around the room. I'm going to ask you questions I don't know the answer to …', says Jack as she clicks the YouTube play button. Once the video is finished, for the rest of the lesson there is the most brilliant discussion of gender representation, America, Trump, the male hegemony …

'Men are quite cruel or they're sidelined. She's damaged. He's confident. The woman has been dumped. Cheaters and players who abuse women. Unfaithful. We don't know he cheated … *He* regrets it. Represented as jealous. Looks and women. Being with another woman … *so* many men in the band. Not ethnically diverse. All people of colour. Different sides of men. Energy. Amongst the students. Rarely see African American men playing instruments in a marching band. We see things we rarely see. Anything about the diversity of men? Marching band guys, before they help them, they single the girl out. More complex … men can be more than one thing. Mixed body types. 100% attention. Girl just cries. Polysemic (one thing can have more than one meaning. Poly means many …) the man just leaves her and walks off. Most dominant person in the video. Still has power. The *o-shou* shot has her out of focus in the foreground. He is more important.'

It was a delicious discussion, and impossible for me to transcribe effectively; all I can do, I think, is give a taste of what was said. Jack says, 'Wow! I thought that would take five minutes. That was an amazing response, and some of you thought there weren't any men in the video! So, there are some voices in the room I haven't heard from yet.' Jack mops up who she hasn't heard from.

They drain the video dry of its connotative meanings. 'Look how much analysis you've collected. You've taught each other. I've just stood here and listened,' Jack exclaims, 'now I want to push you further … Why are men represented? Why are they sidelined? Four bullets …' The responses come flying in. 'That's interesting. Mmmm. Good. To uplift women. Video isn't about men. Focusing upon the empowerment of women. Raising up and the celebration of women. Community and equality. In the band it doesn't matter. Uniform is genderless. Body positivity. Inclusivity.' They go on to discuss ethnicity. The video features Lizzo practising and performing with the marching band and the dancers from Southern University, the Baton Rouge Historically Black Colleges and Universities (HBCU). Loads comes out. There is an amazing energy in the room. Left-my-homework-at-home girl is head down, hands-wringing.

This is all great stuff. Jack then reads an examination question aloud: 'How far have representations of females in music videos changed since the 1980s? Refer to two music videos you have studied, in your answer.' This is where she has been heading. There are six minutes of the lesson left. She shows a still from a 1980s music video. 'See how the women are wearing just their knickers? And look at Lizzo. She's wearing just her knickers too, 40 years on? So, what's changed, if anything? What's the difference?'

Henry says, 'In the '80s, it was all about men. Now it's about women.'

Jack is warm in her praise and then asks, 'Why aren't the men in their pants? Why is it only the women?'

Then, out of nowhere, left-my-homework-at-home girl puts her head, and then her hand, up. Perhaps she has decided she wants to go early to see her head of year. Jack invites her to speak.

'It's all about the lens we're seeing it through. It's about body positivity. Men used to control the story. In the 1980s women were wearing only knickers for the men, but now they're wearing only knickers for themselves.'

Jack smiles and says, 'Wonderful. They are reclaiming the narrative and owning the narrative and so are you my lovely. I love you.'

What the students think

The students file out, except for six of them who are swiftly joined by a couple of sixth formers, to sit round to talk about what makes Jack Bream such a great teacher. I give them some Think-Pair-Share time, before I open up the discussion. One of the boys begins: 'You can tell when a teacher doesn't really want to be teaching, but with Ms Bream, you *know* you're her main priority. She's passionate about her job and what she's teaching.'

Another student politely carries on, 'It's so obvious she's not in it for the money. She teaches because she loves it, it's not about what she's paid. You can tell she wants to do it. She enjoys it. She's focused on us and what we need.'

I go round the room. Each pair offers a different perspective. 'In the end she's just a really nice person. I really want to be taught by her. She treats you, and she teaches you, like a person. She treats you like an equal.

There's a genuine connection with her. And she loves what she does. She wants to get the best out of everyone. She is never mean, you never feel any negativity from her. You just want to be taught by Ms Bream.'

Next stop: 'She's so thorough. She's not going to ask you to do some work and then leave you to do it on your own. Like with the EPQ ... if you needed support outside the lesson, that was fine. She would make the effort to meet with you, whenever she could. What was good about her feedback was how she said exactly what she thought about my work. She was direct when she gave me feedback. It's what you need, especially with an EPQ. You can take that honesty from her because she is kind and you know she just wants the best for you.'

Another pipes up. 'Same. There's lots of coursework in media, and she gave up her lunchtime to show me how I might improve. Every criticism comes from a good place. Her honesty is so important in helping us to improve. You want to impress her. You work hard to try and fix it.' Her peers nod. 'And she's not afraid to talk about herself. We can still all have a chat about things that are off-piste. Especially at the start of the year ... I felt really included in her class.'

The sixth formers are especially insightful. 'She taught me for GCSE and A level. That's four years. She gives such constructive criticism. She offers you alternatives to help you improve. She doesn't tell you. She gives you options. She's *so* good at this. She notices things that no one else does. And I know she's not being mean when she criticises my work. She just wants me to get the best marks possible.' As they talk, I remember how student voice has become discredited in some quarters, but the more I do this work, the more I realise just how perceptive students are about teachers and teaching. None of the interviews with students have contradicted the other sources of evidence I have gathered to form a comprehensive picture of each teacher.

'What about her teaching?' I ask.

'You're not in the classroom to be taught, you're there to learn.' It's an interesting distinction that Emma makes. I push her further. 'Well, it's not just an ordinary lesson. There's no copying off the board. All the lessons are interactive. There's no sitting in silence. Any idea you have she'll be positive about and then develop it so that you feel like you have made a great contribution. She gives practical advice, and we have great debates. It's not just Ms Bream at the front of the classroom, telling us things.'

One of the sixth formers finishes by saying, 'She forms such good connections. And she is clear about what she expects, "These are my expectations of you and are you reaching this level at the moment, and you need to be here, instead …" In the end, we want to please her. That's one of the reasons we work so hard.'

In Jack's case, I think the list of single words to describe the teacher is hugely revealing: inclusive, community, passionate, caring, lively, irreplaceable, humble, brave, strong-minded, independent and kind. *Humble* is noteworthy. It took a lot to persuade Jack to allow me to nominate her for the national teachers' awards, and she has only agreed to feature in this book as a favour to me. Jack is such a great role model for all students, but for the female students especially – look at those epithets: *brave, strong-minded, independent.* Some teachers are just so much more than a teacher.

Testimonials

One of Jack's previous head teachers wrote 'in 37 years of teaching she is the most impressive colleague I have ever worked with.'

Alex Quigley noted how she 'manages to be a great teacher with no grand designs or ideology and without official status or elaborate title … [when she teaches] established routines are executed almost imperceptibly as students' minds are kindled with interest. It is [Jack's] conscious effort to improve that marks out her excellence.'

Jack's newly qualified teacher (NQT) mentor wrote, 'Jack's subject knowledge, imagination, delivery, feedback and style were inspiring, which I think is rare to find in a graduate teacher. She just seemed to be born to be a great teacher.'

Her colleague Karl highlighted how Jack has worked continuously hard at her teaching: 'She has honed her methods over a substantial teaching career that has seen her accept the challenge of teaching subjects outside of her comfort zone.'

One of Jack's students from the beginning of her career, wrote, 'As a teacher now myself … I can only hope that I can leave such an impact on my students' lives as she has on mine.'

'When she explains the task we have to do, she will always go through it a few times to ensure that the whole class fully understands.'

'She always motivated me with my English through her comments by focusing primarily on what I *had* achieved as a student, which gave me an incentive to work even harder, while also giving the detailed feedback a student needs to improve.'

'Ms Bream has a natural encouraging nature about her that helps push students to be the best they can be … I've learnt so much from her.'

'I felt encouraged by her enthusiasm for her subject … without her confidence in me, I probably wouldn't have realised my potential and have got to where I am today.'

So, what can we learn from Jack Bream?

Objectivity is difficult when it comes to writing about Jack Bream's teaching, but I'll try. The first thing that strikes you about Jack is the commitment to the subjects she teaches. She is a scholar herself, and there is a tangible sense that she enjoys learning new subjects, despite the huge effort it takes to be able to confidently teach an A level well. None of which is helpful when we face a teacher recruitment crisis, and policy-makers are trying to make the job of a teacher attractive and manageable. I would argue, however, that the energy Jack has for the job is *increased* by the academic challenges she has faced. She enjoys the job *because* it is challenging: *harder but better*.

Jack's humanity is difficult to beat. When I wrote up the account of her lesson, I hesitated about including the girl who had forgotten her homework. In the end I decided to include her story because it illustrated so much about Jack. She was attentive to the girl throughout the lesson, but you wouldn't have necessarily seen it. Jack trod the fine line all teachers tread when you have a distressed pupil in the room – take the risk and insist they stay in the room in the hope they'll be OK and learn something or play safe and send them to the pastoral office, forfeiting the chance of them learning anything. Jack held her nerve, and the final act of the lesson not only justified her decision, but it was also a moment of celebration. It seemed entirely appropriate to end the account with Jack's declaration of love for the student, even if that love was, perhaps, of the *tough* variety.

The forgotten homework story also exemplified another learning point from Jack's practice: *Don't teach them to ignore you*! I remember Tom Bennett saying that you have to apply the rules, even when the best student on the planet transgresses. The rules are the rules. Now, that doesn't means a zero-tolerance regime, but it does means that for the vast majority of the time, when a student does wrong, they face the consequence. If all teachers took just that piece of advice from this chapter, their working lives would improve, maybe.

Sir David Carter once said to me, 'People think that teaching "rock star" lessons is what you need to do to be judged outstanding. I say that teaching consistently good lessons that are well planned and progressing sequentially from the previous lesson is outstanding.' If that is the case, then Jack Bream is one of the most outstanding teachers you will ever meet. She epitomises all that we might aspire to as teachers: integrity, tolerance, kindness, academic expertise, professionalism and an unrelenting belief in our pupils. She represents a core of teachers who deliver great lessons, day-in, day-out; week-in, week-out; and year-in, year-out, anonymously, in the distant corners of our schools. Thank goodness they do. Ultimately, as the account of her lesson demonstrates, what Jack Bream brings to her classroom is so much more than an ALPS score of 1.16.

Jack Bream's students' progress and achievement data

Jack's exam data are consistently impressive. Her classes' examination progress data for summer 2024 are representative of her students' outcomes year-in, year-out, whether it's a history A level class or a Year 11 English GCSE nurture group. At Huntington, media studies – where results reflect Jack's work and that of Karl Elwell, the subject leader – has been the best performing A level in terms of value added over the last decade and was an ALPS 2 placing those results in the top 10% of the ALPS schools, in value-added terms. Their shared GCSE class had a P8 score last summer of +0.8.

A Truly Great Science Teacher: Jen Lewis

Jen Lewis is the subject leader of science at the Church Hill Middle School, Worcestershire, and is the science lead practitioner for the Central Region Schools Trust (CRST).

The school leadership's view

I know Redditch well, having spent many a day working with CRST. I trust this Trust, and I especially trust Ange Crawley and Sam McGonagle, who are, respectively, the primary- and secondary-school improvement Trust leads. So, when the pair of them recommended CRST's Jen Lewis as a truly great science teacher, I had no hesitation in hurtling down the M42 south of Birmingham, to gather evidence of Jen's true greatness.

'She's an absolute gem', says Ange. 'I've known her of old and new. She's been with the Trust a long time. She was assistant principal in charge of Key Stage 3. She has always been a ray of sunshine. Always positive. And she is, first and foremost, relationships focused. She establishes such positive relationships with the students and gets them interested in the subject by making it relevant and delivering the content in a way that they'll remember it.' We are in a small conference room at Church Hill Middle School where Jen teaches science. There are CRST values posters on the walls. It's great to be visiting a secondary science teacher. She's going to be teaching Year 8, a middle school's senior students.

'What is it,' I ask, 'that makes her pedagogic approach stand out?'

Ange grins. 'Experiments, experiments, experiments … and if what she's teaching doesn't lend itself to an experiment, it's at least a practical demonstration. She takes the content and the main concepts, which are very abstract to many students, and thinks about ways to make the science understandable and memorable for them. It's hard to imagine things like atoms, which are so small, so she uses practicals and demos to make them real.' Jen sounds like my type of science teacher!

According to Ange, Jen also creates a collaborative atmosphere in the classroom. 'She will often say something like, "I find it hard, but this is what helps me remember it. It might help you too", or "I know what things you might find hard and this is how I am linking this up … and giving you a chance of remembering it". It's like she is happy to feign finding it difficult, so the students feel less worried about getting stuff wrong. And she's incredibly enthusiastic. It's like she is saying, "I love what we're learning and you can come on this learning journey with me".'

Part of Jen's success is the classroom culture she creates. Ange explains: 'She manages to pitch it right. She challenges them. She has high expectations but makes it achievable. She uses positive praise, but they realise they are getting a good deal – *this is interesting, Miss is really nice to me, I am doing well and I am learning things I didn't know before* – and they buy into it. She talks to them on their level … "Come on, we've got this guys!" She is such a positive force.'

She has expert subject knowledge, which enables her to be adaptive, in the moment. Ange says, 'Jen reads the room. She sees when they're not getting it and adapts when the lights go out. She genuinely cares. She takes time to get to know what they do beyond school. She remembers things about them that show she has clocked them. And she will always volunteer to do the meet and greet and take the parents on a tour round the school.' We talk about Jen's decision not to be a form tutor. 'She felt she wanted to concentrate on her science teaching. She's a brilliant tutor, but it takes a lot out of her because she takes the role so seriously. Working with young people is a privilege for her.'

We set off to Jen's classroom and her Year 8s. I've never seen her practising her craft, but after my chat with Ange, I'm feeling confident that I'll see some truly great teaching.

Teaching

We walk down corridor after corridor and finally find Jen who greets me, smiling. In fact, she smiles a lot. She seems very happy. 'Hi, we've got Year 8. Digestive system.' We chat as we await the students. It makes me think how everyone gets a bit nervous. She seems supremely confident, but she says, as we converse that she is like the proverbial swan, gliding along whilst her feet are flapping furiously. I reassure her that we will just have some fun and that I am hugely thankful for her agreeing to be in the book.

Another teacher comes looking for a tray of kit. 'No problemo!' says Jen. The students begin to enter the room and Jen greets them at the door. One of them hands Jen a note. 'Thank you, my lovely.' I think 'my lovely' is the Redditch term of endearment, having been called it at both Costa and Waterstones earlier. One of the students asks Jen how she is, and she replies, 'Very well. Thanks for asking!' It is a civilised, calm and happy start to the lesson.

Jen chats briefly with some students about someone's birthday, sets up the retrieval task – 'Four questions on the board' – and proceeds to take the register. 'Good afternoon' tennis is played with every student. The room is so calm and purposeful. It's full of science-related displays and feels like a great place to learn. There's a display about revision and an exquisite set of planets hanging from the ceiling to represent the solar system. There is nothing out of place. A poster exhorts students to, 'Keep Calm and Wear Goggles.' Jen teaches in a beautiful corner of the school, literally. We couldn't be further from the front door. I look out the window. The last few late autumn leaves are left to fall. Rays of a thin sun light up the back of the students' heads. This is white working-class Redditch. The class is full, and every single one of them is completing the starter task. 'Let's go then, beautiful people', says Jen and they work through the starter answers. The lesson is called, 'Gums to Bums'. They are revising the digestive system. They are beautifully focused. Jen asks questions around the room, probing for a deeper understanding and surfacing the students' thinking. There are no hands up. These students are well-trained. 'Why do we need acid in our stomachs?' says Jen and soft midlands accents bounce around the room. There is total and utter attention. 'What's the smallest unit of our body, not including atoms? Think about it in terms of Lego, and the smallest part of Lego, the smallest brick', and they easily list cell-tissue-organ-system-organism. 'This is good, we're developing our understanding of how our digestive systems works', says Jen, encouragingly. She walks the room and works between the desks, glancing at students' work and cold calling, reaching the corners of the classroom. 'What's the difference between mechanical digestion and chemical digestion?' She picks up on a boy that I had noticed had drifted slightly. He gets asked the question. She has that radar on that all truly great teachers possess.

There is a knock on the door. 'Hello Stephanie', says Jen. Stephanie is looking for her pencil case from last lesson. 'Have a look my lovely.' Nothing fazes Jen. She is consistently warm and friendly.

We move on to the practical demonstration. She has them come to the far wall in a semi-circle, where all the resources are carefully laid out.

'Right, we are going to use this plastic bag. It's going to be our stomach.' Off she goes, and she delivers the most realistic demonstration of the digestive system I have ever seen. It is a joy to watch. At the beginning she puts a whole load of stuff into a mixing bowl, which acts as the mouth – crisps, Jacob's crackers, sweetcorn and baked beans. She adds a liquid, which she is calling saliva. One of the students mashes the stuff up. It's a hoot! 'The enzymes help break down the food in this mechanical digestion stage.' She's enjoying herself. She offers a cheeky lad a taste of her mixture … he nearly retches. It does smell pretty gross! 'After you have chewed and swallowed your food, it passes down the oesophagus to the stomach.' The big bowl of chewed up 'food' is dropped from bowl to bag – aka from mouth to stomach. It's grim. The students groan. 'You're welcome, everyone!' says Jen. She massages the plastic bag. 'So, the stomach churns up food and mixes it with acid and enzymes. This breaks the food down into much smaller pieces.' She shows the contents of the bag to the front row. More groaning. She adds further liquids. 'Digestive juices from the stomach and pancreas help the small intestine take in important substances from the food.' One of the cheeky chaps wants to feel the stomach bag. He loves eliciting a reaction from those of a more fragile constitution. She demonstrates how the waste begins to leave the food as the stomach muscles move it into the small intestine. 'So, in the small intestine we mix the food up with an alkaline. Why?'

Hands shoot up. 'To neutralise the acid from the stomach, Miss.' She responds, 'That's great. Yes. And what colour is bile?'

So, the Q&A goes on. Back and forth. Testing their knowledge and applying it to the demonstration. It is lovely stuff. The villi get a mention and all the students hold their hands in the air and move their outstretched fingers in waves. She adds brown bile pigmentation ('made in the liver and stored in the pancreas') and, finally, once she sponges out the water, the remaining mulch is left in the large intestine bag, ready for the performance's climax. It is such an impressive demo. She is talking for 15 minutes. She is faultless. She doesn't miss a beat. But, it's not called 'Gums to Bums' for nothing. She cuts open a corner of the large intestine bag, mentions the word 'rectum' and proceeds to squeeze out the contents, which, in terms of consistency and colour, are remarkably like the real thing! It is suitably graphic … and gets just the revolted response from her audience she was looking for.

They move back to their seats, talking about what they've just seen. One or two look slightly pale. One boy looks green. Two are holding their own stomachs. 'Right, we need to transfer what's in our brains into words.' They label a coloured diagram of the human digestive system. 'Talk in pairs about what might go into those boxes.' Then they have to note down what happens at every stage. 'In your own words onto your sheet.'

'Miss, what's the dangly thing?'

'The epiglottis. Helps you have a gag reflex. A safety mechanism.'

She tours the room. Questions, questions … 'What's a reflux? Dietary? Hereditary? Have you got any allergies?' Jen has such effortless confidence. 'What jobs can you do in this field? Nutritionists. Nurses. Doctors.' Everyone, including Jen, is working hard. 'Remember the word, *enzymes*! It's important that word is in the explanation.'

She says to one student 'All right, boss?' There is total silence as they work. The silence hovers and settles, and is only broken by a request: 'Can you go back to the oesophagus, please Miss?'

'''Sorry, was I a bit speedy?' says Jen. She explains the role of the oesophagus and then says that the small intestine is seven metres long. She asks four students to the front; she has seven one metre rulers. She gives three of the students two of them and the other student gets one. They hold them up so that the seven rulers are end-to-end. It gives a brilliantly graphic sense of the seven-metre length of the small intestine. 'And remember,' says Jen, 'you've got another metre and a half of large intestine.'

Complete silence falls again and is maintained. They are zooming through their work. She recaps the vocabulary: liver, pancreas, lipids, fats, enzymes, carbohydrates, carbohydrase, proteins, protase … teaching it now, in Year 8, rather than waiting until they get to GCSE.

The pupil of the lesson is named as Liam, who gets a round of applause. 'I'm going to throw you a fish, if you keep clapping like that ...' she says with a smile to a friend of Liam's whose clapping is a little over zealous ... She bids them farewell row by row.

James arrives for the next lesson. 'I'm always happy when you're here first', says Jen. Jake shows me his book. It is rammed with great work. Really well-kept. Dates, underlined. High expectations. He is so proud and he looks like he might be a cheeky lad.

Since we are due to go to the meeting room for our chat, Jen has cover for the lesson. But she had promised this class the same demonstration as she has just done. I reassure her that she must do it, and do it again she does, with the same sense of fun, the same gusto, the same sparkling smile, and the same commitment to the students' learning. As we walk away from the class, leaving the cover teacher to oversee the completion of the post-demonstration writing tasks, I tell her how gut-churningly *unforgettable* that was.

What the students think

Back in the conference room and it is soon rammed full of Year 8s. Jen's knowledge about science impresses them all: 'I think she's intelligent. We learn loads with her. Miss has her own way of teaching, her own way of explaining stuff. She goes over stuff so we're not confused. If you ask about a certain topic she will break it down to find out what you're struggling with. And knowing so much about science means she can simplify questions for us if they're really wordy. She knows what she's doing.' They also confirm what Ange said and what I've just seen about Jen's preference for practicals: 'Miss Lewis won't let us forget what we've learnt until it's stuck in our heads. We do loads of practicals. It's not all writing. We mixed iron and sulphur to make iron sulphide. It smells like rotten eggs.'

Jen has the knack of so many great teachers in making the learning enjoyable, of being purposeful and approachable in equal measure. One student says, 'Lessons with Miss Lewis are fun and she's really funny! She helps if you get stuck. If we are all stuck, she goes over it with all of us as a big group. She interacts with all of us individually. Whether it's to have a joke, or if she's being serious.'

In my time, I know I have had to leave lessons to photocopy sheets I'd forgotten to reproduce. It irritates students. Not so with Jen: 'She's really well-organised. She's well-prepared for everything. When I see science is my next lesson, I always like it.' It's as clear as day to me that being well-organised is a trait in teachers that students admire.

All of them recognise Jen's interest in them beyond the academic. 'Miss Lewis is a fun person to be around. You can chat about anything. A teacher and a best friend in one. She doesn't think of us like students, more like a family. As though we are adults. She never has anything bad to say about any of us. She's really caring – if a student is not quite themselves she'll take them aside.'

This is something that I think marks Jen out. I am not sure I have seen a teacher enjoy her work quite as much as Jen. According to these Year 8s, it's not ideal having double science on a Monday, but Miss Lewis doesn't mind … 'The thing is, I think she enjoys it, *even on Mondays!*' It's true. When you are near Jen you can feel the optimistic attitude radiating from her. I don't particularly want to say it, because it would sound a bit gushy, but she does have an aura of positivity about her.

I ask for a single word to describe Miss Lewis: expressive, caring, amusing, loving (she's a 'Big Teddy Bear' in a nice way), friend(ly), inspirational, intelligent and energy. To finish, out of nowhere, one girl says, 'We should have more people like Miss Lewis in the world, then more people would want to come to school and it wouldn't seem like a burden.' Wow! That is some tribute to the truly great teacher that is Jen Lewis!

IRL: Jen Lewis

John Tomsett (JT): What made you teach?

Jen Lewis (JL): I'd done my degree in sport and exercise science. I didn't necessarily know that I wanted to teach. I enjoyed being at school and college, and loved university, so I always had good bonds with teachers but I didn't necessarily realise that I did. When I became a teacher I was able to look back and remind myself, actually, these people were really influential. I was working in public relations (PR) in London, and it was lots of fun, but it wasn't fulfilling. I had a wonderful time, and I lived the dream, but it just got to the point when I felt like I needed to do something that was more purposeful. They offered me a graduate teacher programme (GTP) course in a school near to me at the time. The deputy head, Tracey O'Brien, interviewed me. She's amazing. She interviewed me and I didn't really have a clue what I was doing, but I do have teachers in the family, so I was able to reach out. One of my older sisters is a primary school teacher. So, then I did my GTP and was in at the deep end, so if I hadn't liked it then I was never going to like it, but I loved it. I just *loved* it. I loved the camaraderie of teachers, and the bond and the relationships they forged. When you see how hard people work, it just connects you. It brings everybody together, because everyone knows how hard you're working and how precious your time is, and how precious the children are, and how important the work is. I'd never known that before, and I loved it. With the children there are just times when they make the hair go up on your arms and you feel like, 'I've done something for that child and I've made a difference.' I know that sounds cheesy but it's true. Even recently, just having a student find me to make a disclosure, and you think, 'That's such a privilege that you found me. You wanted somebody to talk to and you found me, and thank God I'm here because that made it possible for you.' Little things like that. It's eureka moments in classrooms and equally the pastoral side too … I'm a people person, but equally I like to care. I like to fix, and I wasn't getting that fulfilment. I was getting the people side, but there wasn't that nurturing side.

JT: **Where did you begin teaching?**

JL: Southfields Community College in a tough old area in Wandsworth. You got lots of students from the local areas, and there were a lot of gang issues. I was in at the deep end. I was born and bred in Ludlow in Shropshire, so it couldn't have been more different from Wandsworth. At the time I think there were 72 languages spoken in the school, so it was as diverse as it could be, and I taught Year 7 to Year 13. I ended up spending 14 years in London in the end.

I worked from GTP to being the head of PE in a large PE department. I think PE's such a great place to start because you don't have the control you have in a classroom. There's quite a lot of freedom, I think, outside, so you've got equipment, you've got children with javelins. You've got them with lots of different equipment. You have to be very organised. The rigour is important. If you haven't got it, you get a javelin in the neck. You work your flow diagram in your head of how this needs to look. To have those skills was amazing.

I then went away and lived in Vienna for about two terms. My sister was moving out there and so I took a sabbatical and went to spend time with her and her family. When I came back obviously things changed. They said, 'Well, there's an opening in science.' So, I began teaching science and quite liked it. I was relearning things that I hadn't ever really touched on since school.

Then I moved to Worcester from south London to be closer to my family. I became assistant head here at one point, which I loved, but I wasn't in the classroom as much. My lessons didn't feel as I wanted my lessons to feel. It became very pastoral because I was leading the Key Stage 3 team, who are amazing, but I was slowly falling out of love with the job. I was slowly finding myself doing things that didn't lead me to teaching, or didn't keep me in teaching as much, and I just needed an overhaul. I needed to re-engage with that.

JT: **Well, whatever you lost, you've found again!**

JL: Yes, and I'm very happy. I'm very happy being in the classroom and being with the kids. I love being with the kids. They make my day on a daily basis. I'm now lead practitioner for the Trust. On a Wednesday I visit other schools in the Trust, to support science teachers.

JT: **You've got deep expertise. Tell me what your principles, philosophies and thoughts are about teaching.**

JL: I think, number one, is to give the children self-belief, because most of the time they can do it, but they don't think they can. I think by telling them that they can do these things we are building relations with the children, and that's so important. I don't think they get that reinforcement. I think that's my number one. The second one is planning and processing. It's asking and answering certain questions: 'What would I want? If I was sat there, what would I want to see? What would engage me? What would help me to remember?' I think picking up a second subject made me re-learn it, so I'm able to uncover the potential misconceptions. That's been a real advantage in that I'm able to pick up on the things that I found tricky, and I had to learn ways myself to remember and recall them, and now I can use that knowledge to shape my teaching. 'What do the kids want to see?' Well, they want it to be interactive. They want to be able to visualise it. If you're not stretching them, they're not going to enjoy your lessons, because without that challenge, they're bored and you lose them. It's that fine line. They're in the pit but they can get their fingernails in to pull themselves up. There is something to hang on to. They know enough to pull themselves up, and they're really enjoying that stretch. It's just that positivity. Regardless of what is happening to me.

JT: You're amazing at that. There's not a single word that wasn't encouraging today.

JL: I just feel that I want them to want to be there and want to learn it. They want to do well for me and for themselves. I don't want them to think, 'I'm going to do this because I'm going to get told off.' I don't want the fear factor, necessarily. There are a few times where you do have to pull them back, but I want them to learn because of a passion, because of feeling they are rewarded for the things they do. That's how I think a classroom should run.

JT: *You want them to do it for you.* Tell me what you mean by that.

JL: I will say to them, 'This is what I want for you. I want you to be the best that you can be, and I want you to go as high as you can, and be as great as you can be.' I want them to think, 'OK, if Miss wants the best for us and we want the best for us, we're going to do the best for us.' I want them to aspire to be their best version of themselves. I tell them that they can be brilliant, and they are brilliant, and what they do is great. I want them to feel that positivity. They walk into the lesson and they know that's what they're going to hear. That self-belief then begins to grow because they're told that they can do it. When they get an answer right it's exciting, it's that feeling inside, isn't it, that you get when you have got something right, which is just lovely? I want to them to feel, 'I'm going to do that'.

JT: **They replicate your mood. One of the things that's emerging in my research is how important teacher behaviour is at every level, and how students mirror it.**

JL: 'Be a fountain and not a drain!' If they walk into your room and you're sat there miserable, it's not helpful. I walk through that door and I have to be somebody else. I can't be that person. I think that's why it's so exhausting, isn't it? At the end of the day, I sit in silence in the car on the way home, because I just need silence.

JT: Could you tell me your thinking behind today's lesson?

JL: I wanted them to be able to hold on to a memory, so that when a question comes up in a test or an exam about the digestive system, the memory hook would enable them to recall that memory. It might come from making the room smell of baked beans, and the scientific vocabulary connected with that memory, like, 'enzyme' and 'saliva'. So, my principle is that I want them to have a hook to remember this when it comes up in their GCSE in two- or three-years' time?

JT: **A student said that. They said about you making sure they remember. I picked up on the smallest Lego piece comparison. They said how you explain stuff so it's really easy to understand. Your explanations are very clear, and you teach between the desks.**

JL: Yes, I'm a walker. I'm such a walker. I can't stand still. That's, I think, part of the show, but I also like to look at the books without being intrusive. I want to know how they are getting on, all the time.

JT: **The books are beautiful. So, James, who seemed to me like a really cheeky little lad, said, 'Look at that, sir.' He gave me his book. He's so proud of it. I begin to look through it and I'm thinking, 'There are three or four pages of neat stuff … five, six, seven … blimey, it's nearly full, and it's only just December.' That's 12 weeks of work, and it's rammed full of really neat learning. He was as proud as anything to show me that. I said 'Wow!' and James said, 'She won't let us forget it. She won't let us forget what we've learned until it's stuck in our heads.' He is so right. You get them to write out the sequence of the digestive system and fill in the blanks. Then they're doing it a second time using the diagram and then they're writing out the function of each one, and then there was a moment**

	in that lesson where it was completely silent, making notes and internalising what you'd taught them.

JL: They are great. They're great kids here.

JT: They're white working class. That's the fourth-worst-performing demographic in the country. That's largely what you've got here, and you have them eating out of the palm of your hand, proud to show me their work, and I haven't seen anybody off task. The one that I did see *slightly* off task, you picked up on him straight away.

JL: [*Laughs*] I do feel so sorry for new teachers, because things that have become second nature to me now are still so new to them. I still remember how tough it was. I'm quite a people person, so I do enjoy interacting and having conversations with people. I think sometimes you're training teachers who really find that interaction quite difficult.

JT: You communicate beautifully. Seven metres long? So, you get seven metre rulers out. Just a really simple, graphic illustration of how long our intestines are.

JL: I hadn't planned it. I just thought, 'Oh, that's a good thing.' It's just those little things, isn't it? 'Oh, I know. Let's do this.' I thought, 'This'll work.' It gets them back in again, and it stops the writing for a second to look at something else. It's just those little breaks.

JT: There's some research by Rosenshine published in 1971 on identifying which teaching behaviours result in good student progress. One of the behaviours was *enthusiasm*, which you have in spades. Another was *variability of teaching approach*. It's about not knowing exactly what's going to happen in the next lesson.

JL: I'm planned. I know what I'm doing.

JT: Completely. But they don't. They're thinking, 'What's Miss going to do this time?'

JL: Yes. I get you. They don't know what's coming when they walk in. 'What are we doing today, Miss?' That's the question when they arrive, because they don't know. I hadn't thought of it like that. Yes. They do ask me that.

JT: *Variability* **is important for children's progress in teacher behaviours.**

JL: Yes, absolutely, and consistency, too? That's another huge principle. They know, day-in, day-out, my human approach won't be any different. I don't give myself a day off the performance in that sense.

JT: **How do you keep it up? You're relentlessly positive.**

JL: I know. It's sickening! I just want it for them. I just think that so many of them don't have anything positive happen to them, and I just think, 'I can't be that person reinforcing that negativity. I want to be the person that shows them that it doesn't have to be like that', and I feel genuinely very happy in their company. I feel very comfortable. I feel very at home. I feel like they deserve it. I feel like they deserve the best version of me, and that's what they get. Yes, it's exhausting, but equally there's no time to forget what we do when we're in that room because they're scientists in there. That's what I want them to believe. I want them to know that.

JT: **You treat them like scientists.**

JL: They *are* scientists, because they're doing science. That makes them a scientist. When they do a practical, they put their lab coats on, and they put their goggles on … I don't need them necessarily to protect their uniform, but that makes them a scientist, and they love it. James … you can only imagine what he's like in his white coat! He gets so excited! We just invested in some lab coats to make them feel like they're scientists *because they are.* So, when they're in there and they're goggled up in their white coat and the Bunsens are going, they're very serious then and they're doing science. That's just brilliant. I love it. 'You are scientists', I tell them. 'No we're not.' But I say, 'The moment you walk in my room, you're a scientist.'

JT: It's part of your expectations.

JL: Yes, of course it is, because they are. When they walk into history they're an historian, and when they walk into English they're writers. They're doing these things, but they don't realise just how brilliant they are. That's exhausting. Six hours, six subjects, with teachers' expectations and the pressure on the teacher to get those grades. So, when they come into my room I don't want them to think, 'Oh, here we are …' I want them to come in and think, 'All right, let's go!'

JT: **So, you've got deep experience and you learned and re-learned the science, and you've got some great principles about what you do. What advice would you give to young people coming into the profession?**

JL: I would say think about why you're doing it, and what you want to get out of it. They must understand just how important they are going to become in the children's lives. Those children will become adults, and if you work selflessly for them, they'll become better people, and they will remember you. There is no greater feeling than knowing that you really impacted people's lives for the better and your influence continues to have an impact on their whole lives. That's really special. There are not many things in life where you can do that. I think you can in nursing. And when it's a bad lesson or a bad day, remember that you're still making a difference. You're still doing it. There's still a child sat in your class who is happy to be in there and pleased to come to your lessons each day. I just think it's making sure that they realise the impact they're going to have, no matter how hard their journey.

JT: What about the evidence-informed stuff? What do you take from that in your teaching, and what do you leave?

JL: I guess I think I've got quite a deep path that I've started to go down in the sense of what I feel I know already, but you're never done. We're not robots. I think there's always information that I can use. I love watching new teachers because they come up with these new ideas sometimes, and I'm like, 'Whoa!' when I'm reading things or I'm watching someone teach.

JT: You mentioned cold calling in your lesson, so, you're deliberate about your teaching, and what you're doing and when you're doing it?

JL: You get your quiet ones who will try and dodge as much as possible … It's a way of saying, 'You'd better make sure you think this through, because I'm going to come and ask you.' I just try and do it in a way that doesn't make them feel bad about it, I just want to ensure that they participate as much as possible, and get them thinking. I don't want them to feel intimidated by the fact that I'm going to ask them a question, but I'm going to because they're part of this journey with all of us. I want to hear what they're saying. I think it's about finding out what they know, in their books, through verbal feedback. Those conversations, I think, are really important for me, just to make sure that we are on the same page.

JT: You're always checking their understanding aren't you?

JL: Yes, constantly. I don't think the books are always the way of doing that, because it's verbalising it as well.

JT: You don't need mini-whiteboards very much, because you know what's going on. You know how they are doing, because you're around the room.

JL: Yes. It's the books, and conversation and questioning, all that … by the end of the lesson I know what I've got to do, so I'll sit

JT: **Is there anything you're working on in your teaching now?**

JL: We have been focusing on modelling and how modelling can aid learning.

JT: **You seem very happy.**

JL: Yes, I am happy in my classroom. I hate it when someone teaches in my classroom, because they kick me out … but that's my stage! [*Laughs*] I find it hard to take my books and mark somewhere else, or sit on a computer in the staff room and plan something, because I'm not on my stage, where I belong …

JT: **Thank you so much, Jen. It's been a joy.**

Testimonials

These first two testimonials, the first from a student and the second from a senior colleague, were given to Jen when she left Church Hill for a brief sabbatical. They encapsulate and confirm what all the other evidence suggests about why Jen Lewis is such a great teacher.

'I really want to thank you for all of the fun times that you have given to Church Hill Middle School during your time working here. Not only have you helped everybody else, but you have helped me through so much these past four years. I really am going to miss your assemblies, watching Grandad and, of course, your iconic singing and dancing at the front of the class. I never used to have much confidence, but you have really helped me to come out of my shell. I can't thank you enough for how much you have helped me through things. I've been truly lucky to have you as a teacher, and everyone else you have taught is extremely lucky too. No other teachers can compare to how awesome you are. Not only are you the best teacher, but you feel like a best friend too. Over these years, I have felt as though I can tell you anything and it will all be fixed. You make me smile every Friday morning with your jokes and assemblies. I hope you go on to have another teaching job, because I know that all of the students will adore you. So, thank you so much for these amazing four years.'

'I just wanted to say a huge thank you for your time that you have given to Church Hill and the team over several years. I have really valued your commitment and support and the huge amount that you have brought to our school as a teacher, a leader and as a colleague. Your impact has been significant and we are where we are today thanks to your fantastic enthusiasm and drive! The children have been incredibly lucky to have you teach them, and I am sure that many will remember you. You really did make a difference. My biggest thanks are for your friendship, which I valued immensely – such fabulous listening ears and such wise words! I am so going to miss you!'

This testimonial is from Jen's time teaching PE in London, and it typifies many I could have chosen from to include in Jen's profile.

'I want to give you the biggest shout out for not only being the best teacher ever, the most supportive teacher ever … the funniest … the diva … the stunner … the caring one … but for being *you*!!! Thank you for taking us in when no one wanted us because we weren't easy and you've done a *fab* job with us! Thank you for believing in us all and you still do, to this day. You've not only taught us how to be good students, but to be young women and to stay true to ourselves (a second mum indeed). Your drive and work ethic are beyond words. We have learnt from the best … you have left a legacy for us to run with, and for that, we will run like the wind! Keep being the rock that you are and shine bright like a diamond. JLew, you deserve nothing but the best in life!'

So, what can we learn from Jen Lewis?

I have never been completely convinced about the middle school system. I have found, in some circumstances, that Years 7 and 8 can become fallow years, where a lack of urgency, because there is no end point accountability measure, can allow students to drift. Not so at Church Hill, and not so in Jen Lewis' classroom, where ambitious, risk-taking teaching, coupled with subject expertise and a challenging curriculum, ensure students make good academic progress. The students I saw seemed more like Year 10s than Year 8s.

So, what is it, then, that marks Jen Lewis out? Well, the subject knowledge, and all that she knows about science in the wider context of the world, is a given. What she has is an undimmed commitment to practical work, which helps her gain the students' attention, the most important prerequisite of the teaching and learning process. There is a good argument, in our quest for efficient use of time, to scrap practical work; opportunity cost principles suggest students learn more in the time available if science teachers stick to direct instruction. I can see the merits of that argument. In science, there is *so* much curriculum content to cover, that faffing about with titrations is not time efficient. Yet … the practical demonstration I saw Jen deliver was suffused with direct instruction style questioning, and, simultaneously, it was absolutely riveting. Every single student had their eyes fixed on Jen's demonstration. She could just as easily, and with far less hassle for her and her science technician, have chalked and talked it, or shown a video from the 1980s explaining the digestive system. But no, she took the trouble to perform the demonstration (twice, with the same gusto the second time as she did the first) and completely bewitched the students. It was just wonderful to watch!

The other thing is Jen herself, and her demeanour. She is so smiley and enthusiastic that it is hard not to feel energised in her presence, and the students ape her positivity. Again and again in researching this book, I have been struck by how far teacher behaviours influence student behaviours. Jen's confidence, her affability, her sense of fun, her determination, her positivity and her love of science are all mirrored by her students. The lad who took so much pride in showing me his book, unsolicited … the laughter that echoed around the room during the demonstration … the silence that fell upon the class as they completed the follow-up writing tasks to embed the learning … are all evidence of the influence that Jen's personality has upon her students.

The last thing I wanted to highlight was her unwavering belief that her students can succeed. I built a significant part of my early career on a simple quotation from Virgil: 'Hos successus alit: possunt, quia posse videntur', which translates, roughly, as, 'Success encourages them: they can because they think they can.' Jen's belief that her students can do well is tangible. Her principle of talking them up relentlessly bears fruit. Her students are making great progress. They believe they can do well because Jen does too. On top of that, they work hard, and, of course, they are taught by a truly great teacher.

Jen Lewis' students' progress and achievement data

As the Trust lead practitioner at CRST, Jen not only develops and implements best practice across the Trust's schools, but also plays a vital role in partnerships that enhance educational opportunities. One of her standout initiatives is a collaboration with The Ogden Trust, designed to foster a passion for physics among students of all backgrounds. Her impact on science education is marked by her unwavering commitment to student empowerment and educational equity.

Year 8 Key assessment 1 data	% achieved	Age related & above
Mastery	28%	84%
Secure	56%	
Developing	13% (mostly SEN)	16%
Emerging	3% (non-attenders)	

A Truly Great Special School Teacher: Mary Cawley

Mary Cawley is a Year 9 teacher at Kingsley High School, Harrow.

The school leadership's view

I'm in the depths of a non-descript housing estate in North West London visiting one of my favourite schools on the planet! Kingsley High School is a community special school. It provides a high-quality education for children with visual impairment, hearing impairment, autistic spectrum disorder, multi-sensory impairment, severe learning difficulty, and profound and multiple learning difficulty. It and its satellite site have 126 pupils aged 11–19 years but, as a special school, is not deemed to be of any phase of education. When I talk about the school, I find it hard not to enthuse. As Mary Myatt has often said to me, 'John,

Stop your tears. These people are just doing their job.' And one of these people who is *just doing her job* is Mary Cawley, the topic of my conversation with Lee Helyer, the head teacher.

'Mary has been teaching for over 40 years and is our most experienced teacher', says Lee. 'She is unconsciously highly competent, but, as with the humble nature of true experts, she won't know she's being so good. People like Mary are very careful not to feel too good about themselves. Trying to get a sense of their worth is incredibly difficult, and, for me, affecting some sort of tangible, repeatable knowledge transfer from Mary to our less experienced teachers is near impossible as it can be with some experts in their field, though I am sure she does this naturally whilst working with staff and modelling.' We talk about the Marxist view of labour, as just another dispensable factor of production, and how it is all too easy to see people reach the end of their career and be dispensed of, and how important it is for leaders to cherish such colleagues, value their vast experience and make the move towards the end of their careers as positive as possible.

Lee is clear-headed about his role: 'There are systems and processes that we follow to make the school run, but Mary will adapt those when necessary to meet the needs of the young people. I just need to get out of the way of people like Mary. When I go to watch her teach, what have I got that I could contribute? Nothing! I just need to give Mary the resources she needs to do her stuff and then just keep out the way, offering development or support where it's wanted or needed.' We laugh in mutual recognition of the limitations of headship. Lee continues: 'Mary's strength is the world she creates in that classroom. The atmosphere she creates is purposeful and meaningful. She supports her colleagues and they work as a well-oiled machine. She has such expertise, she makes it look all so effortless. And these children have complex needs and are so physically active and such individuals need careful care and specific learning interventions.'

'How many children does she have in her class?' I ask.

'At the most six to eight. I think she has four today, all Year 9s, and she has three colleagues supporting her, so, with you, there'll be more adults than children, but it will still be incredibly busy!' I mask my surprise as Lee rises from his seat and we make our way down to Mary's classroom.

Teaching

We knock on the door. Mary unlocks it and lets us in. We shake hands, and she introduces me to her colleagues, Louise, Monica and Veronica. Mary is one of those people who has smiled all her life, and so, even in repose, she looks happy and content. It is a bright and airy, smallish room, with enough tables for 10 people arranged in a U shape facing a big bright screen. I am introduced to Joshua, Adrian, James and Ahmed. We also shake hands. A couple of pupils are away today.

I sit on the corner desk, between Joshua on my left and Adrian on my right. I have to admit, I feel like an interloper. I am not sure I have felt this nervous for years. I have arrived halfway through a writing lesson. I watch Mary with Adrian. He is writing his name but is intent on missing out the first letter. Mary is incredibly patient. She asks him to hold the pen, and, in turn, she holds his hand and scribes the letters so he can feel the direction the pen moves and the shape the letters make. Despite Mary's best efforts, Adrian seems to have embedded into his muscle memory the elimination of the first letter of his name! Mary grins. It is time for two minutes' rest and snack time. Mary asks Adrian to say 'snack' and he obliges with the most beautiful smile.

The boys eat voraciously. Having had two boys myself, I know how much they need feeding and the dangers of letting them get 'hangry'! Whilst they eat, Louise tells me about them and how they understand the zones of regulation, and how Mary and the team know them all so well and all their idiosyncrasies. They now have such great support from parents when, not long ago, there was none. A newly formed parent teacher association (PTA) is 32 members' strong. I look around the room. The mission statement catches my eye: 'We support learning to enjoy and achieve whilst preparing for adulthood, through a broad and balanced, ambitious curriculum with relevant skills and knowledge for all.' I am reminded of Oliver Caviglioli, previously head of a special school, when he said that there was no point in teaching something if the learning did not transfer into something that helped children prepare for life beyond school. 'No transfer? No point.'[1] It seems to me that Mary and her team take every chance to put the onus upon the boys to do things. The snack has calmed them down and Mary says: 'Can you pack up now, please?' And the boys dutifully tidy away their snack detritus. In that short interaction, learning is happening. It is skilful and deliberate.

Adrian takes my prompt sheets, which Mary has given me for my session with the boys later, and puts them in his resources drawer. He thinks it is very funny and Louise insists he hands them back. They begin a brick game, where they match the bricks by colour as they build. Mary is asking Joshua questions relentlessly. When he sneezes, she teaches him to put his hand over his mouth. When he throws a plastic bag on the floor, she asks him to pick it up, and he does. I notice that everything is narrated for the boys. 'I'm going to ask you to tidy up.' 'I'm going to ask you to put your things away now.' Furthermore, interactions are relentlessly agreement-based, with the team asking for the boys' agreement when they decide to do something. For instance, when Joshua gets frustrated and begins hitting out, mainly at himself, Mary says, 'You don't need to hit. I'm going to move away, now. All right?' They also give the boys a choice, because it empowers and calms them. We play a game of guessing your favourite McDonald's meal. Adrian wants, 'chicken nuggets, chips, ice cream and water'. It is fun. The room is full of smiles.

It's time for an exercise break followed by maths. Ahmed is especially enthused. He has tremendous energy to expend. We exercise our neck and shoulders, we run on the spot, stretch and shake and jump. After

---

1 M. Myatt and J. Tomsett, *SEND Huh: Curriculum Conversations with SEND Leaders* (Woodbridge: John Catt Educational, 2023).

20 jumps we are all exhausted. As the session ends, James approaches Mary looking distressed and he appears capable of losing control. Mary takes his arms, puts them by his side, holds his face and narrates what we are doing next. His ire subsides. The whole team is so very assertive. All the boys are physically strong and strong-willed – Ahmed, especially, is big for his age – but the team are fearless, talk calmly, look into the boys' eyes and hold their arms if necessary. It is all done with assertive love.

We are into our mathematics. Mary has put the scheme of learning on the board, and we follow it pretty much verbatim. Joshua drops his sheet. Instead of picking it up for him, Monica asks him to pick it up and to put it on his pile. Each one of us is given a wooden shape, taken lucky dip style out of a bag. We watch a video and when our shape comes up on screen we have to hold it up. First out is a triangle and Ahmed shouts out in his soft voice, 'Me!' and holds his wooden triangle high in the air. We all applaud and he looks the epitome of contentedness. It is a lovely moment. He then gets up and takes two lunch plates from Mary's desk – which she was using as circle representations – and puts them on the draining board next to the sink. I sense the importance to Ahmed of things needing to be in the right place, the need for order. They were, of course, plates and it was recognised by Ahmed that they should have been in their correct place! That's why I am pleased to be able to watch the lesson. The boys seem to have accepted my presence in the room, despite me being out of the ordinary.

We go through all the basic shapes: square, rectangle, triangle, circle, star and hexagon. We focus on the hexagon. Through skilful teaching, we all establish that a hexagon has six sides. When Joshua gets the number of sides right, he gives Monica a fist pump. Ahmed suddenly decides to lie on the floor in the middle of the room, beneath the big screen. Mary moves him back to his seat, with a lot of kerfuffle. The lesson continues. I watch Mary. She is checking in with her colleagues all the time, confirming what they might do, smiling, orchestrating and adapting. It is the most skilful teaching. I also notice that she is signing when she speaks to the pupils. It is understated, but important. They are largely non-verbal, so the signing helps with communication. Louise helps Joshua – with his permission – and he counts all six sides of the hexagon. Then Mary spells out the word hexagon phonetically, and all the pupils say it aloud. It is a moment of success that we celebrate enthusiastically.

Mary produces a decidedly weighty wood/cardboard tree, with eight squares of velcro in the branches. Adrian is asked to hold the tree. As he stands there, grinning, he realises that it's the perfect object to club Mary with! Veronica plays security guard, whilst Louise gives out Velcro-backed shapes. As each shape's name is called out, the person with the shape comes up to the front and attaches the shape to the tree, via the Velcro. It works a treat, until James places his circle on the tree, but then decides he wants to steam around the room. He wants to watch *The Snowman* video, it's his favourite. Mary interrogates James quietly to see if he needs anything else, but, no, just *The Snowman* video. Mary realises that time is up on the tree-exercise and decides that drawing the shapes is the next activity to embed their learning. They have six shapes on one sheet of paper, and they have to copy them across onto a blank, keeping each of them within one of the six empty boxes.

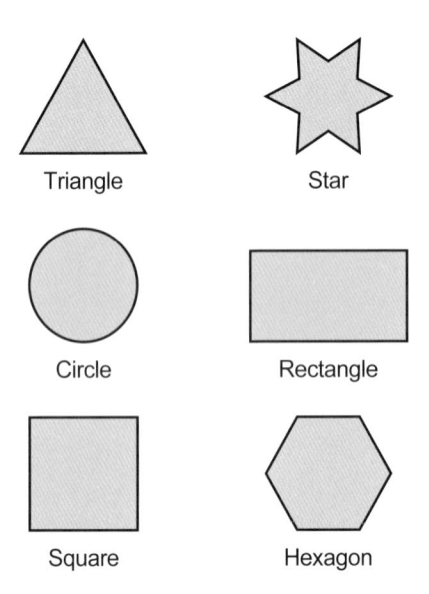

Triangle

Star

Circle

Rectangle

Square

Hexagon

The boys do as they are instructed, and every single one of them is successful. 'That's fabulous', says Mary, 'now write the words underneath the shapes.' Mary sits with Joshua. She understands him so much more clearly than I could ever imagine. James sets off around the room and Monica leads him back to his seat, assertively, talking to him all the time, narrating what is happening, giving him choices. Mary asks Joshua if he would like a book, as he has finished his tasks. But he begins hitting himself, hard, while beginning to yell in despair. Mary says, 'Joshua, you are feeling very angry. What can we do to help? You can show me.' Joshua points outside. They get his coat and he sits outside, exorcising his anger by shouting. Mary says that the book triggered him. It was not one that he was familiar with and he could not read it. They leave the back door unlocked whilst Joshua is out there and James immediately dashes out and away. Veronica sets off to get him and a minute or so later, James is back with us. He wanted to check the bush where they had been blackberry picking a few weeks earlier, to see if there were any berries left.

The final activity of the morning is understanding shadows, which is part of the science curriculum. Each boy is given a torch and we begin to make different shadow shapes on the walls using the torches. Joshua is still in distress outside. He is screaming loudly. The team are all aware of him, but none is distracted from the activity in the room. Veronica is so, so patient with Adrian, who thinks it's fun to keep hold of the torch, even when Veronica has asked him to return it. Ahmed goes into the dark, calm corner where it is great for making shadow shapes. Suddenly Joshua decides he wants to come back in. Mary doesn't hang his coat up for him, but insists he does it himself. Every opportunity to develop the boys' independence is seized upon, even when Joshua has been terribly distressed. Joshua is shown out of the room to hang his coat up, and the door is closed behind him.

Ahmed begins to dysregulate. He lies on the floor again. They encourage him to move, but he immediately returns to where he lay. There is no point trying to persuade him to move. He is given a weighted blanket to *try* to reduce arousal. He then jumps up and heads for the darkened room. He is jumping and shouting. He is probably 5 feet 9 inches tall and weighs about 12 stone. In a moment of behaviour-management magic, seconds later Mary has him tidying up. I could try to explain how she does it, but I don't have the words to describe something so imperceptible, yet so brilliant. Mary is then required to attend to Joshua, to try to interpret what it is he needs to calm him completely.

As the morning's lessons come to an end, and they prepare for my session with them to find out what makes Mrs Cawley such a great teacher, I have a few seconds to think. How does this team anticipate what the boys are going to do next? Where do they get the courage to assert themselves so calmly? Where do they find the energy to do this eight hours a day? How on earth are they so patient? They are terrifically well-trained, for one, and they work in a superbly led school, where Lee acknowledges their expertise and, as he says, gets out of their way. But, without being mawkish, the ultimate answer is, of course, that everything they do for those boys comes from a place of love.

What the students think

The room is finally tidy. As you can imagine (and, to be honest, I didn't until we actually began) discussing with the pupils the strengths of their teacher is challenging. Mary, Louise, Veronica and I sit with Joshua, James and Adrian – Ahmed isn't in the room just at this moment – and we use question sheets that have graphic images that the pupils can circle to express what they feel. All three circle the smiley face when asked 'Are your lessons exciting?' Judging by the way they react to Mary's team and the activities provided for them, that is so clearly true.

They universally enjoy food technology. James likes art. Joshua likes writing. Adrian and Joshua like ICT. Indeed, I had noticed that any opportunity to access the iPad is eagerly taken by all of them, especially Ahmed. James and Adrian then decide that to circle every image on their sheet would be a fun thing to do, so their data are slightly unreliable, as they claim to like everything they do in school! We all laugh! It is a lovely moment. Adrian signs his name (*sans* the letter A, obviously …), quite legibly, at the end of his second sheet, along with the time of day, 12:15 pm, which he copies from the large screen. Joshua finishes the session by writing the title of his favourite website which is, fittingly, www.helpkidzlearn.com:

help kidz learn

Joshua's writing is testimony to the purposeful culture Mary and her team create. The fact that Joshua, who was so troubled a mere 20 minutes ago, is able to sit quietly, answer all the questions on the sheet (without being tempted to join in the fun of circling every image), and then communicate clearly on paper his favourite website for learning, is nothing short of remarkable. I ask Joshua if I might keep his piece of paper and he passes it to me with a smile.

IRL: Mary Cawley

John Tomsett (JT): How did you get into teaching, then?

Mary Cawley (MC): Well, it was probably my last year at school, in the upper sixth. We were asked what we'd like to do. At that time, my mum used to be involved with the local church. Every now and then, they would give parties for people with learning disabilities, and she would ask, 'Do you want to come along?' I would go along, and it would be really good fun. I didn't have any qualms about it. I wasn't afraid, I just slotted in. So, when I met with our careers teacher at school, I said that I was interested in nursing people with learning difficulties in homes or hospitals, which was an absolutely stupid thing to say, because I hate needles and I hate blood. But she said to me, 'Have you ever thought of teaching?' I hadn't thought of teaching because I was unaware of any special schools at the time.

JT: What year are we talking about?

MC: I think it was 1976. From there, I was asked to look up various places and I really liked Wall Hall teacher training college. They had a specific course for special education. I think it was called the Education and Psychology of Mentally Handicapped Children and Young People. That term was still in use, but it had a horrible undertone.

I attended Wall Hall for three years. It was quite a 'hands on' course. There were just four of us on it. It wasn't a degree course, although we had many links with our fellow students!

Our course provided us with various opportunities to learn about many different subjects/areas and relating this to how you would teach those with a learning difficulty. We visited classes in local schools, with a Nursery attached to the college. We visited Harperbury Hospital, which was at that time an institution. I remember going into a long dormitory and walking down long corridors, every door was locked behind us.

JT: **They were like mental institutions.**

MC: They were. That's what it was. It was heartbreaking to see how little control of their lives the patients had. The single beds and just a little locker. There were about 20 beds in the long dormitory that we saw. We were told not to leave the group of people who were showing us around. From Wall Hall College, I found my first job as class teacher in a special school in Ilford. It was a lovely school, and the head/deputy head teacher, in fact all the staff, were friendly and welcoming. The head teacher knew I played the piano, and asked if I would like to be in 'charge' of music. I said I would give it a go. It really only involved playing the piano in assembly and organising the Christmas band. I was there for about eight years, and it was a real community.

I learned such a lot and built some wonderful relationships with pupils and staff. I am still friends with the deputy and head teacher from that time, plus some of the teachers, pupils and parents. We write and exchange cards at Christmas. There are even phone calls from some of my ex-pupils from those days. It's lovely that they've kept in touch. I remember meeting one of the boys at a school Christmas fair

I asked him, 'Peter, what do you actually remember about school? Do you remember your school days when we were in the classroom? Do you remember the first time you could write your name?' He said, 'Well, no, I don't. But I remember when Bryan Young got in trouble and when he was taken out.' That was the thing he remembered. Nothing about the academic part. It was just the fun, the fun that he'd had. He'd made it to living on his own in sheltered accommodation, which was wonderful for him. Other ex-pupils also live in sheltered accommodation or family group homes. It was a real milestone for me to find out how independent they had all become.

I opened a Leavers Unit for 16–19-year-olds as the teacher in charge, roughly four miles away from the main school, in Barkingside. I stayed there for approximately eight years. We had many links to the local community, including pottery classes, weekly work experience on a city farm, horse riding, access to nearby shops, hairdressers, library and swimming pool. There was a wealth of independence skills to gain! It was an amazing time.

I resigned when my son began school. I wanted to be involved more in his life. We had a lovely childminder around the corner from the school where I worked, and I just wanted to take him to school and pick him up. After about 18 months/two years at home, I contacted local authority supply pools, one in Harrow and one in Watford. I put my name forward for special schools. I then wrote to all my local special schools to ask if they were interested in employing a supply teacher. All replied positively. I worked at four different schools. It was a busy but fulfilling time because I learned so much from those different schools. Each school had a different approach to their curriculum and how they approached their students' needs. There was a variety of learning and physical needs, as well as behaviours. It was incredible. When I first worked here (Kingsley) on supply, the school was a very old building. It was called Whittlesea School. I began working here more frequently and eventually took a part-time permanent contract.

JT: **What I really want to pick your brains about today is teaching. How much of what you do is deliberate, and how much of it is deeply unconscious competence, because you've been teaching for 44 years? I'm going to try and unpick what you did today. I'm going to try**

and relate back to you what I think you were doing, some of the principles, and you can then just tell me if I'm right or wrong.

MC: Oh, OK. That's interesting, yes.

JT: **I think you give them as much choice as possible about what they do, about their behaviour, because you always give them an option to do something. What you're working on there is developing their own self-regulation, rather than you telling them what to do.**

MC: Yes, I avoid the 'now do this, now do that' approach. There usually needs to be a negotiation, rather than a demand.

JT: **That seems to me a principle.**

MC: That is. That's right.

JT: **You make the effort to get them to say stuff a lot, as much as you possibly can, and we celebrate when they do.**

MC: Yes, brilliant, but bearing in mind we have many non-verbal students, signing is as important as vocalising, plus the use of symbols, pictures or pointing to an object.

JT: **When Joshua was saying 'triangle' or 'circle'.**

MC: Yes, he was using his voice, which was brilliant to hear, but there are occasions when we may not have understood what he was trying to say, in which case we would ask him to write it down.

JT: **Just pointing, we're just celebrating that cognition. I think you're thinking all the time.**

MC: I think it has to, yes, because if one strategy has not worked, you need to be ready with an alternative. You also need to be aware of pupils that may have reached the end of their ability to focus and need a calming choice of activity or a different task.

JT: About where they are, and what they're doing. You treat them like adults, really. You treat them very civilly.

MC: Yes, I think there has to be respect and an awareness of how each pupil communicates. It may be vocally, signing or both, or taking you by the hand to show you a meaningful object. We celebrate everything!

JT: Yes, so how much of that sounds like some of the conscious principles of what you do?

MC: Most of the above is conscious, but awareness of behaviours for example, or needing a different approach with a task, or the need to do something independently, that has reached an unconscious level for us as a team.

JT: Talk to me about what you do, then. That was an extraordinary lesson I saw today.

MC: Thank you! During a lesson you are aware of the content; you have briefed your staff team; you have a selection of tasks; you have specific communication boards for those students who need them, particularly featuring what is happening 'now' and what will be happening 'next'; you are aware of the different methods of communicating, and if one method has not worked, you try another; and you are constantly anticipating what a particular student might do or might need, for example, when I asked Joshua if he would like to read because he'd finished a task. Often he likes reading specific books, 'reading' to himself. He has memorised the words of his favourite books. The book he chose was not the book he usually chooses.

JT: Is that what triggered him?

MC: I think that's what triggered him. He opened it and he couldn't read it, and even when I said, 'Can I read it to you?', or 'Do you want to change it?' he couldn't cope with this. That's what I feel upset him. But by then it was too late to do anything. Once he reaches that point he has to 'let go' of his frustration and he then needs to calm down by himself. There is no point interrupting him, for example, saying, 'Okay, Joshua, two more or three more minutes' (at the table) because he is unable to continue for two or three minutes longer, but that's OK. We can manage that.

Yes, you do have to anticipate things. For example, James is finishing his task. He will want to watch *The Snowman* film, so if it's not a designated reward at that time, we can turn the computer off when we have finished using it as a teaching tool. I often turn the computer off totally as it can be a huge distraction. Ahmed and Yana, who was not there today, would have an argument about it, because they would each want their choice of YouTube clips!

It's important to treat our students with respect. They are young adults. They're 12/13 years old. Next year they'll be going into Key Stage 4, which is the next step towards leaving school. I think subconsciously they appreciate being treated like adults. We use symbols and pictures a lot, because we are all busy together and some may be walking around. Often our pupils cannot cope with a voice and the use of pictures and symbols is plain and easy. Often that works with Ahmed. We just show him a picture of the chair and he will go and sit on his chair.

JT: **You're adapting every second of the lesson, depending on what you get from them.**

MC: Yes, on what I've got back. And if I see that somebody does something that isn't quite what I'd asked them to do, but they had extended it by themselves, that's fine. I'm not going to go back and say, 'Oh, gosh, you've done that wrong', because that's great. Also, when they use their initiative, that's a real cause for celebration.

JT: **Did that happen today, do you think?**

MC: Yes, I think it happened with James. He was doing something with the shapes that I hadn't quite asked him to do, and Monica had sat back a little bit. That's the other thing that's very difficult. In the past, with some colleagues I have worked with, because they want our pupils to succeed, they may help too much. I have to say that our staff team do not do this!

JT: **But *you* let them either succeed or fail on their own terms, and through their own decision making.**

MC: Yes, and it has got to be that way, because that's the stage that leads to them learning to be independent, which is what we're all about, learning to be independent. I didn't show it today, but we have a list of skills that we would use for that particular lesson, and it belongs in our skills workbook. So, for example, today would have been learning how to use a torch, using it properly, not throwing it. I thought Ahmed might throw it any second, so I was nervous about that, because it's not my torch, but he didn't. He was quite interested in what he was doing, so I think all of that comes into play, as well. There are always skills to be worked on to move towards adulthood and independence.

I think the first thing, in September when we have new classes, is making that relationship. That's the first and foremost interaction that you need. I had Joshua, James and Adrian last year, so we already had a relationship, but I didn't with Ahmed, or Ricky or Yana, that's the first thing. Regardless of what you want them to write, what you want them to learn … you've got to have that relationship and spend time forging it.

JT: **How do you get that? Everybody I've interviewed, and I'll have interviewed 19 teachers for this book by the time I do my last one on Wednesday, everybody says that forging relationships is the first thing.**

MC: It is. I'm glad everybody's saying it!

JT: It's no different. So, how do you get that with these lovely young people?

MC: With ours, you would spend time with them doing nice things, or finding things that they're interested in, sitting on the floor with them, singing with them, playing a hand game with them, maybe just twice or three times a day, or at the same time the next day. Then, they get to the point where they're all ready to sit around a table. James usually has a workstation at the back of the room where he's looking out at us, which keeps him feeling secure and focused. I don't mean secure in terms of him not running away. I mean secure in his head, because it's a safe space, and nobody comes and annoys him there! Lots of the class are still very sensory orientated, so we have a lot of objects that light up, make a noise, feely, touchy.

JT: The dark room.

MC: Yes, so Ahmed sometimes will go in there and just lay down and we have a TheraBrush™ that he puts that under his head and lies on it. Sometimes you have no idea (well, I do know) what they're trying to achieve. They're trying to achieve regulation in their bodies. As you say, looking at Ahmed, it's just constant. That energy flow through him is constant, and I'm amazed he sits at the table for as long as he does.

JT: He does it beautifully.

MC: He's talking, and it's lovely to hear his little voice.

JT: He has got the whispering. He has got the tiniest voice for this big lad.

MC: I know! It's brilliant, and the teacher he had last year, she'd done such great work with him. He has come from a very quiet class where he was able to sit quietly at the table, and so was everybody else. Whereas our class, you know, there's one up, one down. But you give them that time. You build your relationship by being with them. Getting into their world. Finding out about them, finding out what they like, and what they don't like.

JT: It's about having a bit of imagination, is it?

MC: Yes, totally. Yes, going for a walk around the school, you find out lots.

JT: Trying to imagine what the world is like from their point of view.

MC: Yes. My colleague, Julie, who I share the class with, often says, 'I just wish I could see the world as they see the world', because they see it very differently to us. School is one environment and home is another environment, and they've got to adapt to the school environment, which they have done from when they were small. Obviously from reception to Year 6, they've been at Woodlands School, our partner primary school, and then there's the huge transition when they come here. They've got all of that to cope with – new staff, new pupils, new class, new visual things. It's extremely hard when they first come from primary school. The transition moments are difficult but really important, so we have a lot of space to allow that to happen. The transition time is much longer now than it was, and for those that can read symbols, we give social stories to take home, send pictures of the new staff that they're going to be working with, so they have this information to look at throughout the summer holiday. Anything that will help their next journey.

JT: Yes, so you're very deliberate about the choices you give them. You've got your radar on all the time, from a health and safety point of view, I guess, because there's a whole load of things they could do to damage themselves, and you. How do you cope with that?

MC: Well, we have our behaviour strategies, so you wouldn't go towards Ahmed and physically try to move him.

JT: No, because I was going to ask you about whether you ever get to the point that if Adrian hadn't handed the torch over, would you ever take it off him?

MC: I wouldn't try to, because Adrian has got such a strong grip. I have in the past, but he doesn't let go, and then it escalates and he thinks it's really, really funny, and the more attention you give him, the more he carries on. He's like a little boy, really, and so I say, 'OK Adrian … when you're ready, you can give me the torch', and then I walk away.

JT: Yes, so you make it less of a deal.

MC: Then he'll say, 'Mary.' I'll say, 'Yes, when you're ready. I'm not interested yet.' If it was something dangerous, then I would take it from him, but usually it's a torch, or a pen, or your papers, and then he'll giggle, and smile, and say, 'I've got them.'

JT: So, you have procedures for every child?

MC: Yes, so for Joshua, for example, that's the zones of regulation we would use. Ahmed, we try and use pictures or try and use a gentle voice. Once you have recognised that he has got to do his bouncing and jumping or lying down between tasks and then he will come back to the table. You either count down or you use a timer. He loves kinetic sand. I don't know if you saw that.

JT: He's feeling it, because there was still a sand tray, wasn't there?

MC: Yes, so that's his station for when he has his 'leisure' time and wants to build, when he wants to use the sand, even when he wants water play. We say, 'Okay, you can use that now. It's time. You choose what you want to do'; symbols would have been placed on his *Now and Next* board to show him what's happening next.

JT: That's the other thing you do; you narrate all the time. You narrate what's happening in the tiniest interactions.

'Now, now, now', and you're also very agreement-based, it seemed to me.

MC: Agreement?

JT: 'Could we do this? Can we do this?'

MC: Oh, yes.

JT: You ask them for their agreement to do stuff.

MC: Yes, not that they always reply.

JT: No, but they do.

MC: In their own way, yes. If they choose to do whatever they have chosen to do.

JT: Yes, they are accepting your invitation.

MC: Yes, 'Can we do this and that?' Yes, I wasn't totally aware of that.

JT: There's very little forcing them to do anything.

MC: I think it has got to come from them. Otherwise, if you're forcing and they don't actually like or they are not interested in what you're doing, it won't work. You can't make it totally exciting all the time, because then that can escalate, as well. Just a bit of difference, like putting things on a pretend tree. Okay, it's not a great activity ... The next part of the science lesson was going to be showing the light box, which would have been quite a nice activity. But it was great that they were experimenting in the dark room. I saw Ahmed experimenting just by himself, and he'd got the hang of it, and so he was anticipating what was coming.

JT: Yes, that was amazing. You get them to speak as much as you possibly can, and actually, I looked at Joshua and he understands a lot, doesn't he?

MC: Yes, and then the time that you think he has understood what you've said, he hasn't. I can see his eyes and I think, 'OK, Mary, just water it down a bit again to two or three words.' Sometimes he will just hang on to the last word. He is quite 'on the ball' with his films and his selection of what he wants to use on the computer. I think at home, as well, his iPad is important to him.

JT: **Is there anything else you do, consciously or unconsciously, pedagogically?**

MC: I know I try and encourage our students to speak as much as they can, but if not, we would use symbols, but I also think, probably unconsciously now, you're just aware, totally aware all the time … 'OK, he has finished that. I need to go over there', or 'I can see he has moved his hand. He may be about to get up from his seat.'

JT: **Yes, do you become able to read them?**

MC: Yes, you do, and I don't know if that's just a thing with me or everybody. I don't think everybody can, because sometimes you have agency teaching assistants come in to cover planning, preparation and assessment (PPA) time, and, for example, Ahmed gets up, and they'll say, as soon as he gets up, 'No, sit down, sit down.' We will say, 'He's going for his movement break. It's okay. He knows what he needs to do.' 'Oh, but he needs to sit down at his table.' And we say, 'But he doesn't. He will come back. You're escalating him.' For some people, it has got to be that they sit at their tables all the time, which not many of our pupils can do. They can't focus for very long. They sat for half-an-hour, I think, each time this morning.

JT: **That was pretty impressive.**

MC: Which I was surprised about. It might not have happened if Ricky was there. He would probably have been in his own space. He has his own space to explore things.

JT: **Ahmed, it seems to me, gives you very little facial messaging about what he's thinking, but the others were much more expressive.**

MC: Yes, he does.

JT: **I thought James gives you everything.**

MC: Yes, and then he has got that little smile.

JT: **Yes, this lovely smile, but then he can look really angry.**

MC: Oh, very. It changes.

JT: **Ahmed's is almost quite blank.**

MC: Yes, and he will push you if he doesn't want you standing near him. He might accept what you've said, but he can push you away medium hard, and if you're standing in the way of something that he wants, he may push you. Our behaviour strategies with Ahmed will come into play, though, and all staff will be aware of what might happen.

JT: **You're communicating all the time, so you sign a lot.**

MC: Yes, so that's just another addition, because we're a total communication school.

JT: **Right, tell me about that.**

MC: It's signing, it's speech, it's symbols, it's pictures, it's objects of reference for some of the PMLD class, or even in our class, to explain what you're going to do. I had used different shapes. OK, a plate was one of them, and, of course, for Ahmed that wasn't supposed to be with the shapes. It was supposed to be there.

JT: **Yes, he was obsessed with putting those plates on the draining board.**

MC: Because why would I want a plate on my desk?

JT: **Why would I want a plate on the desk? I want a plate on the draining board, because that's where they go.**

MC: Which is where it should be.

JT: **Fair enough.**

MC: Yes, that was great. He has got that. So, we sign, and it just helps them to focus more on what you're saying, because you're doing something, and sometimes they will sign back. Joshua probably won't, because he's too busy talking.

JT: **He's quite verbal, isn't he?**

MC: Not always clear though. Which is frustrating then for him, because we haven't understood what he said, which is why we started asking him to write down, which was another wow moment, the first time that he did. I thought, 'He can write what he wants, look!' That was fantastic. We have communication books, and we have separate communication boards, say, in art for colours. 'Can you choose what colour you want and which paint brush? Okay, you go and get it from the cupboard or from where it is over there.' It's another enablement to independence, I think. The relationship between you is crucial, because communication is the be all and end all, the key thing to everything, and all the behaviour is a way of communicating to us.

JT: **Yes, because what's happening to them in their head affects what they do, doesn't it?**

MC: Yes, absolutely, and also they are looking around them. Ahmed, even though he wants to do what he wants to do, like putting the plate back, he's also attached to the timetable. As soon as we finish something he takes it off the plan for the day.

JT: **I felt I massively impinged on their world today.**

MC: They accepted it.

JT: **They were quite good, weren't they?**

MC: Yes.

JT: I was surprised, because I thought, 'I feel massive in this room in terms of an alien presence.'

MC: Oh, I think Ahmed is bigger!

JT: I know! I felt like a big thing in the corner, which is not usually there. But you put visitor up on the plan for the day, so you anticipated me.

MC: Which brings us back, doesn't it, to the unknown of when you first meet somebody with learning difficulties, and because you don't know them, you don't know what they're going to do, or what they're capable of doing.

JT: Is there anything else that you and your team do deliberately? You're running that whole group of people, aren't you? You've got four adults in there.

MC: Yes, you couldn't do it without a team, they're so important. I think we make sure that whatever resources we use are tailor made for them. Deliberately, as well, we ensure that they can use whatever resources we have. It's hard to say deliberate, because I think we just know now. Using our knowledge of them to enable them to enjoy their day is deliberate. It's about fun and it's about providing the right resources for lessons to make it that little bit more exciting or different. Not doing hundreds of worksheets, with lots of writing on them. Just plain, simple stuff, but making it harder each time they go along. I think that physical side of things is deliberate and the building of the relationship is, and remembering what it is they like. You're constantly thinking about the next thing that you can try to enable that person to do his best or her best.

JT: Would you ever have done anything else?

MC: No. Honestly. By the end of that first year, we'd been on holiday together, some wonderful trips out, I was caught. By the time we had the post-16 unit, we were in a fantastic place in Barkingside. We managed to teach students to go to a shop and buy a pint of milk using the zebra crossing. We were on tenterhooks, but they did it.

JT: **It's like when you let your own kid go to the shop for the first time on their own.**

MC: Yes, one of the girls went to the hairdresser, with her mum's permission of course. She came back with this huge perm! All of this was fostering independence. No, I couldn't have seen myself doing anything else.

JT: **Passing on the baton, Mary, to a new generation of young people going into teaching, what advice would you give them?**

MC: I would say go for special, because it's not standing in front of a class of 30. Some of ours have homework, so we do have just a little bit of marking to do, but not all do, because home is home to them and school is school. Why on earth would you be doing what you do at school at home? Some do not understand. So, I would say go for it, because there's such a lack of special needs teachers in mainstream, as well as in special schools.

JT: **What is it that has made you stay at it for 44 years?**

MC: I think the excitement and the surprises. There are always surprises, and always something happens that you never thought would. Like James finding the letter S for snowman and walking around with his snow picture, and us not getting it at all for a long, long time.

JT: **In the end, he communicated.**

MC: In the end, I think he was desperate. He was desperate to communicate this, or Joshua writing what he wanted to know. There are always behavioural challenges, and it's about getting into that person's world to find out what is it that's making him tick? What is it that's causing him this pain? What is it that I can do to help? What can I do to help make that person's life a bit better, a bit easier? It's just so interesting. There's never a dull day. Never a day the same.

JT: The days fly by.

MC: They do! It's just exciting. You meet so many interesting people, as well. Some agency teaching assistants who come in have gone on to want to be teachers, because of what they've seen, which is the best way forward, isn't it? Go for special needs teaching.

JT: Is there anything else you think I ought to know about you before I write this chapter in the book?

MC: Just how much I enjoy it. OK, we get tired, I know, and sometimes we 'moan' because there's another task to do, where we would rather be in class doing what we need to do. I do enjoy being in class and, although our PPA is so important and I *so* appreciate it, being in class is, I think, the absolute. Just being around your little group and your staff, obviously, because I want to recognise them and how much they do.

JT: They're so brilliant, aren't they?

MC: They do so much ... without our class teams, we would not be able to function properly in the classroom, we would not be able to support our pupils and we would not have access to their brilliant ideas

My friends say, 'Oh, when are you going to retire?' I say, 'Well, maybe next year. I'll see how I feel in May', because physically I'm fine. I'm still able to jump around and chase somebody down the corridor, which is necessary sometimes.

JT: Yes, that's just brilliant. Well, thank you so much. It has been a real pleasure.

MC: I've enjoyed it!

Testimonials

'I have had the privilege of working alongside Mary for over a decade. During all these years, I have known Mary as a colleague with strong work ethics. Mary is an incredible professional with excellent communication and listening skills, who collaborates, adapts, and has empathy and patience.

The specific characteristics of her effective teaching include an engaging classroom presence, value in real-world learning, exchange of best practices and a lifelong love of learning. Her strong passion for teaching inspires both students as well as fellow teachers.'

'Mary always displays patience and understanding, and creates a calm happy learning environment. She manages chaotic behaviours extremely well. No matter the incident she has a way of remaining softly spoken and peaceful. I watch in awe, and remember thinking "I want to be like her". Mary is both supportive and encouraging of me. I am now an unqualified teacher, and Mary continues to cheer me on to gain my QTS. She asks my opinion when we share lesson ideas and she happily takes on board my views. This will always surprise me, as she is such an experienced teacher, with a wealth of knowledge. She is a dedicated, understanding, caring, professional, and friendly individual who is always on hand to offer me any support or answer any of my concerns.'

So, what can we learn from Mary Cawley?

It's an easy thing to say about colleagues, but I've never been more genuine when I write that watching Mary teach was truly humbling. That said, trying to surface the expert features of her teaching that have been so entirely embedded in her person, that even she is hardly conscious of them, is pretty difficult. But in the interview I managed to highlight some aspects of her practice that any teacher might learn from:

- Spending time finding out about each child helps establish the foundations for the learning relationship with individual pupils.
- Giving pupils choices at every opportunity is hugely beneficial. It enables them to develop their independence and helps them feel a modicum of autonomy.
- Using an agreement-based way of communicating makes for calmer classrooms.
- Narrating the day, through the *Now and Next* cueing process, provides certainty and a degree of safety for pupils.
- Having your *anticipating-what-might-happen-next* radar on in a very deliberate way is crucial to effective behaviour management.
- Communicating closely with fellow adults in the room, in the moment, and giving them the autonomy to take actions that might prevent behaviour issues escalating, seems to be an obvious learning point from Mary's classroom practice.

Now, there is much more that we might learn from Mary's practice, but these six observations are a decent starting point. That said, if there is one more thing that struck me about how Mary goes about her work, it's this … in her fifth decade of teaching, she is never without a smile!

Mary Cawley's students' progress and achievement data

2023–24 SEMH: 54% target achievement (compared with the ASD 47% average target achievement).

2023–24 Learners' personal learning plans (PLPs), our main sources of progress targets: 96% achieved or partially achieved, (compared with 93% for all ASD, 92% for whole school).

2023–24 Community and Independence: 92% targets achieved or partially achieved, in line with general school and Key Stage data, taking into account the complex needs of the learners in the class.

A Truly Great Science Teacher: Mariam Sankar

Mariam Sankar is the subject leader of science at the Frederick Bremer School, Walthamstow, London.

The school leadership's view

It's a decent walk from Walthamstow Central to Frederick Bremer School, especially in the sharp spring sunshine. I am heading there to spend a day with Mariam Sankar, the subject leader for science. I arrive to find it is *Harmony Day*, where everyone wears clothes to reflect personal pride in their cultural roots. As I walk through the gates I am met by a riot of colourful garb. Stewart Hesse, the relatively new deputy head teacher, greets me in a kilt and a New Zealand rugby shirt. He wears them well.

In the conference room Stewart tells me about Mariam. 'When I arrived here in September and I was talking to the rest of the staff and middle leaders about the curriculum, the SLT were confident about the improvements in science. They were effusive about Mariam's leadership qualities and her fierce desire to improve the quality of teaching as well as the quality of the curriculum content for the students. She was off last year on maternity leave. She returned this year, and has just begun the subject leader role. With all the stresses and strains of being a new parent, she has picked it up and is running with it really well. She is a positive advocate of the teaching developments that we're making at the school, and she is a great teacher.'

Kelly, Mariam's line manager, is also with us. 'She is relentless with those students. She does lots of assessment for learning in her lessons; she's constantly checking where they're at. She addresses misconceptions. And I think she really knows her students well.' Kelly continues, 'I think she has very high expectations and the students rise to that. Every time I see her teach, I comment on the academic challenge in the lesson; the thing is, it doesn't feel like challenge because she scaffolds the teaching so well, it allows all pupils to succeed, and that's why she can have genuinely high expectations of them. On top of that, she has high energy all the time. She's a powerhouse. What you see of her as a teacher is exactly how she is as a leader. She leads by example. She models everything. She gets stuck in. She would never ask anyone to do anything that she isn't doing herself. She's thinking ahead constantly.' Kelly chuckles, 'I mean, she looks at the progress data before we do!'

Everyone around the table is nodding in agreement, including Jenny Smith, head teacher at Frederick Bremer. I ask Jenny what she would add. 'She has an infectious and relentless positivity. She believes in everyone, both staff and pupils. She's a member of staff I've never seen have a bad day. Ever. She is the epitome of relentless optimism and I don't know where she gets that unwavering positivity, all day, every day. Pupils know that she absolutely expects them to be successful and believes in them unconditionally, so they enter her classroom knowing there is a high bar in terms of expectations, both behaviourally and academically. And if pupils aren't living up to those high standards that she's setting in her classroom, then it will be made known to them, in such a lovely way that no one ever feels like they're being told off. Mariam's so skilled at raising the bar with care. They like being successful, but they know what is expected, and as a result, they go in with that mindset for success. It's all led by those expectations, building people up and helping them believe that they can do it.'

I ask about the pedagogic hallmarks of Mariam's teaching. Jenny says, 'She can deconstruct quite complex things to make the pupils believe that they can access it. *All* the pupils. She explains things in real detail, so that she keeps them all with her. She has a deep understanding of the subject matter, but she can approach it as if she's not a specialist. She can deconstruct the science in a way that means anyone can understand and then rebuild it.'

'What do you think of Mariam's leadership of science?'

'Well, she's only been head of faculty here since the beginning of the year, but I see that infectious positivity has really begun to spread across the team. It's like you can't *not* get enthused by that buzz that surrounds her work. She's got such a "can do" attitude so that people find ways of being able to work with her rather than putting up obstacles. I always like to think that I'm relentlessly positive and optimistic, but she's on another level!'

I give Jenny a final chance to reflect upon Mariam's practice. She pauses, 'Well … she's really reflective. She's always willing to learn and improve her practice. She's got a radar and it's finely tuned as to where those tweaks in her teaching need to be made. You always feel with her that she's got a clear sense of what her pupils' learning should look like at the end of the unit or scheme. It's so finely tuned that she makes sure that they've *all* got it before they move on. She creates a sense that everybody feels like they're treated equally in her class. And she'll take no nonsense!' More laughter. 'And the science labs she teaches in don't make it easy. She's a small woman and it's hard to be visible but she finds a way of being *really* visible in that space. I don't quite know how she does it, but you always know where she is.'

Jenny's passion for ensuring her teachers provide the best possible learning experiences for the pupils is clear. She says, 'With Mariam, it's a case of what I'd call that old school charismatic teacher who has the pupils in the palm of their hand because they've got such a compelling narrative, with those expert pedagogical skills underpinning it all. The pupils learn because they really like the teacher and they really want to succeed, but they don't quite know why they're doing so well! They know they're well taught and they're just working hard for that teacher.'

It's time to go and watch Mariam teach. As we stand to leave, I point out how incredibly modest and self-effacing I find Mariam. It seems to me that she does everything with genuine humility. She presents herself professionally, in a way that embodies her high expectations. In so many ways, she is a role model for the profession.

Teaching

I first saw Mariam teach in my role as The Frederick Bremer School's Improvement Partner. Five minutes in, I noticed a student I had seen earlier in the day in another lesson, where *he could have been working harder*. In Mariam's lesson he was industry personified, completely focused upon her explanations and engaged in the challenging tasks she set. I asked him what he thought of Ms Sankar, and he said, 'She's an amazing teacher.' Mariam's teaching confirmed the boy's testimonial. She had relentless energy, she was fierce in her insistence upon every single student thinking hard about the content she was teaching, and she did it all with humour and charm. She had a pedagogic toolbox where every technique was well-practised and used appropriately. If you were one of her students, you couldn't afford to let your concentration lapse. Another boy – someone I would call a *cheeky chappie* – tried to evade giving an answer to a question about hydrocarbons. He knew the answer but hid behind a faux 'Don't know' response. He was quite funny, but there was no way Mariam was going to let him off the hook. What was interesting, as she pursued a constructive response, was how the rest of the class were on Mariam's side. He certainly didn't elicit any sympathy from his peers. This was a class where students knew they were there to work hard and *learn*.

Walking down the corridor, chatting, I remind her of that moment. She laughs. 'He wasn't ever going to get away with it!' She's about to teach a challenging Year 9 class of thirty-plus pupils. The context isn't easy. For most of the spring term, they've been taught by the trainee teacher. This is Mariam's first lesson with them for a while. Some of the behavioural norms she'd established early in the academic year have frayed. They need re-*Sankaring*! It's Wednesday, the lesson before lunch at the end of a long term, which means the pupils are tired. And it's *Harmony Day*, with all the implicit informality that that brings. To top it all, the day before, when she had intended to plan the lesson, the school's computer system and internet access suffered catastrophic failure!

I settle in the corner of the room and watch while Mariam meets the pupils at the door. She greets them, using each pupil's name, and checks if they're OK. 'Books out, bags on floor.' They have three recall questions on the board and they get on without fuss. There's a school-endorsed sign on the wall: 'Be the best you can be.' It might as well be there just for Mariam. It's the mantra she lives by. Near me, a girl flops down in her seat. Let's call her Maddie. She clearly isn't interested in being anywhere near her best. Not today. Mariam notices and when she asks Maddie to raise herself from her slouch, Maddie says she can't be bothered. It's too hot. She's tired. But Mariam is insistent and eventually Maddie sits squarely in her seat. There's no conflict, just persistence.

Once she is at the front of the class, Mariam secures 100% attention and reminds them of the work on ionic bonding from last lesson. 'We're going to build on that knowledge. You were great last lesson. I know all of you can do this.' She addresses the recall questions, without fuss:

State the three different types of bonding.

- Draw a structure of an atom, label all its parts and explain its function. (As an aside, I tacitly admire the correct [non] use of apostrophes …)
- Explain the difference between groups and periods on the periodic table.
- Challenge: Draw the ionic bond in lithium fluoride.

As the pupils work, Mariam teaches between the tables. She walks around the room, encouraging, cajoling, praising, prompting. She is a ball of 'can-do' energy. 'Sit up, put your chair in.' 'Give 100%, come on!' 'I don't want to hear "I don't know", cos I know you do.' She thanks the pupils individually for good learning behaviours. There is a great level of industry, driven by Mariam's insistence that they get their heads down and concentrate. She ensures she speaks to Maddie twice before she brings the class together. It's clear that Maddie is capable; Mariam won't tolerate her not trying.

Mariam's response to her situational assessment of who is doing what across the class is deliberate and impressive. At the front of the class, she goes through the answers swiftly. She doesn't tarry where she doesn't need to. She knows who has answers and who needs to be checked on because she has been teaching between the desks. She invites a boy up to the board to answer the challenge question because, 'I want everyone to see what you did.' She reassures him, 'I'll help you through it if you get stuck' but she is not needed – he does well and she pushes him to use the word 'orbiting' when talking about electrons in their shell 'orbiting' the nucleus.

There follows an intense session of checking who understands what, using mini-whiteboards. 'No flappy boards. No cheating. I want to know what you know. If unsure, I still want you to try it. 3-2-1 – be patient.' It is clear that she has bellwether pupils – if those pupils know the answer to a question, it is likely that everyone in the class will do too. She walks the room, enthused, positive energy personified. Her very own proton. Indefatigable.

She explains how, for the next few minutes, she is going to explain the next thing they need to know about sharing electrons, and how they need to give her 100% attention.

'Hannah, I need your attention.'

'Sorry, Miss.'

She's not afraid to teach from the front. She talks about diatomic molecules. She questions the pupils to check for understanding. No one can afford not to pay attention. If you want someone to demonstrate direct instruction, Mariam's your woman! There are high levels of attention. They behave well, are fully engaged and work hard. I am struck by how she thanks them for making a contribution. She is intense and relentless. I sit there, wondering where she gets her energy from. She sets them the following task to consolidate what she has just explained and says, 'I know you guys are going to get this right.'

Draw the molecular structure of the following:

- Hydrogen and chlorine
- Hydrogen and fluorine
- Methane
- Hydrogen and oxygen
- Carbon dioxide

Mariam makes a beeline for Maddie. Of course she does. She hears some off-task talk and those pupils won't be off-task again. And when she returns to the front of the class, cold calling pupils, no one refuses to answer, no one declines the invite to come up to the board. To do the work is the norm in a Mariam Sankar class; it's cultural. She has high expectations. Content is chunked up perfectly. What is so interesting is that Mariam has learnt to teach like this through reflecting on her practice and adapting her teaching depending on whether the pupils have learnt what she wants them to learn from the way she has taught.

I watch these Year 9s – sat here together in a single classroom in London, their dress proclaiming personal pride in their diverse backgrounds, learning about the formation of chemical bonds, taught by a British woman whose Indian parents are both professors, one in India and one in England – and I am suddenly overwhelmed by a sense of awe. It is a humbling, extraordinary privilege to see tolerant, modern Britain working in harmony.

She ends by introducing the double bond of CO_2. It's where they are heading for the next lesson. The pupils have stuck at it and worked hard. Mariam dismisses them as she greeted them – with a smile and her best wishes. Before she leaves, I ask Maddie over. I ask her why she did the work even though she wasn't feeling it today. She smiled and said, 'Well, I like this teacher.'

What the students think

I sit with five wonderful young people. One of them is wearing an England football shirt, one a Belgian football shirt, one a Pakistani cricket shirt, one a grey tracksuit and one is dressed in magnificent traditional Somalian dress. I explain I am writing a profile of Ms Sankar, and they open up straight away. 'She's very nice. She's always welcoming to students when they come into class. She's always there at the door. She's always happy to teach us. That makes me feel welcome in the class and makes me want to learn.'

So, she develops positive relationships with pupils. What else, I ask? Another pipes up. 'I think Miss Sankar is really good at reinforcing knowledge. We'll always spend a lot of time on a topic, so that *everyone* in the class gets it. I think she's very fair in that way. She takes everybody with her.' I ask him how she does that. 'She's very big on exam questions when we reach the end of a topic and she explains how to apply what you know to answer those questions. You learn the *application of knowledge* in class, as well as the knowledge, which I think is effective.' I am struck by the pupil's perceptiveness. For a nano-second I think about introducing the notion of metacognition. 'In our tests, we nearly all get high grades; there isn't a stark difference between the highest and the lowest in the class, really.' I don't point out how that is almost certainly down to the quality of teaching, rather than some quirk of nature that brought together 30 individuals of very similar academic ability.

Is there anything else they want me to write about Ms Sankar? 'She is so enthusiastic about the science,' says one.

Another comments upon how she, 'comes round and ask us all how we are, and to see how we were doing with our work. If we're learning something, she goes through it very thoroughly. Right now we're learning about electron configuration. We've had a lot of lessons on it, so the whole class understands it well. She's really good at explaining things.'

'That's right', interrupts another, 'the way she presents information makes it easy to remember.' I ask him to tell me more. 'With the starters, she asks questions about stuff we've done in the previous lesson to help us remember what we've learnt. And she explains why we're learning what we're learning and how you apply it. She's really direct like that. I have a good idea of how Miss Sankar teaches and I think, you know, if that sort of teaching works for a lot of us, which it does, I don't see any reason to change that.'

To wrap things up, I ask them if there is anything else they would like me to write about Ms Sankar. 'Well, three of us have a two hour lesson on Tuesdays in the afternoon, which is quite difficult. So she tries to give us as many practical lessons and fun stuff to do as possible. And I think she's quite honest. So this new topic that we're doing, she's straight-up told us it's very wordy, and it's going to be hard. She's quite realistic, if that makes sense. Some people were tired, as it was Ramadan, and she was very aware of what people were going through and why, maybe, the energy was lower in the class than usual.'

Before we finish, one of the quieter boys suddenly says, 'I feel like when we come to the class, she's very happy, and I feel like she's happy to teach, but also she's challenging people in their work and making sure they do their best by asking questions about stuff they may not be sure about. And she cares about us.'

It's a truly great moment to end on. And I forget to ask them for a single word to describe Ms Sankar. D'oh!

IRL: Mariam Sankar

John Tomsett (JT): So, Mariam, what did you do before you went into teaching?

Mariam Sankar (MS): I was a biomedical scientist. I did my Master's in biomedical science. I worked in a hospital and moved on to doing my teacher training. I've always been passionate about teaching. My mum and dad are both professors. My dad is actually a retired head teacher of two schools in India. He's currently doing a lot of education work in boroughs in India and every holiday I've had since childhood, I've always visited my dad. And any time I'd go to his school, I'd ask him, 'Can I can I just teach a lesson?' I loved it, teaching Year 7s, Year 8s. I'd plan the lessons as though I was a teacher, because I've always seen my mum planning her lessons, so I knew what to do.

JT: What does your mum teach?

MS: Mum's specialisms are biology and chemistry, and Dad's is physics. I've always enjoyed teaching, but my mum said to me that since everyone in the family is a teacher, I should do something different. That's why I went into biomedical science, but even then I was looking for opportunities to train others on how to do experiments. I thought to myself, 'I've always had a passion for teaching, why don't I just try teaching? If it doesn't work, it doesn't work. It wouldn't matter.' And I used to get a lot of compliments from the parents of the children I taught, who would say, 'My child really enjoyed that lesson. Have you ever considered teaching?' And so my passion for teaching has always been there. I've always enjoyed it. If I wasn't in India during my holidays, I'd be asking my mum, 'Can I mark some papers?' I guess at the root of it is my upbringing where education was so important. That's how it all started.

When I did my NQT year, I really enjoyed it. I did my teacher training at University College London (UCL). I then moved on to doing my NQT year at another school. Again, I really enjoyed it. Every time I got positive feedback, it motivated me even more. I wanted to do even better. I took on a leadership role in my NQT year as Key Stage 3 coordinator, and then, within a year, I moved on to another school to be in charge of Key Stages 4 and 5, and was head of biology and chemistry. And in every role, I was learning something new. I realised that my passion lay in teaching and learning, and how to identify certain areas of weakness in pupils' learning and how to address them. And then I got lucky coming here as deputy head of department. And then, when I returned from maternity leave last September, I became subject leader.

JT: That's an impressive CV.

MS: Well, I enjoy teaching students more than anything. But I've also enjoyed tremendously the subject leadership role, and looking at what works best in the classroom when we teach science. When I see that work transformed into results and pupils making progress, it's extremely rewarding. I feel so much joy from that.

JT: I spoke to the pupils earlier. They all feel successful in science. They love being taught by you.

MS: That's really nice.

JT: You're steeped in education. How have you developed your pedagogic understanding about what works in classrooms?

MS: It's always been through student feedback. I'm not a person who reads loads of research. I've just developed approaches based on what my students can and cannot do. You probably think I read educational research and apply what I read about in the classroom, but that's not me at all, John!

JT: That's so interesting.

MS: There's probably evidence out there about what works, but I begin with the energy that I get from students. Do they understand it? Do they not understand it? How can I make them understand it? What can I do differently? What technique works with which pupils? What technique does not work with certain pupils, because there are some that would fly through certain tasks, but some that just don't understand difficult concepts, and how can I make them understand? It's all based on the students and the feedback they give me.

JT: So it's based on pupil feedback and your growing experience of what works and what doesn't work in your own teaching, and reflecting upon what you do constantly, and refining your practice in the light of your own learning.

MS: Even if there's *one* student that's not learned something in the class, that's something I really hate. I go back and ask myself, 'What can I do differently so everyone in that class can actually understand what I have taught them?'

JT: That's so interesting. One of your pupils said, 'We always spend a lot of time on topics so that *everyone* in the class gets there. I think she's very fair in that way. She takes everybody with her.'

MS: That is so important for me.

JT: You may not read the research papers, but you're doing research in the moment, in every lesson aren't you? You're finding out what works through experience. And you're coming to the same conclusions, probably, that educational researchers are coming to about what works best in the classroom.

MS: I'd never thought about it like that, but, yes …

JT: Tell me, then, what are the pedagogic hallmarks of your work?

MS: When I think about planning a lesson, I begin by establishing the absolute fundamentals that they need to know. What are the key ideas that I want them to understand? What does it say in the specification or the national curriculum? I go all the way back to the drawing board. What are the key things I want them to know? I also have an understanding of the assessment objectives (AOs) and know exactly what they need for exam purposes, but, ultimately, I want them to enjoy the science. I want them to have a love of the subject because if they don't love it, they're not going to engage with me. And this is crucial too, it's all about having that positive working relationship with students. The very first lesson, before I start any topic, I just want to build that relationship with every student. I identify who my key characters are – who my naughty ones are, who my cheeky ones are – and I go to them first. They're my key targets. I get them on board first. Ultimately, it all comes down to relationships, because they're the foundation for learning.

Once I have a clear idea of all the main ideas and the concepts, and what I want them to learn, I then explain my plans to the class: 'This is what I want you guys to do. This is my long-term plan. This is my short-term plan. If it doesn't work, we're going to do it again in a different way.' We keep going until I get *every single one of them* understanding what I have taught them. I always strive to get to that point where they can all confidently answer exam questions independently.

And I say this quite regularly in my class: 'I don't mind you making mistakes in front of me and you shouldn't be embarrassed when that happens. I want you to be confident in making mistakes; when you make mistakes, it's only in front of me – I can correct you, so you won't make those mistakes in your exam. Your examiner doesn't see you, they don't know you. It's important you get it right then.' It's about instilling confidence in your pupils, because everyone can achieve a GCSE grade, but there are some pupils who just don't have that confidence to even get to that stage. Building that trusting relationship is so important, just having that simple conversation when you're on break duty, outside of their lessons.

JT: **So, you've forged that positive relationship, you've decided what you want them to learn. What have you learned about pedagogy that allows you to take everybody with you?**

MS: I think having high expectations is really important. So, although I'd be very supportive, very nice, very encouraging, at the same time they cannot mess about in the lesson. I want their full attention until that lesson finishes. They have to be concentrating for every single moment in the lesson. I don't tolerate background chatter. I don't like low-level disruption because the minute I start letting that happen, then it all just falls apart. And I have a lot of conversations with them. When they're getting on with a task, I check in on them: 'How are you getting on? How can I help you?'

JT: You teach between the desks, in amongst it all?

MS: Yes, always. And if someone does disrupt things, I won't discourage them by challenging them in class – it's always quietly, but firmly, in the corridor, never in front of the class.

JT: How useful has all your experience from before you became a teacher been? You've got your Master's in biomedical science. How does that help when you're teaching a concept?

MS: I always link the content to real-life applications. I always make it very relevant and relatable to students. That stops the 'Why do we need to know this?' attitude from the pupils. Take exothermic and endothermic reactions, which is a really nice topic, where we talk about energy changes and heat energy. We'll get all the pupils in the classroom who are into sports talking about how they use ice packs when they get an injury. They need to understand how ice doesn't put cold into where you are injured, it withdraws the warmth from the injury, and that's why the ice melts, and the injury cools down and the swelling reduces. It's a really hard concept to get their heads around, but the sport injury context makes it more relatable to the pupils. The real-world context is also about building the relationships with pupils. There are pupils who just won't work if you don't build that relationship.

JT: And what do you mean by *that* relationship? I'm really interested in how you characterise that relationship?

MS: Take James. He works in the lesson only because I engage with him on a human level at the start: 'Hi James, how are you doing? Are you okay? How was your weekend? Come on now. I want you to get on with the work today. I want you to try and focus on the lesson. Remember what we're here for. Remember what you're going to get out of this. Right? I want you to do really well in the future. I want you to get really successful outcomes. I'm saying this for your benefit. Think about yourself.' And he'll reply, 'Sure, Miss. I understand, Miss. I'll do it. Thanks, Miss.' He's thinking, 'OK. There's someone that cares for me. They're telling me for my own good. I'd better focus.' Just that simple conversation is all it takes. It's the same with so many students. They can be naughty, but the minute you pull them aside and you just have an encouraging conversation, it's all they need to convince them you're on their side. They just need someone to check-in with them.

JT: **That is such a detailed description of what *that* relationship is and how it works. Science is surely the most fascinating subject on the curriculum. How free do you feel to go off-piste?**

MS: Obviously, I do allocate time for it. We do have space in the curriculum. And this is one of the things I love about working at Frederick Bremer. There's a lot of teachers in our department who are passionate about certain things. Here we get the opportunity to experiment. If we want to collapse the curriculum for a day to do something special, we can. At Bremer, we get that liberty, as long as we have a rationale behind it. We need to know why we're doing it. What is the intended outcome? What are we getting out of it? What's the takeaway message for the students? For example, we had a debate about polycystic ovarian syndrome. It's not part of the curriculum, but it's a common problem that affects a lot of women, and pupils really enjoyed that. There were different skills they developed from doing that campaign. They've learned so much, how it affects women, the treatments, the symptoms, how we can manage it with diet and lifestyle. And students really enjoyed that.

JT: **So, how do you manage everything?!**

MS: I cannot *not* do this. I can't imagine *not* being involved in teaching. I feel like I'm better organised when I've got so much on. But I manage, mainly because I enjoy teaching. It's just the passion that I have towards teaching, knowing what I am going to do next, how I am going to do it better, how I am going to make that lesson better. I've taught covalent bonding so many times, I've taught it for so many years, but I know for a fact that that lesson I taught earlier needed to be adapted for this specific set of students. I planned the lesson yesterday like I was doing it from scratch. I obviously had an idea of what was going to work. I knew which key AOs were going to be the focus. But I had to adapt that lesson to meet the needs of the students in that class.

I've always allocated time towards my lesson planning, and allocated time for family life and work life, and I've always had that balance. Ultimately, I want my students to make progress. I can have a very difficult day if I don't have a well-planned lesson!

JT: **That raises big questions, doesn't it, about bought-in schemes of work. What you're saying is that you can't just pick up the content and teach it.**

MS: You can't. You've got to think it through. You've got to think what order you're going to teach the content in. What's the sequencing of the lesson? How are the pupils going to understand it? How are you going to build that challenge from early on? How are you going to start off simple? How do you make it very relatable, make it relevant? And how are you going to build the challenge?

JT: **What do you think your strengths are as a teacher?**

MS: My main strength would be identifying the needs of all pupils and addressing them. Knowing who my students are. Knowing the data, knowing my pupil premium students. Who are my EAL students? Who are my target groups? Who are the students that need my support? And who are the ones I need to stretch? How much am I going to stretch them? How am I going to adapt the lesson so that every single pupil in that class makes progress? That's what I would say my strength is. I might have a grade 8 student – how am I going to get them to get a grade 9? At the same time, how am I going to scaffold the learning, so my low attainers make great progress, or those who are potentially disengaged – how am I going to get them on board, so they get the best outcome?

JT: **Teaching and learning is fundamentally human processes. And this work on truly great teachers has come to reject some of the formulaicness that's seeped into the school system, and returned to the humanity that is, actually, at the heart of teaching. You pushed every single pupil in that lesson today!**

MS: Yes, it was hard, because I had to do so much recall work before we pushed on with covalent bonding. In an ideal lesson where they've had a series of lessons where they've been building up to today's lesson, I could have just focused on covalency itself. I could have done exam questions stretching the higher prior attainers, but at this point, I decided to dedicate a future lesson to that. Today I just wanted them to understand how to draw the basic covalent structures. That was the key learning point. Without those foundations, you can't go on to look at double covalent bonds and really stretch them, but I can now, after what they all learnt today. Next lesson I will do a little recap and then straight into double bonds and on to giant covalent structures diamond, graphite.

JT: **Then you can ask, 'Why are diamonds so hard?'**

MS: Exactly! But they would not be able to answer anything to do with giant covalent structures if they didn't have today's understanding. But now they will be able to say that carbon has four bonds. And I will emphasise stability, but before we then go on to melting points and boiling points, they need to understand why something has a high melting point, for instance. And it's because it's got a strong covalent bond, and the components are difficult to separate. It's got a high melting and boiling point. It needs more energy to break that bond.

JT: They need all of this knowledge from today to be able to understand and then apply that knowledge to new problems. One of your students said earlier that Miss Sankar is great at showing us how to apply the knowledge that we've got. But they need that knowledge in the first place, don't they? And you can't do much exploratory learning without understanding covalent bonds, you just need to teach them directly, explain clearly, ask them questions to check their understanding, be relentless in ensuring every single student has a confident grasp of the fundamentals. I loved how you insisted on their attention.

MS: And that's all I wanted. I wanted them all focused. I don't care that it's the lesson before lunch. It doesn't matter. When it gets to lunchtime, you can have your lunch. Until then, you're going to be focused … I absolutely love that class. But they're a really challenging group. There's a lot of characters in there.

JT: I could tell! You had thirty Year 9 pupils, two days before the Easter holidays, last lesson before lunch, *Harmony Day* and a really dense theory lesson on covalent bonding … But you were relentless and unapologetic about the need to learn this stuff.

MS: There's no other way. That's my job.

JT: At one point, you asked a tricky student to pay attention, and she replied, 'Yes, sorry Miss.' It was brilliant!

MS: But that is all possible because of the relationships I have built. And that's where the energy comes from to make them work.

JT: And you can be slightly sharp with them. When you've got that relationship, they don't react badly. They apologise. Because they know you care. It seems to me that the fundamental element is the purposeful relationships, but then it's having the highest expectations, then your expert subject knowledge which is at the heart of your fabulously clear explanations. All supported by your commitment to providing assistance to individuals, and then the way you demonstrate how to apply their knowledge to solve new problems. And it's an unbeatable formula!

MS: Thank you. I've learned some things about myself through this conversation. It's good to understand what's working. Although I reflect a lot on my teaching, I've never thought about it in this way and what it is that's actually enabling them to learn. When you put it this way, it makes sense.

All I would say, reflecting on that lesson now, is that I could have done a lot more. I could have still done the double bonds. I could have still done a bit more on exam stretch questions.

JT: But you couldn't have done … you got exactly where you needed to get to, and you'd have been pushing things too far if you had tried. You responded to the context of the room and the context of these children at this point of the year. And I think it was absolutely perfect. They end up caring about stuff they didn't care about at the start of the lesson. Take Maddie. She didn't care about covalent bonds at all when she walked in the room.

MS: She really did not care! But in the end she cared that she got it all right, and was quite proud of what she could do at the end of the lesson.

JT: I asked her over at the end and said to her, 'You weren't feeling up for this at all when the lesson began. What made you do all that work?' She smiled and said, 'Well, I like this teacher.'

MS: That's amazing.

JT: That exemplifies the challenge you face every day and you are driven to meet that challenge, in a positive way. The pupils are fortunate to have you in their corner.

MS: Thank you.

Testimonials

'From the start of Year 7, I always struggled with science. It was my worst subject. But since you started teaching me, my grades have improved, and I have started to really enjoy Ms Sankar lessons! It's always a joy. Even *I* am beginning to get science – you are the best teacher!'

'You made me go from a 3 to a 5 in a single year. C'mon!'

'I love your lessons so much Ms Sankar. You always teach in a way I understand. You helped my grades go up so much! ♡'

'Thank you for being my teacher for the past year. You've helped my grades in biology improve drastically and made me actually want to aim for the highest grades. I love our little chats at the front of the class and thank you for letting me talk about all the stresses of life.'

'I just wanted to say how much I loved having you as my science teacher this year. You have a way of making even the hardest topics make sense. You have genuinely made me enjoy science so much more and I love having you as my teacher because of how confident you make me feel!'

'Mariam, you have been absolutely brilliant and I want to thank you so much for your mentorship this year. You have taken on so much more than your share and have done it all with a smile and I am truly grateful for that. You have been a shining example of what a great mentor looks like and it has been such a pleasure to work with you over the past few years.'

And, to finish, a poem from a Year 13 pupil:

'It hurts to think we must unwind, break bonds, and part ways;

This cannot even be blamed on the DNA helicase.

This triple hydrogen bonds between guanine and cytosine we thought were so strong,

Can also break easily and will not last long.

We got on so well and made memories that shine bright,

We were complementary, like substrate at the enzyme's active site.

No catalysts were needed, our lessons were so lively,

We appreciate the content you have taught us so nicely.

I hope you continue to be successful and stay amazing and wise,

But for now let us go and say our goodbyes.'

So, what can we learn from Mariam Sankar?

In terms of triangulating the evidence, there is a level of consistency in what people say about Mariam's teaching and what she does in the classroom, that is quite remarkable. When I proofread this profile, it was so obvious that what she does, she does every day of the week, lesson-in, lesson-out, in the corners of the school, when no one is looking.

I am a fully paid-up member of the researchED club, having been there at the very first conference at Dulwich in 2013. I was the head teacher of one of the first tranche of Research Schools. My teaching was enhanced – even *transformed* – by what I learnt from research evidence about what has the best chance of helping pupils learn. So, counterintuitively, I found it incredibly impressive to learn from

Mariam that her teaching – which has all the hallmarks of someone deeply versed in Rosenshine's 'Principles of Instruction', Daniel Willingham's learning model, etc. – has been developed over time purely in response to how easy or hard her pupils have found learning what she has taught them. It does make perfect sense, when one thinks about it. Mariam's whole array of teaching techniques is the result of her adapting her teaching so that her pupils can learn better. Extreme adaptive teaching, if you like.

I did wonder whether her approach to improving her practice – looking at what assessments tell her about who has learnt what (*evidence* of pedagogic efficacy) and then adapting accordingly – derives from her being a scientist and the scientific method. She teaches in a certain way, tweaks one variable, sees how that affects the outcome, then tweaks another variable and another, until she gets the outcome she wants.

It will come as a relief, then, to many people, that you don't have to spend the corners of your weekend reading Graham Nuthall's *Hidden Lives of Learners* to become a better a teacher – you just have to learn how to improve your practice from how effectively your pupils learn when you teach them in this way or that way. That said, the word 'just' is doing a great deal of heavy-lifting in that last sentence. Mariam is extremely intelligent. Teaching is in her family's blood. Like all great teachers who reflect upon their practice and then adapt what they do, being the best teacher she can possibly be matters to her in her soul. She cannot tolerate her pupils underachieving. And it is from those sentiments that her high expectations derive. She has a right to teach with a hint of fierceness, because this stuff really matters to her.

Another striking thing is the precision of Mariam's pedagogy. Her expertise in the generic fundamentals of pedagogy free her up to make what she is teaching seem irresistible. She can bring her spellbinding personality to the classroom, without the lesson being all about her, because her checking for understanding, her probing questions, her use of mini-whiteboards, her 'I do, we do, you do' are flawlessly executed. She reminded me of Dylan Wiliam's pithy aphorism, 'What makes some teachers more effective than others is that they make learners care about stuff they didn't care about when they stepped into the classroom.'[1] She made that happen so brilliantly in her lesson, cajoling Maddie to work when the girl really didn't want to engage at all. And she did it without conflict.

Which brings me to my last point. As the nineteenth, and last, truly great teacher I visited during this incredible project, she confirmed as strongly as any of her predecessors, that forming positive working relationships with pupils is the bedrock of the teaching and learning process. She was able to challenge Maddie and others in her class because they knew that she worked hard, that she cared and that any chastisements were coming from the best possible place.

Mariam Sankar's students' progress and achievement data

At Frederick Bremer there is a substantial KS4 triple science cohort and Mariam teaches biology GCSE. In the last few years, Mariam's GCSE classes have averaged a Progress 8 score of + 1.07, over one grade higher than expected, on average, for every GCSE entry, with 63% of pupils gaining a 7+ grade.

---

1 D. Wiliam, Curriculum, Pedagogy and Assessment, in that Order. Speech at the Osiris World Education Summit (25 March 2025).

What Might We Learn from these Truly Great Teachers?

This final chapter begins with a huge caveat. I certainly don't consider these eleven teacher profiles to be irrefutable research evidence, or what I say in this chapter to be definitive. Despite the caveat, I do think there are things we might learn about teaching from these teachers. All I intend to do in this final chapter is identify the major common features of the teachers' practice and highlight aspects of their work that seem to me to be both extraordinary and useful. Before that, however, it is worth explaining the particular lens through which I have looked at these teachers. For the past decade or so, I have thought about classroom practice within the context of a model for learning and a closely linked model of the curriculum, both of which are detailed below.

A model for learning: Daniel Willingham's Memory Model[1]

I once purchased a vintage leather satchel as a colleague's leaving present. The stitching was rotten, so I ripped it all out. I bought a proper needle and thread for stitching leather, found a YouTube video on the subject and spent three nights repairing the satchel. When I had finished, it was as good as new. But I hadn't learnt how to stitch leather satchels. If I had wanted to repeat the feat, I would have had to revert to watching the video again. My brain had merely enacted the leather stitching technique *temporarily*, through in-the-moment mimicry; it hadn't assimilated it. In essence, then, learning is a *permanent* change to the long-term memory.

---

1 D. T. Willingham, A mental model of the learner: teaching the basic science of educational psychology to future teachers, *Mind, Brain, and Education*, 11(4) (2017).

Over the last decade, I have come to understand a simple truth about teaching, namely that it is difficult to teach in a way that has the greatest impact upon pupils' learning, if you don't have a model for how pupils learn in the first place. According to Dr Anita Devi, 'You need a model of learning. It gives you the questions to ask when a child is not learning.'[2] And answering those questions is key to progressing pupils' learning.

To gain a fundamental understanding of how pupils learn, Daniel Willingham's memory model is a good 'best bet'. It is clearly not definitive. When it comes to how the brain works, we have a distinctly limited understanding. Willingham's model can only ever be a work in progress. Nevertheless, it has some avid fans: esteemed educators such as Sarah Cottinghatt,[3] Tom Sherrington[4] and Josh Goodrich[5] subscribe to Willingham's thinking about memory and learning.

In essence, Willingham's research suggests that pupils have a working memory and a long-term memory. The longer pupils pay attention to, and struggle cognitively with, what we are teaching them in their working memory, the more chance there is that there will be a change to their long-term memory and learning will happen. We need pupils to regularly retrieve what we have taught them, in order to embed that change in the long-term memory. To learn how to stitch together leather satchels, I would need to repair quite a few, over an extended period of time.

A crucial, additional element to understanding the learning process is recognising the importance of building upon what we already know to extend our learning. It is difficult to understand negative numbers, for instance, if you haven't got a fluent understanding of the basic number

---

2 M. Myatt and J. Tomsett, *SEND Huh: Curriculum Conversations with SEND Leaders* (Woodbridge: John Catt Educational, 2023).
3 S. Cottinghatt, *Ausubel's Meaningful Learning in Action* (Woodbridge: John Catt Educational, 2023).
4 T. Sherrington, *The Learning Rainforest: Great Teaching in Real Classrooms* (Woodbridge: John Catt Educational, 2017).
5 J. Goodrich, *Responsive Coaching: Evidence-informed Instructional Coaching that Works for Every Teacher in Your School* (Woodbridge: John Catt Educational, 2024).

system. We extend our understanding by assimilating new learning with schema that already exist in our long-term memory.

Ultimately, there is no learning without remembering and, as Willingham famously claims, 'memory is the residue of thought'.[6] If we can encourage pupils to attend to, and think hard about, what we are teaching them, the better chance there is of learning happening.

This graphic, taken from Josh Goodrich's book on instructional coaching, illustrates Willingham's learning model and the kind of questions we might ask about where teaching might be adjusted to increase pupils' progress in their learning.[7] (see page 284).

A learning model is crucial for teachers to plan their teaching and for them to adapt it if their pupils aren't learning. It is equally important, perhaps, for anyone like me, who watches people teach, to have a model of learning. Josh Goodrich's questions are a helpful *aide memoire* for beginning to evaluate whether the visible teaching you have seen might lead to pupils learning (which is, of course, invisible). Only when you hear or see what pupils produce as a result of the teaching that has happened, can you even begin to gauge whether learning has taken place.

While I saw a very limited sample of teaching, the lesson visits recorded in this book are hugely detailed. I wanted to be able to give a sense of what it was like to be in the lessons, and some indication of whether learning was taking place. At best, perhaps, all we can glean from the lesson visits, using the Willingham memory model, is that there is a decent chance learning was taking place.

---

6 D. T. Willingham, What will improve a student's memory? *American Educator* (Winter 2008–2009): 17–25. Available at: http://www.aft.org/sited/default/files/periodicals/willingham_0.pdf.
7 Goodrich, *Responsive Coaching*.

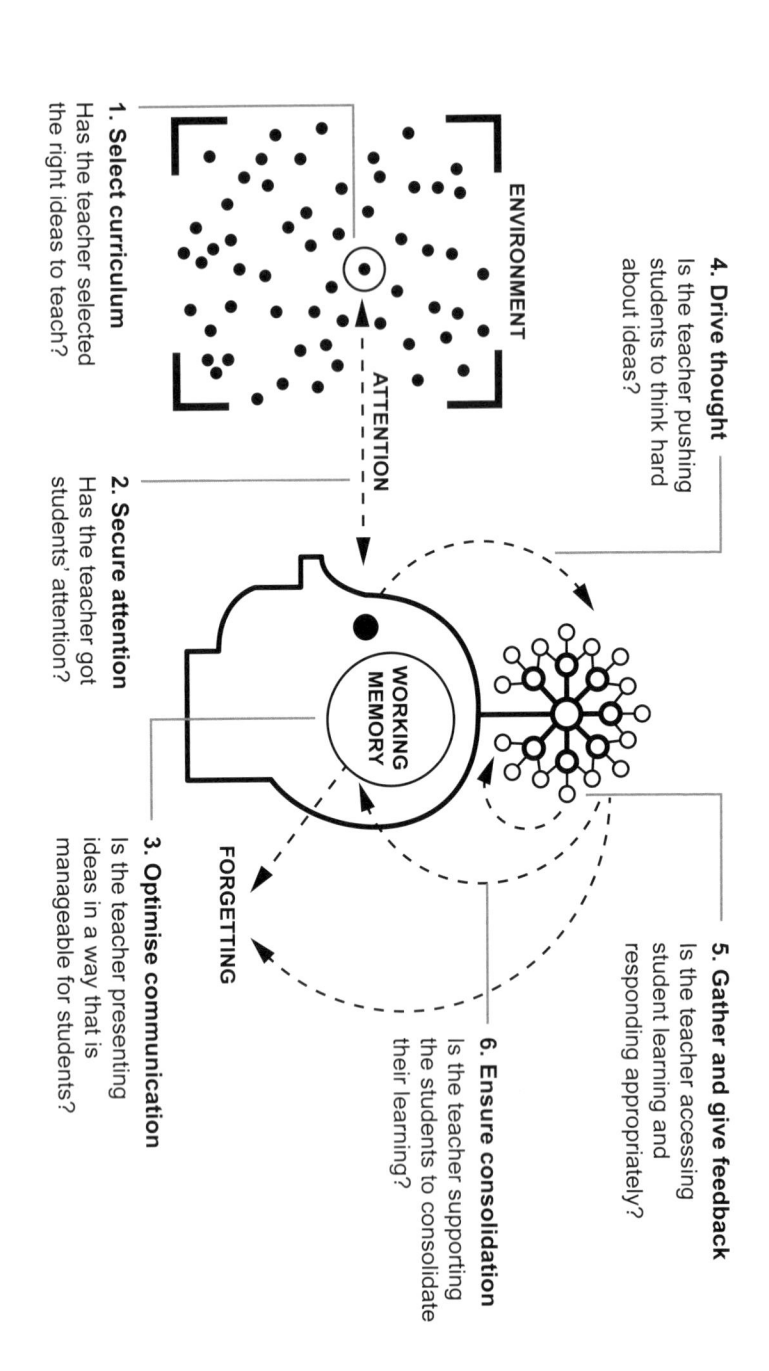

1. Select curriculum
Has the teacher selected the right ideas to teach?

2. Secure attention
Has the teacher got students' attention?

3. Optimise communication
Is the teacher presenting ideas in a way that is manageable for students?

4. Drive thought
Is the teacher pushing students to think hard about ideas?

5. Gather and give feedback
Is the teacher accessing student learning and responding appropriately?

6. Ensure consolidation
Is the teacher supporting the students to consolidate their learning?

ENVIRONMENT

ATTENTION

WORKING MEMORY

FORGETTING

A model of the curriculum: the curriculum triumvirate

The focus upon developing the curriculum in England has led to some unintended consequences, one of which has been an obsession with content over the two other elements of the curriculum – pedagogy and assessment. The quality of pupils' classroom experiences depends on both *what* is taught and *how* it is taught, all underpinned by short-cycle formative assessment. The three elements of curriculum – content, adaptive pedagogy and assessment – I have dubbed the curriculum triumvirate. When they work together in harmony – when the content is rich and ambitious, the teaching is vibrant and expert, and the teacher's formative assessment ensures no pupil is left behind – they provide all pupils with irresistible learning experiences.

Now, when I watch colleagues teach, I use my knowledge of all three aspects of the curriculum to help me get a sense of whether the pupils are participating in the lesson in a way that is likely to result, at some point, in learning. So, is the content they are being taught rich, challenging and ambitious, pitched at the Goldilocks level of academic demand – that is, not too hard that they have no hook to begin engaging with the content at all, but not too easy that they can complete what is asked of them without having to think – where it challenges them to wrestle with the content and builds on what they have learnt before? Is the way the content is being taught clearly explained, in a way that makes it irresistibly interesting to the pupils? Is there sufficient time allowed for checking conclusively whether all the pupils have at least begun to grasp what has been taught? The relationship between the curriculum triumvirate is dynamic.

When developing the curriculum, all three elements of the triumvirate need to be considered simultaneously. What we have seen, however, is content privileged over pedagogy and assessment.

Arguably, two key figures laid the foundations for redesigning the curriculum in England: Dylan Wiliam and Michael Young. In 2013 Wiliam wrote that, 'A great intended curriculum badly taught is likely

Content
What should my pupils learn?

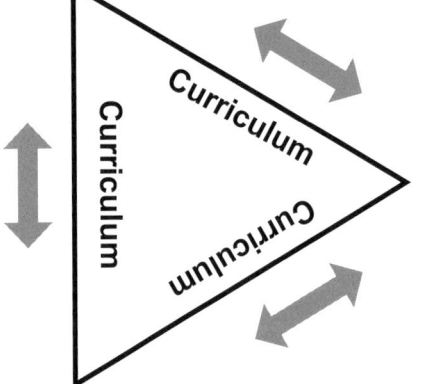

Adaptive teaching
How do I teach this subject specific content so that my pupils learn it?

Assessment
How am I assessing whether my pupils have understood what I have taught them?

Curriculum · Curriculum · Curriculum

to be a much worse experience for young people than a bad intended curriculum well taught. Pedagogy trumps curriculum.'[8] Wiliam was clear that content alone is not enough.

Michael Young's book, *Knowledge and the Future School: Curriculum and Social Justice*, published in 2014, was highly influential in the drive towards a knowledge-rich curriculum.[9] It is important to point out at this point, that I am not arguing against a knowledge-rich curriculum. What concerns me is merely *giving* pupils content, without thinking about how to present the content so they find it irresistible.

Knowledge organisers and glue sticks are a modern educational curse!

In an important, yet little noticed, article Michael Young reflected upon the development of the knowledge curriculum in England, some eight years after publishing his seminal book.[10] His comments – cited at length below – seem incredibly important to me:

'Lev Vygotsky [wrote] that acquiring knowledge in school has to be the voluntary act of a learner. You can't actually teach anybody anything; they have to learn it. You can help them, but they've got to have that desire to know. If you haven't encouraged pupils to engage in the process of acquiring knowledge, which is a very difficult process, then all you get is memorisation and reproduction in tests. I think this is why a lot of kids actually lose the desire to know during their time at school, whereas if we somehow found a way of enabling kids to discover that desire, which is inherent in all of them, schooling would be quite different. It would be a lovely thing to be a teacher, and not a struggle for much of the time. That's been quite a revealing thought to me. The current interest in the curriculum overlooks this point. It's so concerned with saying, 'Have we got the knowledge?' that it forgets to ask, 'How is the knowledge being acquired?' The curriculum is not just

---

8 D. Wiliam, *Redesigning Schooling: Principled Curriculum Design: 3* (London: SSAT (The Schools Network), 2013).

9 M. Young, D. Lambert, C. Roberts and M. Roberts, *Knowledge and the Future School: Curriculum and Social Justice* (London: Bloomsbury Publishing, 2014).

10 G. Duoblys, Michael Young: What we've got wrong about knowledge and curriculum, *TES* (21 September 2022). Available at: https://www.tes.com/magazine/teaching-learning/general/michael-young-powerful-knowledge-curriculum.

a body of knowledge; it's a group of communities we must encourage our students to join. That's how we have to look at it. We have to keep open the idea of a curriculum that is pedagogic, in the sense of it being accessible knowledge. It's difficult to access, but accessible nonetheless.'

Our education system is suffering, post-COVID, from low pupil attendance rates and poor pupil behaviour, and parents and children no longer live by the imperative that pupils must attend school. This is a world where a university education is no longer a guarantee of meaningful employment and where the internet is seen, all too often, as the easy-to-access source of all knowledge. Is it possible we have forgotten just how crucial it is to entice pupils into the learning process; that we no longer feel an obligation to encourage them to join our learning communities; that we think we can just give them a knowledge organiser, a glue stick and five hours of low-level administrative tasks and call that *teaching*?

Both Wiliam and Young emphasise the importance of teachers' pedagogy in the learning process. They trust the content specialists to know how to teach the nuances of the subject.

The thing is, you have got to make learning irresistible, and one way to do that is to let the expert teachers fly. I go fishing with my mate Tom. He is a truly great teacher. He has his own highly successful methodology. His students love his teaching style and they make great progress, evidenced in their GCSE progress scores. When I told him about this project, and one teacher in particular whose pupils have astronomically high progress scores, Tom said, without hesitation, 'I bet they are just left to get on with it.' And, of course, he is right.

The *well-trained, professionally thoughtful, and evidence-informed* truly great teachers featured in this book have earned a level of autonomy. None is fettered by pedagogic diktat from above. They have fun, they enjoy what they do, and their pupils learn a great deal. As Tom

Sherrington says, 'Teaching has to be joyful – and it can be if we let it.'[11] And what comes next was true for these secondary teachers as it was for the primary teachers I feature in its accompanying title (*This Much I Know About Truly Great Primary Teachers*), namely, that being in those classrooms was – and I hesitate to use the word because I think it is overused to the point of redundancy, but I genuinely mean it and will use it anyway – an absolute *privilege*. Not once did a lesson drag, not once did I lose interest, and rarely did I ever see a pupil off-task. The learning process is joyful. Watching them teach, one can only conclude that it is 'a lovely thing to be a teacher'.

The major common features of these truly great secondary teachers

Much of what we can learn from these truly great teachers comes from the detail of the lesson visit records and the interviews. That said, I thought it would be useful to position my suggested findings within an evidence-based context. Barak Rosenshine's meta-analysis, Research on teacher performance criteria, written with the help of Norma Furst in 1971, identified eleven teacher behaviours that led to high levels of pupil learning:[12]

- Clarity
- Variability
- Enthusiasm
- Task-oriented and/or Business-like Behaviour

---

11 T. Sherrington, Evidence-informed teaching has to be built around each teacher's personality and desire for autonomy; let's celebrate that, *Teacherhead* [blog] (7 January 2024). Available at: https://teacherhead.com/2024/01/07/evidence-informed-teaching-has-to-be-built-around-each-teachers-personality-and-desire-for-autonomy-lets-celebrate-that/.

12 B. Rosenshine and N. Furst, Research on teacher performance criteria, In B. O. Smith (ed.), *Research in Teacher Education* (Englewood Cliffs, NJ: Prentice Hall), pp. 37–72, cited in R. K. Barrick and A. C. Thoron, Teaching Behavior and Student Achievement: AEC582 WC244, 1 (2016). EDIS 2016 (1). Gainesville, FL:6. https://doi.org/10.32473/edis-wc244-2016.

- Student Opportunity to Learn Criterion Material
- Use of Student Ideas and General Indirectness
- Criticism
- Use of Structuring Comments
- Types of Questions
- Probing
- Level of Difficulty of Instruction

I would argue that the first four in Rosenshine's list are common features of our truly great secondary teachers. The most obvious is how every single teacher taught with unbridled, infectious *enthusiasm*. It's impossible not to share Jack Bream's delight in seeing her struggling student break through at the very end of the lesson with her incredibly perceptive and articulate comment. It's hard to be disinterested in Jen Lewis' smelly, gut-turningly brilliant practical demonstration of the human digestive system! Only a cardboard cut-out could fail to be excited about making bread rolls with Garry Littlewood. What they were teaching was, according to their enthusiastic selves, irresistible. Now, they were, of course, putting on their best children's TV presenter personas; yet it is possible to act as though you are enthused. I would argue that you *have* to be enthused, it's part of your job to be enthused; if you're dulled by what you're teaching, what chance do the pupils have? Pritesh Raichura, in his spellbinding talk at the researchED London conference, acknowledged that you needed to learn how to have presence, how to perform in the classroom, how to vary your voice and exaggerate your facial expressions in order to appear enthused and make what you are teaching appealing to the pupils. He was certain you could learn to develop that elusive thing called 'classroom presence' and I cannot help but agree. Watching our truly great teachers, I wonder whether being enthused becomes a habit. These teachers are *actually* enthused. Chris McGrane's energy for challenging mathematics, Tom Fraser's joy at one of his least academic pupils identifying a fine example of a symbol, Suzy Marston's verve for theatre studies, Mariam Sankar's sheer delight in the act of teaching itself, are all – it seemed to me as I sat in their classrooms – genuine.

Many enthusiasts would make poor teachers, however, because they would not be able to explain the object of their enthusiasm with any *clarity*. Not so with these truly great teachers, whose teaching is characterised by clarity in two main ways. It appears that narrating the direction of the lesson creates a safe environment for children. It was clear, in so many classrooms, exactly where we are now, what we are doing next and where we will end up. Mary Cawley, who, more than most teachers, needs to create a classroom that is a psychologically safe place, outlines the tasks for the day before they begin, with each activity on a small card, velcroed to the metal cupboard at the front of the room. Every time an activity is completed, Ahmed will take down the corresponding card. Garry Littlewood, who, with an oven at 220°C and razor-sharp knives all around the room, narrates his lesson to the letter to ensure the pupils in his food technology room are all in one piece.

Rosenshine suggested that teachers who were able to explain content and frame questions with clarity, were more effective.[13] Indeed, clarity in communicating curriculum content is a crucial element of effective teaching. Without exception, the teachers modelled their thinking to the class. One extraordinary example was Chris McGrane, who modelled his thinking in an '*I do, we do, you do*' process when he taught some demanding mathematical processes. Michelle Goodger's modelling of the factorising process was equally clear, as was Tom Fraser's demonstration of how to complete the recreative writing process. Live modelling characterised by high-quality metacognitive talk clarifies for pupils – *makes visible* for them – the thinking processes of the teacher expert. Indeed, what Rosenshine called *student opportunity to learn criterion material* sound suspiciously like teaching children how to think their way through applying what they know to new problems: 'student achievement can be increased by teaching students how to resolve problems they encounter that are related to the content of the course

---

13 Rosenshine and Furst, Research on teacher performance criteria.

but are not specific regurgitations of facts taught in the course.'[14] After watching these teachers at work, I have become utterly convinced that making our thinking visible is central to effective teaching and learning.

There is much to be said for *variability* when thinking about what constitutes a truly great teacher. Rosenshine suggests that, 'variation in the teacher's cognitive behaviour or the richness and variety of classroom materials and activities' were consistently significant in relation to student achievement.[15] That said, it is understandable why school leaders might prioritise consistency over variability, especially in a world where recruiting teachers is challenging. A vacancy cannot remain unfilled once term begins, because a vacancy cannot stand in front of 30 children and teach them. Yet a sentient human being with a set of slides, a script and a DBS can make a passable attempt to teach a class, but they are not going to be a truly great teacher. Pupils enjoy variability; in pedagogic terms, variability helps secure and maintain their attention. Take Mary Cawley's lesson, where, in 90 minutes, we had reading aloud, experimental learning, physical exercise, phonics, use of video, writing, speaking and listening, sign language and … and … Now, Mary's special needs class requires the ultimate in adaptive teaching where varying what you do, frequently and regularly, is essential. But, as Gary Aubin has often said, 'There are things that teachers can do that are useful for all pupils, while being particularly useful for some'.[16] Louise Booth's lesson on the Church in the Middle Ages included, amongst other things, teacher exposition, paired talk, teacher live modelling, questioning, drawing, using the textbook, writing and playing a game. Louise's students' joy at recalling her clothes rail and dressing up to re-enact moments in history is rooted in the varied approach to teaching and learning that characterises her practice. When you speak to them, variability in lessons is important to the pupils; turning up every day to the same old, same old, is hardly likely to make learning irresistible.

---

14 Barrick and Thoron, Teaching Behavior and Student Achievement, p. 4.

15 B. Rosenshine, *Teaching Behaviours and Student Achievement*, no. 1 (IFA studies) (Slough: National Foundation for Educational Research, 1 November 1971), p. 147.

16 M. Myatt and J. Tomsett, *SEND Huh: Curriculum Conversations with SEND Leaders* (Woodbridge: John Catt Educational, 2023), p. 209.

Business-like behaviour, aka *being organised and purposeful*, is an essential feature of the truly great teacher. Rosenshine found 'a consistent, positive trend in favour of' achievement-orientated or business-like teacher behaviour.[17] Pupils especially enjoy being taught by someone who is well-organised and wants them to achieve, who focus their teaching on what is needed for pupils to be successful. They invariably commented upon the focused, organisational skills of their teachers. Take what one of Louise Booth's pupils said of her: 'When you get in her lessons she's always ready to go, really well-organised. All sorted.' Louise's pupils could have been talking about any of the other teachers featured in this book; for instance, according to one of his past pupils, Tom Fraser 'has an extraordinary ability to create an organised and welcoming classroom for his pupils to learn and thrive in'. There is no point being enthused, clear and varied when you teach, if you cannot organise yourself and your resources to target your pupils' achievement.

While the teachers profiled in this book demonstrate many aspects of the other behaviours identified by Rosenshine and Furst, *enthusiasm, clarity, variability,* and *being organised and purposeful* are the main ones. Beyond those, there are five further common traits that emerged as I reflected upon what makes these teachers truly great. They all had *genuinely high expectations* of the pupils, both behaviourally and academically. Expectations of pupils is a complex area of research according to Rosenshine, who says, nonetheless, that there is 'significant correlation between teacher attitudes towards student achievement and actual student achievement'. This might be influenced by who teachers are teaching. It may be affected by the quality of curriculum materials; poor curriculum materials mean poorer achievement.[18] What I have come to know in my travels, is that it's easy to assert, quite glibly, that you have high expectations of those you teach; it is another thing entirely to see high expectations riven through classroom practice like the words through a stick of seaside rock. Take Suzy Marston, for example. Her teaching of practical drama, with improvisations of an intensity you would normally encounter in the professional theatre

---

17 Rosenshine, *Teaching Behaviours and Student Achievement*, no. 1, p. 96.
18 Rosenshine, *Teaching Behaviours and Student Achievement*, no. 1, p. 218.

world, was extraordinary and elicited from her pupils performances that they themselves could hardly believe they were capable of. Or Jack Bream, whose pupils grappled with issues of gender representation as if they were first year undergraduates, not GCSE students. Or Garry Littlewood, who treats his Year 8s as though they are chefs working in the kitchens of York. These truly great teachers epitomise what it is to have high expectations of their pupils.

Whilst I have named the third triumvirate of the curriculum, 'assessment', the term encompasses any activity which *checks for understanding*, something these teachers do relentlessly. Someone like Chris McGrane, who teaches between the desks, has excellent situational assessment. He has his radar on *all* the time, building an insight map across the class as to what learning is happening, pupil-by-pupil. Moment after moment sees these teachers check whether their pupils have learnt what they have been taught. The way Jen Lewis detected the only boy who might have been drifting off-task and brought him back into the lesson via a probing question was impressive to watch. Suzy Marston is constantly assessing who needs to be asked a question and when so she can keep them in the lesson. And then there's Mariam Sankar, whose whole pedagogic approach has been developed over years through adapting her pedagogy according to how well her pupils have learnt what she has taught them. All of which brings us back to the dynamic relationship between content-adaptive pedagogy-assessment. Whether it is via teaching between the desks, disciplined use of show-me boards, expert questioning techniques, or the responses of bellwether pupils, truly great teachers have a forensic understanding of who can do what and, consequently, the direction in which they need to take their teaching next.

Closely linked to checking for understanding is the commitment to give *help to individual pupils*. Such precisely targeted support takes huge amounts of teacher energy, but watching these teachers (and those I feature in its accompanying title, *This Much I Know About Truly Great Primary Teachers*, help the individual pupils who need just that little extra guidance, I swear they were energised rather than depleted by the process. Michelle Goodger's pupils, for example, were hugely praiseworthy of her efforts to support them: 'If we mess up, she helps.' To the accusation that such individualised support fosters learned helplessness, I would merely say that when these teachers provide a pupil with support, that is all it is, support. They don't tell them the answers, they clarify their thinking. In fact, the individualised help is more like *probing*, another of Rosenshine's identified behaviours: 'probing; that is, teacher responding to students with further clarifying questions ... may lead a student towards a more comprehensive answer than the initial one s/he gave.'[19] Individualised support is most often part of extending pupils' thinking and not telling pupils the answer. I liked what Lousie Booth said about providing individual support, in class. 'It's a big group there, with differentiated needs. I went around, and asked, "Do you want this support?" Some said, "Yes"; some said, "No". I'm also aware that you can't overdo that because you've got a TA in the room.' The impressive level of *measure* in the support allocated to pupils is something that comes with deep experience.

Truly great teachers have a *confident understanding of the content* they are teaching – indeed, it is a prerequisite for intellectually challenging the pupils. Rosenshine found that 'achievement gains were higher in classes of teachers who provided intellectual emphasis (over whether students enjoy themselves), something only possible if the teacher is confident about their curriculum content'.[20] So many of these teachers are subject experts. Take Jack Bream, who has taught four different subjects to A level, and has willingly done all the academic work to prepare herself for teaching her pupils. Chris McGrane's understanding of mathematics is extraordinary and allows him to design the curriculum in a way that caters for the full range of pupils' prior attainment. Suzy Marston is fiercely bright and treats the whole endeavour of teaching GCSE theatre studies as though she is producing an RSC production of *King Lear*. Michelle Goodger's hunger to learn and learn and learn is awesome. Louise Booth brings her academic learning to the classroom to create a sense of playful scholarship with such skill it is striking. I would argue that the way Garry Littlewood insists upon

---

19 Rosenshine, *Teaching Behaviours and Student Achievement*, no. 1, p. 136.
20 Rosenshine, *Teaching Behaviours and Student Achievement*, no. 1, p. 93.

treating food technology as an academic subject that just happens to have a practical element is at the heart of his success as a teacher. Mary Cawley's determination that she teach her pupils with the most challenging additional needs how to read and write is humbling. Jen Lewis' insistence upon using the correct scientific terminology during her digestive-system demo ensured that the whole enterprise was intellectually demanding. How my own truly great teacher Dave Williams knew every word of all our A level texts always amazed me. Tom Fraser's determination to share his love of literature with teenagers from Hull is inspiring. Not one of the teachers I visited relied on a bought-in scheme and a clicker.

The final common feature of all the truly great teachers featured in this book, is that they take time to find out about each child and *build positive working relationships*. Tom Fraser treats every one of his pupils with unconditional positive regard (UPR) to an extent I have never seen before (if that isn't contradictory, as all UPR is unconditional by definition). What was extraordinary in Tom's case is how his core relationship with his pupils is manifested in how he teaches, in that he asks them questions about the work as though they are solving problems together. It feels like learning in Tom's classroom is an entirely collaborative process between teacher and pupils. His pupils adore the way he is with them. One said, 'that's just how it feels. It's not him and us. We do the work for each other. He's learning as we're learning.'

The primacy for these teachers of building foundational relationships with their pupils is open to challenge. The famous line by Rita Pierson from her TED talk, 'Every child deserves a champion, an adult who will never give up on them, who understands the power of connection, and insists that they become the best that they can possibly be', is sometimes derided.[21] But teacher after teacher mentioned the importance of building those foundational relationships with pupils. Pupils taught by Mariam Sankar were utterly clear – in the interviews and in their testimonials – that Mariam cared about them. When

---

21 R. Pierson, Every kid needs a champion, *TED* (3 May 2013). Available at: https://www.youtube.com/watch?v=SFnMTHhKdkw.

Mariam takes on a new class, the first thing she does is forge deep, trusting relationships. Michelle Goodger said, 'create the supportive, trusting relationships, and they'll let you teach them'. One of Garry Littlewood's pupils said, 'He's a nice person. He cares about everyone individually. He properly takes time to help you if you need it.' Forging positive relationships with her pupils is central to Louise Booth's view of how she teaches: 'Everything is based on the relationships I have with the kids. Forget how clever I might be about history. I could be teaching anything. I could be teaching geography, RE. The main thing is the mutual respect. I'm never going to humiliate you; I'm never going to bully you, but I'm going to be firm and you're going to feel safe in my classroom.' As Chris McGrane says, 'I just want them to know I care, because I really do.'

It's hard to argue with Michelle – and Garry and Louise and Chris and Mary and Jen and Suzy and Jack and Dave and Tom and Miriam – because they all are truly great teachers and they all subscribe to the notion that, without getting to know your pupils as people and forging respectful, trusting relationships with them and their parents, it is difficult to teach as well as they do and for their pupils to learn as much as they possibly can.

Final reflections: two sides of the same coin, or something more?

So, here are nine behaviours of the eleven truly great teachers featured in this book:

1. *Teach with enthusiasm*
2. *Explain things with clarity*
3. *Vary your pedagogic practices*
4. *Be organised and purposeful*
5. *Have genuinely high expectations*

6   Check for understanding

7   Have a confident understanding of the content

8   Help individual pupils

9   Build positive working relationships

Many readers will say that they could have listed these nine behaviours of truly great teachers for me before I began my work and saved me the days spent beetling around the country visiting schools and the hours it has taken to write this book. I am sure that Professor Rob Coe, both my collaborator and provocateur, will point out that all I had to do was look at these teachers' pupils' progress data to know that they must be truly great teachers who do the nine things listed above on a daily basis. But, as Rosenshine says, 'student achievement is inadequate as a sole measure of teacher effectiveness,'[22] a sentiment supported by Matthew A. Kraft, who wrote recently in the *TES*: 'We know that we can't boil down a teacher into a simplistic uniform measure of their performance. It is much more complex.'[23]

That said, are my findings and Rob's single pupil progress data point just two sides of the same coin? They probably are, to a great extent. That is, if you exhibit those nine teacher behaviours, as night follows day, your pupils will make good progress; and if your pupils have made good academic progress, it is highly likely that you will be exhibiting those nine teacher behaviours. But it is nuanced and it is, as Kraft says, *complex*. The thing about the Rosenshine book, is that it begins by saying this field of research is damned tricky. I led Huntington School in York, which is a Research School. I know, through bitter experience, how tracking the golden thread from teacher behaviours to pupil outcomes is complexity personified. I remember asking my last Year 13 Economics class, in their final lesson, what it was they liked best about the way I taught – was it the pre-reading process, questioning, modelling answers, the role play to illustrate the law of diminishing

---

22 Rosenshine, *Teaching Behaviours and Student Achievement*, no. 1, p. 13.
23 Z. Niemtus, Matthew A. Kraft: The struggle to spot (and develop) effective teachers, *TES* (6 November 2024). Available at: https://www.tes.com/magazine/teaching-learning/general/how-to-spot-and-develop-effective-teachers.

returns of the factors of production, group presentations, research tasks …? And the lad who went on to attain an A* grade at A Level in the summer examinations replied, 'I liked it best when you read through the text book and explained it to us.' All that effort, and that was all I needed to have done! But what the Year 13 student was actually saying, was that he liked clear explanations and the work to be targeted precisely upon what he needed to know to be successful. Since the textbook was endorsed by the examination board and written by the chief examiner, his reflection made complete sense.

But education has to be about more than examination outcomes. Whilst I can see the sense of Rob's quest to find a single pupil progress data point to represent individual teacher efficacy, teachers do more than just help pupils make academic progress. They create communities. So, I think, there are a couple of further learning points to be taken from these teacher profiles.

I was very clear that I wanted to enjoy myself at work. As a head teacher I was in school for 10–12 hours a day, every day, for 18 years. The core part of my waking life was spent at work. I needed to enjoy myself. I never subscribed to the concept of a work/life balance. If work is the opposite of life, then work is logically, being equated with death. I called it a work/home balance since both are part of my life; it acknowledged how important my work was as a major element of who I am.

When at work, you have to be yourself and enjoy being there. The teachers I visited were visibly enjoying their lives in the classroom. Both teachers and pupils were happy to be there. Truly. These teachers were being themselves. Pupil behaviour was great. I never heard a teacher shout. Those foundational relationships that Michelle Goodger et al. talked about were established so very firmly in all the classrooms I visited. They responded to individual need and they cared deeply about every single child. They were not limited by a regimented, didactic teaching and learning policy; indeed, the way these teachers were happy to adapt what they did within a loose pedagogic framework surely raises questions for the current practice in some settings where the approach to teaching and learning emphasises consistency beyond all else. As my mate Tom suggested, these truly great teachers were trusted to get on with it.

Schools are, arguably, the most important social centres in our crumbling neighbourhoods and their output goes beyond an examination value-added score. They are comprised of classroom communities built by truly great teachers like those featured in this book. The sense of obligation to each other that these teachers create in their classrooms leads to great things, one of which is the way pupils mimic their teachers' behaviours and attitudes. When those foundational relationships are established, whatever the teacher does, the pupils will do too. Most importantly, it was as clear as one of Chris McGrane's explanations of gradient that every single truly great teacher worked demonstrably hard for the pupils. Sharon Watson's comments about Chris are pertinent here: 'The pupils work hard because of his investment in them. It's so obvious he wants to be there, in front of them teaching them maths, and they respond to his commitment – which is total – with their commitment.' Chris' pupils were equally clear about one of the main reasons they worked hard: 'He would email us solutions if we were stuck with something. Late at night he was still up, working … If he puts the effort in, then we have to. I didn't want to let him down.' I have always harboured the odd doubt about what you can actually learn from pupil voice exercises, but the conversations with the pupils were utterly illuminating. So many – if not all – of them said that they worked hard because their teacher worked hard and they didn't want to let their teacher down. I had a sense that this was important; I knew that I worked hard for my old English teacher, Dave Williams, some 40-odd years ago, because he cared enough to work hard for me. I once met one of my former A level media students, now in his forties, who said his class had worked hard because Karl Elwell, my co-teacher, and I had worked hard, but I never thought the level of reciprocity was quite so marked. Consequently, if we need a final teacher behaviour to make it a neat ten, it would be *work hard for your pupils*.

Providing a high-quality education for every child in our country is an amazingly ambitious endeavour. I marvel at the whole enterprise. It depends upon dedicated professionals – like the teachers featured here – in the corners of our schools, in villages, towns and cities across the land, maintaining high standards, giving their all for our children, day-in, day-out, when no one is looking. The whole thing is selfless heroism, personified. If it were easy – as some of the cynics might crow – the profession wouldn't have a recruitment and retention crisis.

I will end with Jack Bream, who, when I asked her if she had ever thought of doing anything else other than teach, said, 'No. I just want to do teaching, that's all, that's it. And yes, I'd do it again in a heartbeat. I've done 28 years and I still love my job. How many people can say that?'

Select Bibliography

Andrews, B. (2025). How 'efficiency' derailed education, *TES* (25 February). Available at: https://www.tes.com/magazine/teaching-learning/general/how-efficiency-derailed-education.

Barrick, R. K. and Thoron, A. C. (2016). Teaching Behavior and Student Achievement: AEC582 WC244, 1 2016. EDIS 2016 (1). Gainesville, FL:6. https://doi.org/10.32473/edis-wc244-2016.

Barth, R. S. (1991). *Improving Schools from Within: Teachers, Parents, and Principals Can Make the Difference* (San Francisco, CA: Jossey-Bass).

Coe, R. (2014). Classroom observation: it's harder than you think, *Cambridge Insight* [blog] (9 January). Available at: https://www.cem.org/blog/classroom-observation.

Coe, R., Aloisi C., Higgins S. and Elliot Major, L. (2014). *What Makes Great Teaching? Review of the Underpinning Research* (London: Sutton Trust). Available at: https://www.suttontrust.com/wp-content/uploads/2014/10/What-Makes-Great-Teaching-REPORT.pdf.

Coe, R., Rauch, C. J., Kime, S. and Singleton, D. (2020). *The Great Teaching Toolkit: Evidence Review* (Sunderland: Evidence Based Education). Available at: https://evidencebased.education/great-teaching-toolkit-evidence-review/.

Devine, D., Fahie, D. and Mcgillicuddy, D. (2013). What is 'good' teaching? Teacher beliefs and practices about their teaching, *Irish Educational Studies*, 32(1): 83–108. https://doi.org/10.1080/03323315.2013.773228

Duoblys, G. (2022). Michael Young: What we've got wrong about knowledge and curriculum, *TES* (21 September). Available at: https://www.tes.com/magazine/teaching-learning/general/michael-young-powerful-knowledge-curriculum.

Husbands, C. (2013). Great teachers or great teaching? Why McKinsey got it wrong, *IOE blog* (10 October). Available at: https://blogs.ucl.ac.uk/ioe/2013/10/10/great-teachers-or-great-teaching-why-mckinsey-got-it-wrong/.

Kirschner, P. A. and Hendrick, C. (2020). *How Learning Happens: Seminal Works in Educational Psychology and what They Mean in Practice* (Abingdon and New York: Routledge).

Kirschner, P., Hendrick, C. and Heal, J. (2022). *How Teaching Happens: Seminal Works in Teaching and Teacher Effectiveness and What They Mean in Practice* (Abingdon and New York: Routledge).

Lemov, D. (2021). *Teach Like a Champion 3.0: 63 Techniques that Put Students on the Path to College* (San Francisco, CA: Jossey-Bass).

McCourt, M. (2019). *Teaching for Mastery* (Woodbridge: John Catt Educational).

Muijs, D. and Reynolds, D. (2010). *Effective Teaching: Evidence and Practice* (London: SAGE Publications).

Myatt, M. (2016). *High Challenge, Low Threat: How the Best Leaders Find the Balance* (Woodbridge: John Catt Educational).

Myatt, M. (2018). *The Curriculum: Gallimaufry to Coherence* (Woodbridge: John Catt Educational).

Myatt, M. and Tomsett, J. (2021). *Huh: Curriculum Conversations Between Senior and Subject Leaders* (Woodbridge: John Catt Educational).

Myatt, M. and Tomsett, J. (2022a). *Primary Huh: Curriculum Conversations with Subject Leaders in Primary Schools* (Woodbridge: John Catt Educational).

Myatt, M. and Tomsett, J. (2022b). *Primary Huh 2: Primary Curriculum Leadership Conversations* (Woodbridge: John Catt Educational).

Myatt, M. and Tomsett, J. (2023). *SEND Huh: Curriculum Conversations with SEND Leaders* (Woodbridge: John Catt Educational).

Myatt, M. and Tomsett, J. (2024). *AP Huh: Curriculum Conversations with Alternative Provision Leaders* (Woodbridge: John Catt Educational).

Niemtus, Z. (2024). Matthew A. Kraft: The struggle to spot (and develop) effective teachers, *TES* (6 November). Available at: https://www.tes.com/magazine/teaching-learning/general/how-to-spot-and-develop-effective-teachers.

Nuthall, G. (2007). *The Hidden Lives of Learners* (Wellington: NZCER Press).

Rosenshine, B. (2012). Principles of instruction: research-based strategies that all teachers should know, *American Educator,* 38(1): 12–19, 39. Available at: https://www.aft.org/sites/default/files/periodicals/Rosenshine.pdf.

Rosenshine, B. (1971). *Teaching Behaviours and Student Achievement,* no. 1 (IEA studies) (Slough: National Foundation for Educational Research).

Rosenshine, B. and Furst, N. (1971). Research on teacher performance criteria. In B. O. Smith (ed.), *Research in Teacher Education,* pp. 37–72 (Englewood Cliffs, NJ: Prentice Hall).

Sherrington, T. (2017). *The Learning Rainforest: Great Teaching in Real Classrooms* (Woodbridge: John Catt Educational).

Sherrington, T. (2019). *Rosenshine's Principles in Action* (Woodbridge: John Catt Educational).

Sherrington, T. and Caviglioli, O. (2020). *Teaching WalkThrus: Five-Step Guides to Instructional Coaching: Visual Step-By-Step Guides to Essential Teaching Techniques* (Woodbridge: John Catt Educational).

Sherrington, T. and Caviglioli, O. (2021). *Teaching WalkThrus 2: Five-Step Guides to Instructional Coaching* (Woodbridge: John Catt Educational).

Sherrington, T. and Caviglioli, O. (2022). *Teaching WalkThrus 3: Five-Step Guides to Instructional Coaching* (Woodbridge: John Catt Educational).

Sherrington, T. and Caviglioli, O. (2024). *Learning WalkThrus: Students and Parents – Better Learning, Step by Step* (Woodbridge: John Catt Educational).

Siegel, M. A. (1977). Teacher behaviors and curriculum packages: Implications for research and teacher education. In L. Rubin (ed.), *Curriculum Handbook: Administration and Theory* (Boston, MA: Allyn & Bacon Publishers) (ERIC Document Reproduction Service No. ED 134 932).

Tabberer, R. (1994). *School and Teacher Effectiveness* (Slough: NFER and Staffordshire LEA). Available at: https://www.nfer.ac.uk/media/2lgkpzs4/school_and_teacher_effectiveness.pdf.

Tomsett, J. (2015). *This Much I Know About Love Over Fear … Creating a Culture for Truly Great Teaching* (Carmarthen: Crown House Publishing).

Wiliam, D. (2016). *Leadership for Teacher Learning* (Blairsville, PA: Learning Sciences International).

Willingham, D. T. (2021). *Why Don't Students Like School? A Cognitive Scientist Answers Questions About How the Mind Works and What It Means for the Classroom*, 2nd edn (San Francisco, CA: Jossey-Bass).

Young, M., Lambert, D., Roberts, C. and Roberts, M. (2014). *Knowledge and the Future School: Curriculum and Social Justice* (London: Bloomsbury Publishing).

This Much I Know About Love Over Fear …

Creating a culture for truly great teaching

ISBN 978-184590982-6

This Much I Know About Love Over Fear is a compelling account of leading a values-driven school where people matter above all else. Weaving autobiography with an account of his experience of headship, Tomsett explains how, in an increasingly pressurised education system, he creates the conditions in which staff and students can thrive. Too many of our state schools have become scared, soulless places. Tomsett draws on his extensive experience and knowledge and calls for all those involved in education to find the courage to develop a leadership-wisdom which emphasises love over fear. Creating a truly great school takes patience. Ultimately, truly great schools don't suddenly exist. You grow great teachers first, who, in turn, grow a truly great school.

There is a huge fork in the road for head teachers: one route leads to executive headship across a number of schools and the other takes head teachers back into the classroom to be the head teacher. John strongly believes that if the head teacher is not teaching, or engaged in helping others to improve their teaching, in their school, then they are missing the point. The only thing head teachers need obsess themselves with is improving the quality of teaching, both their colleagues' and their own.

An authentic personal narrative of teaching, leadership and discovering what really matters. It gets to the heart of what is valuable in education and offers advice for those working in schools.

This Much I Know About Mind Over Matter …

Improving mental health in our schools

ISBN 978-178583168-3

John Tomsett's second book, *This Much I Know About Mind Over Matter,* is replete with truths about the mental well-being of children in state schools, about creating a school culture where everyone can not just survive, but thrive, and about life around manic depression. With his typical mixture of experience, wisdom and research-based evidence, Tomsett explains how he manages the pressure of modern-day state-school headship. He interweaves his authentic personal experience of a childhood traumatised by his mother's manic depression with his strategies for turning the tide of students' mental health problems and surviving as a head teacher in a climate where you are only as good as your last set of examination results. He addresses the growing issue of children's mental health issues with refreshing honesty, offering up a plan for averting a mental health crisis in our schools. The autobiographical narrative modulates between self-effacing humour and heart-wrenching stories of his mother's life, blighted by mental illness. His professional reflections are a wisdom-filled blend of evidence-based policy and decades of experience in teaching and school leadership. Tomsett writes with genuine humility. His prose is beautiful in its seeming simplicity. When you pick up one of his books you will find you have read the first fifty pages before you have even noticed: surely the hallmark of truly great writing.

This much I know About Truly Great Primary Teachers

(and what we can learn from them)

ISBN 978-178583745-6

Foreword by Professor Rob Coe

Through a set of in-depth case studies, *This Much I Know About Truly Great Primary Teachers (and what we can learn from them)* by John Tomsett dissects the complex and beautiful art of classroom teaching.

Covering a range of school types, social contexts, pupil ages and subjects, it brings to life how nine outstanding primary teachers engage, inspire, nurture and motivate their pupils. Each detailed vignette, based on observing the teachers teach, and discussions with them, their colleagues and pupils, brings the qualities of truly great teachers to life.

Each teacher is unique in the way they teach and in how they talk about teaching. But they also have some common behaviours and attitudes that make them truly great, which John draws together, summarising what we can learn from their unbridled enthusiasm, skill and dedication to giving their pupils the very best foundation for a bright future.

Essential reading for all primary school teachers, school leaders, teacher trainers and education researchers.